Covenant Marriage

Staying Together for Life

Covenant Marriage

DR. FRED LOWERY

HOWARD
PUBLISHING CO.

Our purpose at Howard Publishing is to:

• *Increase faith* in the hearts of growing Christians

• *Inspire holiness* in the lives of believers

• *Instill hope* in the hearts of struggling people everywhere

  Because He's coming again!

Published by Howard Publishing Co., Inc.
3117 North 7th Street, West Monroe, Louisiana 71291-2227

02 03 04 05 06 07 08 09 10 11   10 9 8 7 6 5 4 3 2 1

Edited by Michele Buckingham
Interior design by Stephanie Denney
Cover design by LinDee Loveland

ISBN: 1-58229-232-9

To Leigh,
my one and only,
to whom my heart cries—
I want you, I need you, I love you

She has stood by me, loved me, prayed with me and played with me, laughed with me and cried with me, parented with me and grandparented with me, ministered with me and sought God's will with me. Her personality has put the celebration in our marriage; her faith has made it sacred and solid. I can't imagine life without her.

It is with a grateful heart and personal joy that I dedicate this book to my covenant bride, my precious wife, Leigh Lowery.

Many women have done excellently,
but you surpass them all.
—Proverbs 31:29 RSV

The Covenant Marriage Movement

The Covenant Marriage movement is a collaborative effort to further strengthen the institution of marriage. Participating in this movement are leading national organizations that are already impacting marriages, such as Focus on the Family, Moody Bible Institute, Promise Keepers, and Lifeway Christian Resources.

The stated mission of Covenant Marriage is to restore churches and society to an understanding and practice of marriage as covenant by applying timeless principles of God's Word.

The challenge is for every couple in America to examine their definition of marriage with the understanding that it must be more than a contract or even a commitment; it must be a covenant.

To learn more about this movement, see their website at www.covenantmarriage.com.

CONTENTS

Foreword: by Kay Arthur ix

Acknowledgments xi

Introduction: What Do You Want for Your Marriage? xiii

Chapter 1: Marriage American Style 1

Chapter 2: When Marriage Is Not What You Expected . . . 19

Chapter 3: Making "I Do" Harder to Undo 29

Chapter 4: What Is Covenant? 41

Chapter 5: The Blessing of Covenant Marriage 59

Chapter 6: Is Your Marriage a Contract or a Covenant? . . . 81

Chapter 7: Is "I Do" Your Final Answer? 97

Chapter 8: A Covenant Wedding 117

Chapter 9: The Power of Covenant Love 143

Chapter 10: Do You Have a Purpose-Driven Marriage? . . . 159

Chapter 11: Covenant Companionship 167

Chapter 12: The Critical Role of Communication 177

Chapter 13: Learning How to Manage Conflict 201

Epilogue: Would You Do It All Over Again? 225

Appendix 1: A Covenant Wedding Ceremony 229

Appendix 2: A Covenant Recommitment Ceremony 235

Appendix 3: Recommended Reading 239

Notes 241

Foreword

BY KAY ARTHUR

How wonderful to have an entire book that helps you understand marriage from the aspect of covenant! Nothing is more transforming than knowing what it means to be in a covenant relationship with God and with your mate. If you understand the covenant aspect of marriage, your relationship cannot help but take on a whole new, wonderful depth of commitment. And isn't that what we all long for—a true, unshakable commitment with a lifelong mate?

There's nothing stronger than a covenant commitment. Covenant is the anchor that holds you and your marriage through any storm—and this book will help you drop anchor. The precepts and principles of covenant laid out in these pages will radically transform your commitment to your spouse. When you've finished reading, you'll have a fresh understanding of the gravity and the blessing of saying "I do."

ACKNOWLEDGMENTS

My heartfelt thanks to the following people who contributed so much to the writing of this book:

Above all, my wife, Leigh Lowery, and our daughters, Christy Faciane and Shelby Koch. Each day you give me a thousand reasons why working on my marriage should be a sacred and never-ending journey. I love each one of you so very much. And girls, thank you so much for marrying wonderful, God-desiring guys and for choosing covenant marriage. No dad could feel more blessed. And of course, to Laura Leigh: Thanks for bringing so much joy into our lives.

My wonderful sons-in-law, Ky Faciane and Jon Koch. Wow, you guys are the best! Thanks for walking with God and for loving and cherishing my daughters. Thanks for choosing covenant marriage.

My parents, Fred and Esther Lowery. Before my father died in 1993, I thanked him for being faithful to Mom and to us kids and for finishing well. His example, spirit, and humor are with me forever. Thank you, Mom, for loving me unconditionally and for praying for me without ceasing. I owe you so much. I can never thank you and Dad enough for staying married.

Terri Williams, my secretary, a woman of many talents, one who has worked tirelessly on this project, and one who always goes the second mile. Terri, you are always there when I need you, and I could not have done this book without you. Your support and computer skills are priceless to me.

My secretary, Terry Perdue. Thanks for protecting me in my fight for time to do this book. Thanks for encouraging me and making me smile when I needed to.

My friends at Howard Publishing. It has been a true pleasure working with you. Your spirit and Christian witness have blessed me.

Michele Buckingham, my editor at Howard. It was a joy to work with you. Without a doubt, you made it a better book.

Denny Boultinghouse, without whom there would be no book. Thanks for believing in me.

Philis Boultinghouse, whose encouragement, suggestions, and help along the way were invaluable. Thank you!

Dennis Swanberg, my friend. Thanks for telling me about Howard Publishing and encouraging me to go forward with this book.

Cecil and Barbara Perkins. Thank you for all you do to encourage me.

Ed and Bobbie Gatlin. James and Peggy Harris. Thanks for giving me a "model" of what a good marriage and a happy home looks like.

Introduction

WHAT DO YOU WANT
FOR YOUR MARRIAGE?

Yesterday more than three thousand couples divorced. Today there will be thousands more.

In the past four decades, a cultural sledgehammer has attacked the American family, and the evidence of collateral damage is everywhere. Since 1960 the number of couples getting married has declined by one-third, while the number of couples getting divorced has more than doubled. In 1994, for the first time in American history, divorce replaced death as the principal cause of family dissolution.[1]

What's my point? You and I are in a *divorce revolution,* and it appears no couple is exempt. I have friends and family members who are divorced, and no doubt you do too. If divorce can happen to other people—even high-profile Christians—it can happen to you or me. There is not one marriage in today's culture that is not vulnerable.

Why? Because we've allowed the culture to seep into our souls. The stigma against divorce is gone. The laws are lenient. The lines are blurred. That means every marriage is in danger. Yours. Mine.

Let's not kid ourselves. For years marriage therapist and researcher

Blaine Fowers has been asking married couples, "How likely is it that your marriage will end in divorce?" You know what most people answer? "No chance!" When it comes to our marriages, Fowers says, most of us are under a "positive illusion."[2] In other words, we're just not realistic!

You probably remember the explosion of the space shuttle *Challenger* in 1986. I know I do. The picture is literally engraved upon the minds of most Americans. It was a horrible tragedy and one that perhaps could have been prevented. According to Joe Brown in his book *Battle Fatigue,* at least one prominent publication blamed the disaster on the double-whammy of pride and stress. Brown writes: "It is reported that a group of top managers failed to listen carefully to the warning of subordinates who were concerned about the operational reliability of certain parts of the booster rocket under conditions of abnormal stress, such as those present on the day of the launch."[3]

Now I don't know if pride and stress were the culprits in the *Challenger* accident. But I do know that pride, coupled with the unique stresses of married life, has caused many seemingly high-flying marriages to crash and burn. The Bible reminds us that "pride goes before destruction, a haughty spirit before a fall" (Proverbs 16:18). Today an estimated 65 percent of new marriages will end in divorce.[4] That means we can't assume that divorce will not happen to us. On the contrary, we have to assume, based on statistics, that we *will* divorce—unless we proactively do the things necessary to prevent it.

But what are those things? The world, it seems, doesn't have a clue! In her July 3, 1975, column, advice guru Ann Landers wrote: "The sad, incredible fact is that after thirty-six years of marriage, Jules and I are being divorced. As I write these words, it is as if I am referring to a letter from a reader. It seems unreal that I am writing about my own marriage." The title of the column? "Ann Has No Answer."[5]

In fact, during the past thirty years the world has had a one-note response for divorce prevention: marriage therapy. But the divorce rate has not been slowed one iota by all those hours logged in counseling sessions. Now, in the face of continued high divorce rates, some marriage therapists are publicly admitting that marriage counseling has failed to deliver. Diane Sollee, who has spent most of her professional life as a marriage and family therapist, is one who no longer believes therapy to be the answer for troubled marriages. She has formed an organization called Smart Marriages that teaches couples the necessary skills to build marriages that will go the distance. Perhaps you have heard about the little Chinese village where the doctor is only paid if he keeps the people healthy? Sollee says she and others would like the same deal for marriage counselors: "Pay the experts if the divorce rate goes down."[6]

But the divorce rate shows no signs of slowing down, and marriage as we've known it is fast becoming obsolete. A cover story in *Fortune* magazine noted that "while there used to be pressure to stay married, at least for appearance's sake, today we are pressured in the opposite direction." Author Helen Singer Kaplan pulls no punches when she says, "There is no longer a prejudice against divorce and remarriage—almost the reverse. In some cases, the man with the old, nice, matronly wife is looked down on."[7] In other words, "Why can't he do better for himself?" Some researchers, including Christian pollster George Barna, predict that "Americans will soon believe that a life spent with the same partner is both unusual and unnecessary."[8] Instead, they will tailor their relationships to fit their own circumstances and preferences.

Clearly we can no longer pattern our marriages after the people around us—if we ever could. Not only does the world not know how to divorce-proof its marriages, it is well on the way to making broken relationships the norm!

If we don't want our own marriages to fall by the wayside, we have to find a better pattern to follow. Fortunately, we don't have to look far. God, the inventor of marriage, gives us everything we need to know about marriage in his Word, the Bible. Better than any earthly marriage counselor, he offers "divine therapy" guaranteed not to fail: "I will instruct you and teach you in the way you should go; I will counsel you and watch over you" (Psalm 32:8).

For the sake of our marriages, we have to get with God, study the Scriptures, and begin to understand marriage as he created it to be: a sacred, permanent, *covenant* commitment. We have to get back to God's original plan and work his plan. We have to be willing to die to ourselves and put our marriages and our mates above our own self-interest. Nothing less will do.

A COVENANT RELATIONSHIP

From Genesis to Revelation the Bible draws a clear link between the everlasting covenant between God and his people and the marriage covenant between a husband and wife. Our human marriages are designed to mirror God's marriage to Israel and Christ's marriage to the church in both purpose and permanence. As David Atkinson writes in his book *To Have and to Hold,* "The primary purpose of marriage is to be found in the acceptance of God's will that the covenant relationship of man and wife, both made in the image of God, shall be an image of his covenant relationship with his people."[9] Bible scholar R. J. Ehrlich agrees: "Marriage, which is the supreme expression of the togetherness of male and female in differentiation and relationship, [reflects the image of God and] represents the covenant by which God has bound himself to his people, his church, to man."[10]

Another theologian, G. R. Dunstan, offers these five marks of comparison between God's covenant with his people and the covenant of human marriage:

- Both are an initiative of love inviting a response and creating a relationship.

- As God's covenant of grace is made sure by oath, so the essence of the marriage covenant is the vow of consent—a vow that guards the relationship.

- Both are obligations of faithfulness.

- Both include the promise of blessing to those remaining faithful to their covenant obligation.

- Both require sacrifice.[11]

In fact, sacrifice is at the very heart of covenant. In both the Old and New Testament, the covenant of Almighty God with his people was secured by blood—by the laying down of life in death. Likewise, the security of the marriage relationship is based on a "walk of death"—death to certain freedoms, death to dependency on parents, death to prior relationships, and death to self, all of which are necessary for the marriage to have a life of its own and a new wholeness as two become one.

Ultimately, this kind of sacrificial "blood covenant" is the secret for divorce-proofing your marriage. It is the antithesis of the self-serving, you-can-have-it-all individualism espoused by the world's so-called marriage experts. Marriage, according to these folks, is all about personal rights, personal feelings, and personal pleasures. Sacrifice? No way! Die to self? You've got to be kidding! But individualism is a death blow to marriage. Consider the case of so-called expert Barbara DeAngelis. She has made millions of dollars giving conventional, individualism-based advice through eight best-selling books and a TV infomercial called "Making Love Work." Yet DeAngelis is on her fifth marriage—one of which was to none other than relationship expert John Gray, author of *Men Are from Mars and Women Are from Venus.* Hello?

As marriage researcher Blaine Fowers says, "Professionals, rather than discovering and describing ultimate truths about marriage, are captivated by contemporary ideals of marriage."[12] But the grim statistics make it painfully clear: When it comes to marriage, the world has got it all wrong. Covenant is the only adequate foundation on which a lasting and fulfilling marriage can be built.

Strangers to Covenant

Two years ago I preached a series of sermons on covenant marriage that also aired on television and radio. The overwhelming response from Christians—including Christian leaders—was, Why haven't we heard about this before? And how can we find out more?

Great questions. Hundreds of books, tapes, and videos have been produced to tell us everything we want to know about marriage—everything, that is, except that marriage is a binding blood covenant. Even in Christian bookstores, where we *can* find some good tools for learning how to tend our marriages and communicate with our spouses, we're hard-pressed to find a single chapter that describes marriage in covenant terms. As a result, the average Christian does not understand the burdens, blessings, and benefits of covenant as it applies to marriage. We are "strangers" to the idea of covenant, to use Paul's term in Ephesians 2:12 (NKJV)—even though covenant is and always has been God's design for marriage.

The good news is that if you're a Christian, you are already in covenant with Christ through your faith in him, and your marriage is a covenant whether you understand it that way or not. But in this case, ignorance is not bliss! The understanding of marriage as a covenant has the potential to revolutionize your relationship with your spouse. It holds the promise of making a bad marriage good and a good marriage great.

In Ephesians 2:12, Paul reminds the Gentiles of their identity before they knew Christ. They were "foreigners [strangers] to the covenants of the promise, without hope and without God in the world." But now, says Paul, "you who once were far away have been brought near through the blood [covenant] of Christ" (v. 13). What the Law with its commandments and regulations could not do, Christ did by his blood covenant, destroying the barrier between Jew and Gentile and making the two one (see Ephesians 2:11–18).

Salvation, Paul explains, is not about keeping the rules and regulations of the law. The law does not work to bring people together. The only way the Gentiles could become one with the Jews, and the only way they could become one with God was through the blood covenant cut by Christ on the cross. It is a basic biblical principle: The only way anyone can become one with God and one with another human being is on the basis of covenant.

Let's take what Paul says and apply it directly to marriage. How can two very different, imperfect, innately selfish people become one—and stay one? Certainly not by viewing their marriage as a legal contract. A contract is all about rules and regulations. It stays in effect until the rules are broken.

A covenant, on the other hand, is all about relationship, and it stays in effect until death. Without a covenant relationship with Christ, Paul says, we are "without hope and without God in the world." Likewise, without a covenant relationship with your spouse, your marriage is *without hope.* Something is bound to happen someday that will severely threaten your relationship; and without an understanding of covenant, without a commitment to die to yourself and put your marriage first, all hope of saving the marriage will be dashed. Once hope is lost, separation and divorce are inevitable.

Without covenant, your marriage is also *without God.* You and your spouse are a company of two. You're a duet, not a trio. When conflicts come—and they will—the two parts will not hold together. But in covenant marriage, there is a deeper commitment, a stronger love, and an abiding hope because God is the senior partner. He is the third part of the trio. By willingly taking covenant's "walk of death," you become one with God; and by his Spirit at work within you, you become one with your mate.

CHANGING OUR VIEW OF MARRIAGE

As I write about marriage and the importance of covenant in the pages that follow, I will try to be straightforward, simple, and practical. I will use real-life examples from my own marriage and from the marriages of couples I've counseled during forty years of ministry. I will also take you directly to

God's inerrant Word so you can see for yourself that the Bible portrays marriage as a sacred and permanent blood covenant, witnessed and protected by God himself.

I'm writing not as an expert but as a fellow struggler who wants to put the brakes on the divorce revolution. But even more than slowing divorce, I want to put the blessing back into marriage! After all, marriage is supposed to be a demonstration and an illustration to the world of what God's covenant relationship with his people is really like. As professor Samuele Bacchiocchi says, "The marriage covenant provides us with a clue to understanding the heart of God. It helps us understand what God has done, is doing, and will do for us. It tells us that God's covenant love is a love 'that will not let us go.'"[13]

I'm convinced that every bride and groom past, present, and future needs a clear understanding of marriage as a covenant relationship. You and I need to know the difference between a legal marriage and a biblical marriage; between a marriage based on contract and a marriage based on the blood covenant of Christ. We need to know that marriage is a covenant to be kept, not a contract to be broken. Divorce is a sin to avoid, not an option to embrace. And in marriage, the best way *out* is *through*.

Changing the way we look at marriage will result in changing the way we look at our mates. When we come to see marriage as a covenant, we are able to love our spouses in ways and at levels we never expected. But we must do more than simply *understand* covenant; we must begin to articulate covenant promises on a regular basis. And more than simply talking the talk, we must walk the walk. By applying the principles of covenant on a consistent basis, our marriages will become stronger, deeper, and more fulfilling than we ever thought possible.

Is that what you want for your marriage? Are you ready to do marriage God's way and learn how you and your spouse can stay together for life? Then read on.

Chapter 1

MARRIAGE AMERICAN STYLE

> The strength of a nation lies
> in the houses of its people.
>
> —*Abraham Lincoln*

The church is beautifully decorated with flowers, greenery, candles, and tulle. Familiar wedding music fills the room with the sounds of tradition and love as the white runner is rolled down the center aisle. The five bridesmaids and five groomsmen are in their places; the minister and the groom stand at the altar, waiting for the bride to appear. Anticipation is in the air as the guests twist and turn in their seats to get the first glimpse of the bride.

Dressed in flowing white, the lovely bride has looked forward to this day since she was a little girl. In her mind, she has rehearsed her walk down the aisle hundreds of times. This is the climax of her dream, a fairy tale coming true. On her father's arm, she steps into the doorway, and the first chords of the "Wedding March" are struck. Slowly she moves toward her waiting husband-to-be, fully expecting to say her vows and live happily ever after.

This is a typical wedding scenario that takes place thousands of times every week in this country. It is the dream and desire of every human being to be known, accepted, and loved by another. And since marriage is the obvious place to get those needs met, more than 90 percent of Americans will marry at least once during their lifetimes.

But what happens after the wedding?

Somebody has said that if the wedding is the dream, marriage is the alarm clock. There is nothing like marriage to wake you up! Unfortunately, marriage in America doesn't live up to its wedding hype. In the ceremony we just described, at least six of the bridesmaids and six of the groomsmen do not believe the marriage they're witnessing will make it. In fact, statistics say that 64 percent of the friends involved in a wedding believe the couple will eventually divorce.[1] And they are right on target; 65 percent of new marriages don't make it. Another 10 percent of couples will stay together for various reasons but will be miserable. In other words, a typical marriage today has a 75-percent failure rate![2]

If airplanes had a 75-percent failure rate, would you let your son or daughter fly? Would you fly? If 75 percent of cars crashed and burned, would you place one of your children inside one of those death traps? Would you get in? No, that would be suicide. Yet people get married every day without premarital counseling, without taking any kind of compatibility test or temperament analysis, and without paying attention to the vows they are about to speak. Does it seem strange to you that it is easier to get a marriage license than it is to get a driver's license? At least with a driver's license, you have to take a competency test!

DIVORCE: A LETHAL WEAPON

"But marriage doesn't kill anyone," you say. No, but what happens when a marriage crashes and burns is worse than death. Divorce is the death of a relationship and carries with it the horrible pain of failure and rejection. Nothing hurts worse. Compounding the deep hurt is the nagging fear that the wound will never heal. And the husband and wife are not the only ones drawn into the suffering. "Divorce," writes Jim Smoke in his book *Growing Through Divorce,* "is the death of a marriage and is usually surrounded by a cast of players that includes the husband and wife as combatants, the children as the mourners, and the lawyers as the funeral directors."[3]

Children, in fact, take some of the hardest hits in a divorce. "Children raised in single-parent households," write Linda Waite and Maggie Gallagher in *The Case for Marriage,* "are, on average, more likely to be poor, to have health problems and psychological disorders, to commit crimes and exhibit other conduct disorders, have somewhat poorer relationships with both family and peers, and as adults eventually get fewer years of education and enjoy less stable marriages and lower occupational statuses than children whose parents got and stayed married."[4] According to Judith Wallerstein, who published the first definitive studies on the impact of divorce on kids, "the children of divorces are twice as likely to drop out of school and three times as likely to conceive a child while still a teenager."[5]

Of course, "The absence of a stable marriage is a risk factor in a child's life, not a prophecy of certain doom," Wallerstein adds. There *is* hope and help available for children who struggle because of the breakup of their parents' marriage. However, she continues, "when parents divorce, they do put their children at risk of long-lasting damage. On average, children lucky enough to have married parents lead emotionally and physically healthier, wealthier, longer, better educated, and more financially successful lives as a result."[6]

Researchers Paul Amato and Alan Booth agree with Wallerstein's assessment. They tracked two thousand married people for fifteen years and determined that "over the long haul, parental divorce led to more problematic relationships between parents and children, increased the likelihood that adult children would divorce themselves, and lowered children's future education and career success…. Low parental marital quality lowers offspring well-being, and parental divorce lowers it even further."

Interestingly, Amato and Booth's data showed that fewer than one-third of divorces involve highly conflicted marriages. Just 30 percent of divorcing spouses reported more than two serious quarrels in the previous month. This means, according to Amato and Booth, that "the majority of divorces occur in low-conflict marriages." In other words, we are experiencing an epidemic of unnecessary divorces in which the children are the major losers! The researchers boldly conclude: "Spending one-third of one's life in a marriage that is less than satisfactory in order to benefit the children—children that parents elected to bring into the world—is not an unreasonable expectation. Especially since 'many people who divorce and remarry find their second marriage is no happier than their first.'"[7]

Cultural Suicide

We must face the fact that divorce and the sweeping pain it causes have become part of everyday life in America. In her book *The Divorce Culture*, Barbara Whitehead writes that divorce "is embedded in our laws and institutions, our manners and mores, our movies and television shows, our novels and children's storybooks, and our closest and most important relationships." With each passing year, she notes, the culture of divorce becomes more deeply entrenched.[8]

This increasing entrenchment does not bode well for our country. According to Census Bureau information, the 1990s saw a marked increase in every kind of household except one: the traditional two-parent family. At the same time, the number of households with "unmarried partners" rose 72 percent. Noting these statistics, Christian commentator Chuck Colson warns, "By any measure, the rise in the number of children being raised in 'unmarried households' is a disaster waiting to happen. For example: A cohabiting boyfriend is thirty times more likely to abuse a child than a father married to the child's mother.... You name the problem, and it's much more likely to occur in single-parent homes and step-families than in two-parent families."[9]

Ralph Steed, the Executive Director of the Christian Coalition, told *USA Today:* "The problem today is that our central institution, the family, is in a state of crisis. One of two marriages ends in divorce; one of three children is born out of wedlock; there are epidemic rates of child abuse. It used to be that no matter how tough times got, the family somehow managed to hang on and stick together. Now that isn't so anymore."[10]

Perhaps we shouldn't be surprised to hear Christian analysts make such statements. But consider this excerpt from a report released in 1995 by the Council on Families in America, a nonpartisan group of scholars and analysts:

> America's divorce revolution has failed. The evidence of failure is overwhelming. The divorce revolution—by which we mean the steady displacement of a marriage culture by a culture of divorce and unwed parenthood—has created terrible hardships for children. It has generated poverty within families. It has burdened us with unsupportable social costs. It has failed to deliver on its promise of greater adult happiness and better relationships between man and woman. We believe it's time to change course. The promises of the divorce revolution proved empty, its consequences devastating for both adults and children. It is time to shift the focus of national attention from divorce to marriage. We must reclaim the ideal of marriage permanence and recognize that out-of-wedlock childbearing does harm.[11]

Wow! What a painfully true and revealing portrait of marriage in America—painted not by conservative preachers or evangelical theologians, but by secular scholars and analysts whose conclusion—that American society would be better off if people got married and stayed married—is right on target!

Listen carefully: *A 75-percent failure rate for marriage in America is totally unacceptable.* If this trend continues, according to the Council on Families in America, it will constitute nothing less than an act of "cultural suicide."[12] America will not survive unless there is a social revolution that reestablishes marriage as the union of a man and a woman in a sacred and permanent relationship.

The Marriage Critics

Of course, not everyone agrees with the council's report and recommendations. Traditional marriage has many critics. As prominent demographer Kingsley Davis points out, "at no time in history, with the possible exception of Imperial Rome, has the institution of marriage been more problematic than it is today."[13]

Some critics believe the institution of marriage is so archaic and unworkable, so restrictive and unliberating, that it should be abandoned altogether. Nancy Saunders, a psychologist who maintains a family practice in Philadelphia, views traditional marriage, with its admonishments against sexual infidelity and its old-fashioned ideals of honor and affection, as "a failing anachronism incapable of binding couples in a lifetime of love and equality." Says Saunders, "Society can no longer support what we think of as marriage." She favors doing away with traditional matrimony and replacing it with individualized contracts that would allow couples to design their own relationships with the full support and recognition of the state.[14]

Not long ago Fox talk-show host Bill O'Reilly told viewers that out of all the controversial things he wrote in his book *The O'Reilly Factor,* he got the most grief over his chapter on marriage—especially his statement that "marriage is vitally important to having a successful life."[15] Both O'Reilly and his guest that day, researcher Maggie Gallagher, agreed that marriage has become a controversial subject in America. The statistically proven facts that married people live longer, lead healthier and happier lives, have better sex more often, and are better off financially seem to be lost on Americans. All lifestyles are equally good, the marriage critics say; there is no one way of living that is better than another.

But the culture is wrong! Marriage is a divine institution, not a mere human invention. Granted, if marriage were no more than a human invention or a social experiment, then different types of marriage could have equal value. But that is not the case. Marriage is God's creation, and that means that God defines what it is. As human beings, we do not have the right to decide the kind of marital relationship we want—although that doesn't stop us from trying.

Recently I read that a London jeweler had designed a wedding ring that is round but not quite closed. It is purposely not the symbolic "unending circle"—implying that the wearer can always get out of the relationship if things become difficult or boring. That such a ring is available in Britain is not surprising, given that two new magazines being published there are devoted to advice on how to dump a spouse. Publishers of *New*

Era and *Divorce* magazine insist that the market is begging for periodicals on divorce! According to a press release, both publications promise to deliver legal and financial advice to help a person survive a marital breakup and keep confidence and bank balance intact—plus fashion and beauty tips to ensure a fruitful search for new love.

Does anyone doubt America is headed down the same road? In her new book *Spiritual Divorce,* popular author Debbie Ford calls divorce "a catalyst for an extraordinary life." She defines a *spiritual divorce* as one in which "we use our divorce to improve our lives, and our experience becomes one of gain rather than loss."[16] With such glorification of divorce, I suppose we shouldn't be surprised that one Los Angeles jewelry store has posted the sign: "We Rent Wedding Rings."

A few weeks ago, while getting dressed for work, I heard a teaser promoting a segment on "divorce ceremonies" that would be aired later on the CBS *Early Show.* So I set my VCR to record the program and watched the tape that evening. It turns out that Phil and Barbara Penningroth were promoting their new book *A Healing Divorce,* in which they claim that a divorce ritual can help end the acrimony between ex-spouses. (I suppose the marriage vows are said in reverse, and "I do" becomes "I won't"? Come on! In my opinion, that is about as realistic as the man who keeps watching the video of his wedding in reverse, just so he can see himself walking out of the church a free man!) I watched in disbelief as CBS ran a video clip from the former Mr. and Mrs. Penningroth's divorce ceremony, which included a heartbreaking marital highlights video and (you guessed it) an exchange of *nonwedding* rings as a symbol of the *reversal* of their commitment.[17] The chilling words, "I release you as my husband" and "I release you as my wife," reverberated in my mind for hours afterward.

I refuse to be conned by "friendly" divorce rhetoric! No ceremony or ritual can erase the hurt, horror, and hell that accompany the breakup of a marriage. I agree that couples who divorce should practice forgiveness and work at being amicable, especially if children are involved. But I resent any effort to honor divorce with a ceremony that mocks marriage by reversing the vows of commitment and "unsealing" them with a ring.

Christians Are Not Immune

Perhaps you're saying at this point, "But what does all of this have to do with me? Surely you are talking about non-Christian marriages, not Christian ones. Only one in a hundred Christian marriages ends in divorce." *Hello?* Wake up! The truth is, the divorce rate in the Bible Belt is higher than in any other area of the country. Baptists have the highest divorce rate of any Christian denomination—29 percent—and are more likely to get a divorce than atheists and agnostics, according to a national survey. "While it may be alarming that born-again Christians are more likely than others to experience a divorce, that pattern has been in place for quite some time," says George Barna, President of Barna Research Group.[18]

Something is radically wrong with this picture! Divorce is just as rampant in the church today as it is in the world. Marital breakdown is not only a serious national problem; it has become a church dilemma. There are few, if any, Christian families that have not been touched directly or indirectly by the hurt and horror of divorce.

HOW DID WE GET HERE?

A quick glance at some well-known trends during the past fifty years is quite alarming:

- People are marrying less and cohabitating more.
- People are waiting longer before they get married.
- The divorce rate has skyrocketed.
- Families are having fewer children.
- Out-of-wedlock births have dramatically increased.
- More families have both parents working outside the home.

- More latchkey children are being raised by television.

- Same-sex marriages are more widely accepted.

What has happened to marriage in America, and how did we get here? "Beginning in the late 1950s," writes Barbara Whitehead in *The Divorce Culture,* "Americans began to change their ideas about the individual's obligation to family and society. Broadly described, this change was away from an ethic of obligation to others and toward an obligation to self."[19] According to author William J. Bennett, modern marriage has been "detached from any objective foundation" and is now generally viewed as "possessing little or no intrinsic worth but as being a means to an end: the end, that is, of 'personal happiness' or 'fulfillment.' In the quest for fulfillment, spouses and children are often looked upon not as persons to be loved and valued for their own sake but as objects to be acquired, enjoyed, and discarded."[20]

During the past fifty years, we have *trivialized* divorce, claiming that it's no big deal; *privatized* divorce, saying that it's no one else's business; and *glorified* divorce, promising freedom and happiness. Lies. All lies! Divorce *is* a big deal, leaving behind it a path of broken hearts and broken lives. It fails to deliver on its promises. According to research, fewer than one out of five divorced women claims to be happy.[21] Divorce is a colossal ripoff! It solves nothing. It merely exchanges one set of problems for another.

Unfortunately, we live in a day when personal rights have won out over responsibilities and wants have won out over needs. We have deified self and humanized God. As a result, our culture is skeptical of any institution, including marriage, that tends to restrict adult behavior. Bowing down to individualism and free choice, we have moved from a marriage culture to a culture of divorce and unwed parenthood. The leading mantra of our day is "Be happy; do your own thing." "Till death do us part" has been replaced by "as long as I'm happy."

Changing Standards

The liberal media has bought into this destructive view of marriage and puts an unholy spin on everything that has to do with marriage or family. As recently as 1970, it was considered too controversial to have a divorced man as the leading character in a weekly television comedy.[22] Today prime-time television appears to be 90/90: 90 percent of couples divorce, and 90 percent of sexual encounters are premarital or extramarital. Didn't someone say, "What we laugh at we soon tolerate, and what we tolerate we soon accept"? Steven Bochco, co-creator of *NYPD Blue,* admits, "There is no such thing as broadcast standards today. It is really what you can get away with. Then it becomes a standard."[23]

Several years ago Microsoft introduced its Windows 95 software with a two-page magazine advertisement featuring two children running with a kite. Smiling brightly, the little girl and boy romped across a deep green field with no fences in sight. Emblazoned on the pages were two words that promised what every human being has desired since Adam and Eve: "No limits!"[24]

I fear that in America today, the only standard is that there are no standards. The only rule is that there are no rules. The fences are down. The limits are gone. The boundaries are fading into the distant past.

Consider the fact that more and more Americans are choosing cohabitation over marriage. "Living in sin," as it used to be called, was illegal in every state before 1970. But today, more than 50 percent of newlyweds live together before tying the knot, compared to 10 percent in 1965. While it may be true that unmarried cohabitators have sex more often than married couples (once more per month), they also experience more cheating by partners, more domestic violence, and more cases of depression. Furthermore, couples who live together before marriage have a much higher divorce rate—almost double—than those who don't.[25] Cohabitation may offer short-term benefits and pleasures, but it is at exorbitant long-term costs. No wonder even secular sociologists are urging young adults to reject the notion that cohabitation is a good preparation for marriage. It is not!

In fact, if sex is a motivating factor, the latest research shows that married sex is better sex. In marriage, sex means something. It is tied to commitment. Authors Waite and Gallagher reason this way: "Every time a married couple make love, they may be reminding each other of the marital promises: to love, honor, cherish, and care for each other—and their children—until death do they part. If the great theme of marriage is union, the counter riff of cohabitation is individualism."[26] For cohabitating couples, there is no commitment, no vow of permanence. Sex takes place on very shaky ground.

A Paradigm Shift

My parents' generation had a strong understanding of marriage as a covenant commitment that should never be broken. It was forever. When they said, "till death do us part," they meant it. It was a given. Circumstances, conflicts, and catastrophes played themselves out, but the marriage went on. As a result, I grew up in an era when the marriages of all my friends' parents went the distance. Divorce was not talked about or tolerated. It was considered a terrible sin.

My generation is an entirely different story. For us, the givens are gone, and the vows are negotiable. Today marriages fall apart simply because somebody gets bored. They fall apart because the chill bumps are gone or somebody feels unfulfilled. They fall apart because money gets tight, responsibilities become burdensome, or freedom seems restricted. The odds that children today will experience the traumatic divorce of their parents are twice as likely as they were a generation ago.

In other words, *in one generation* the selfishness of society has knocked the teeth out of the marriage commitment. Marriage is now convenience-based rather than commitment-based. And the results, as we have already seen, are devastating. My children are touched by divorce on a daily basis.

Many of their friends' parents are divorced. A young schoolteacher told me that every child in her second-grade class was from a broken home. A football coach with one of the best records in college football told me that 60 percent of his players had no dad at home. In one generation, divorce has moved from nonacceptance to acceptance and from last resort to first choice.

If we are going to stop the deterioration of marriage in this country, we have to examine these trends and reverse them. As adults, we must become more responsible and consider more than our own personal happiness. We must reaffirm marriage as a viable institution and reestablish the traditional, biblical concept of marriage as a sacred and permanent covenant. We must acknowledge that every child needs and deserves the love, protection, and provision of both a mother and a father. The two-married-parents family still has no equal when it comes to rearing children.

THE GOD FACTOR

More than any of these things, however, we must acknowledge our need of God. America suffers from a pervasive lack of reverence for moral values and honorable institutions. We mock the sacred and worship the secular. We seek wisdom from no one, trusting only ourselves. As a result, we are a nation that has lost its moral compass, moving at lightning speed on a downward slide that appears to have no bottom. We are as morally and spiritually confused as a termite on a yo-yo!

At the beginning of my marriage seminars, I ask people two questions: Do you have a daily quiet time? And do you pray daily with your spouse? About 10 percent of the participants typically say they have a daily quiet time, and about 5 percent say they pray daily as a couple. What sad but telling statistics! Clearly, we are trying to do marriage without God—and it is not working.

Marriage is designed to be a triangle. The best connection with our mate is meant to be made through our connection with God. "The house of the righteous stands firm," the Bible tells us (Proverbs 12:7). That implies that the house of the unrighteous will fall.

Whatever Became of Sin?

My dad pastored for more than fifty years and built a large library in the process. After his death I went through his books, looking for some classic writings on marriage, but I couldn't find anything. At that point I realized that most marriage books have been written in the past few decades. It may well be that more books have been written on marriage in the past thirty years than in the previous two thousand! The good news is that many of these are wonderful tools that place practical help and spiritual advice at our fingertips. The bad news is that despite this inundation of resources, our marriages are more frail and flawed than ever.

Information alone—even when combined with inspiration—will not fix our marriages. It is not enough to understand the differences between husbands and wives; it is not enough to know each other's love language, temperament, or primary needs. We can read all the latest books and follow all the latest recommendations, but the fact remains that *our marriages reflect our relationship with God.* If we do not walk in covenant with God and choose to die to ourselves, our marriages will not last. When it comes to marriage, it does us no good to know more about "Mars" and "Venus" than about the Garden of Eden and the Cross. Men are from God and women are from God, and the root problem in struggling marriages is as ancient as Adam and Eve: plain old, garden-variety *sin.*

Mind you, divorce is not the unforgivable sin; but as an editorial in the September 2000 issue of *Christianity Today* clearly states, it *is* sin, and we have to face that fact head-on. In "The Christian Divorce Culture," author Barbara Whitehead writes: "To be sure, divorce is sometimes the lesser of two evils, but it nonetheless nullifies God's intent. God joins people together; he doesn't pull them apart." To treat divorce as a therapeutic problem doesn't go far enough, she says. We must raise the stakes and make it clear that "divorce is also a moral issue." We must send "a strong signal that except in the most dreadful circumstances, divorce is not an acceptable alternative for Christians."

Whitehead concludes that if we are going to dismantle the divorce culture, we need to "treat divorce as a morally as well as socially conse-quential event...that creates ripples of moral and social consequences." We also need to drop our euphemisms. "Divorce is more than a 'tragedy,' a 'painful experience,' or 'great loss,'" Whitehead says. "It is the thwarting of God's will. It is something that tears at the fabric of our moral universe."[27]

In his book *To Have and to Hold*, David Atkinson defines divorce as the breaking of a sacred covenant:

> If marriage is understood in covenant terms, then the possibility of divorce must be discussed as the possibility of breaking covenant. The covenant structure of marriage...is not a metaphysical status, which cannot be destroyed; it is rather a moral commitment, which should be honored.... The partners cannot therefore simply be free to dis-solve their marriage at will: The covenant which they make on "get-ting married" is a moral commitment to a permanent relationship and is known as such by others. The tragedy is that marriage relationships do in fact fail, and that society may agree that covenants are in fact broken. When they are, they signal a failure in keeping moral obliga-tion; in these terms, to initiate divorce is not impossible, but sinful.[28]

Today more than ever, problems in marriage do not come from a lack of knowledge but a lack of love. We have full heads but empty hearts. We are controlled by our own lusts rather than God's love. We get with each other, but we don't get with God. We work on our relationships with each other but neglect our relationship with our heavenly Father.

The only solution for the sin problem that started in the Garden of Eden and continues in our marriages today is the Cross of Jesus Christ. Because Jesus died for our sins, we can die to our sins. Underlying every marriage conflict is the sin of selfishness and self-will. The Bible makes clear that self cannot be controlled; it must be conquered. Educated self is still self. Dressed-up self is still self. Street-smart self is still self. Self has to die, and its death has to be confirmed on a continual basis.

To be joined at the heart in covenant involves the process of dying to self. This does not mean a loss of identity, but only the false identity that is based on self-will. It does not mean the loss of freedom, but only the illusion of freedom that is based on selfishness. It is in covenant that our greatest freedom to be who we are is realized.

A Game of High Risk

During summer vacation, our family likes to play a game called Jenga. It is a tower of blocks, and the object is to pull out individual blocks without toppling the tower. Sooner or later, someone always pulls out a block that causes the entire tower to come crashing down.

If society is the tower, then marriage is the basic building block. When it is pulled out, the entire superstructure of home, school, church, government, and business begins to crumble. That's what we're witnessing in America today.

Paul Stevens is right on target when he says, "What is missing in most marriages today is what the Bible identifies as the heart of marriage: a covenant." Says Stevens:

> Everything else is superstructure. Understanding expectations, developing good communication (especially sexual), gaining skills in conflict resolution, discovering appropriate roles or creating new ones, making our marriages fun and free, becoming spiritual friends and sharing a ministry—these are all walls, the roof, the wiring, the plumbing and the heating. They are essential to the whole. But if there is no foundation, they will collapse with the whole being.[29]

As Christians, we must not surrender to the culture. Instead, we must discern the times and reestablish a biblical view of marriage. We must replace our failing, secular view of marriage with its clear and compelling alternative: covenant. We must put God back in his rightful place in our lives and choose to live up to his covenant standards for marriage and family. And we must challenge others in a clear and unmistakable way to do the same.

As well-known marriage expert Gary Smalley says, we must begin to honor the Lord, honor our spouse, and repair the damage when we have dishonored either one! That way, we can build marriages that "last today...tomorrow...and always."[30]

Everything that God does in our lives that is eternally important is done on the basis of covenant. Covenant is the only way we get into heaven, and it's the only way we get heaven into our lives and marriages. I'm convinced that covenant holds the cure for every conflict, the nurturing for every need, the forgiveness for every failure, the blessing for every burden, the triumph for every tear, and the love for every longing. Covenant exchanges a piece of paper for a piece of the rock—the solid rock, Jesus Christ. And absolutely and unequivocally, that's the secret to marriage success.

Recently I read that Bill Bright of Campus Crusade for Christ, James Dobson of Focus on the Family, and Jimmy Draper of Lifeway were going to use their organizations to promote a covenant marriage movement in this country. Dobson, whose *Focus on the Family* radio program reaches three million listeners daily, said that covenant "is an idea whose time has come. We're going to do everything we can to support covenant marriage."[31] Wonderful! It is my prayer that every pastor and church leader across this country will join me in making a concentrated effort to promote covenant marriage and lower the divorce rate in our churches. We can do it, and we must do it.

It is also my prayer that every Christian couple in America will renew their marriage vows and sign the covenant pledge card that Dobson and others are making a key element of the covenant marriage movement:

> Believing
> that marriage
> is a covenant intended by God
> to be a lifelong fruitful relationship
> between a man and a woman,
> we vow to God, each other,
> our families, and our community
> to remain steadfast
> in unconditional love,
> reconciliation, and sexual purity,
> while purposefully growing

> in our covenant marriage
> relationship.

Today you can join this movement by making this pledge with your spouse and declaring with Joshua of old, "as for me and my household, we will serve the LORD" (Joshua 24:15)—regardless of what the rest of the world does. Together with your spouse, say, "We will follow God's original plan for marriage and family. We will forsake selfishness and put our sin on the Cross. By God's grace, we will keep covenant with one another, and neither tiffs, tangles, nor even trysts will change the bottom line. We will be always faithful. We will stay together for life."

A STATISTICAL SNAPSHOT OF MARRIAGE IN AMERICA

The following statistics are those that keep popping up in my research. The work I do with couples leads me to believe they are reliable:

1. The median age for divorce is twenty-eight.

2. Eighteen percent of divorced persons say they are "very happy."

3. Bible-Belt states lead the nation in divorce.

4. One out of two marriages ends in divorce.

5. Sixty-five percent of new marriages will end in divorce.

6. Marriages have a 75-percent failure rate.

7. Christians in mainline churches are divorcing more rapidly than non-Christians (27 percent to 23 percent).

8. Fifty-five percent of children will see their parents divorce before they leave home.

9. Young women whose parents divorced are three times more likely to have an out-of-wedlock child than women whose parents stayed together.

10. Young men and women whose parents divorced are more than twice as likely to cohabitate before marriage.

11. The number of unmarried partners living together increased 72 percent in the last decade.

12. Sixty-two percent of today's "twenty-somethings" believe living together before marriage is a good way to avoid future divorce.

13. Half of currently married stepfamilies with children cohabitated before tying the knot.

14. Grown children of divorced parents are less likely to be happily married and more likely to divorce than children whose parents stayed together.

15. By the year 2010, it is estimated that America will have more stepfamilies than traditional nuclear families.

16. Eighty-one percent of divorced and separated Americans still believe that marriage should be for life.[32]

Chapter 2

WHEN MARRIAGE IS NOT WHAT YOU EXPECTED

If you think that the quality of your happiness is going to change dramatically once you march down the aisle, you are wrong.

—Iris Krasnow

Have you ever wanted to run away from your marriage? To just get in the car and head down the interstate? I have. Perhaps we all have. In the blockbuster movie *Runaway Bride*, Richard Gere and Julia Roberts play the parts of Ike and Maggie. Ike is a newspaper columnist who comes to town to do a story on the bride who keeps running away. Maggie, who works at the local hardware store, has left three men at the altar, making her the talk of the town and the subject of many cruel and insensitive jokes. After a painfully rough start, Ike and Maggie fall in love with each other, and a wedding is planned. But on the wedding day, to the surprise of no one, Maggie runs again. Hurt and humiliated, Ike returns to New York. The story concludes with a contrite Maggie going to New York, where she and Ike are finally married in a private ceremony.

My favorite part of the movie is when Maggie, on her knees, repeats back to Ike the very words he had originally spoken to her: "I guarantee there will be tough times. I guarantee that at some point one or both of us will want to get out of this thing. But I also guarantee that if I don't ask you to be mine, I'll regret it for the rest of my life, because I know that in my heart you are the only one for me."

Simple. Beautiful. Realistic.

Our Story

Leigh and I had been married for six months when we began to question our marriage. It was good, but it was not what we had expected. It was hard, and we had thought it would be easy. It was work, and we had thought it would be a "walk in the park." Leigh and I had seemed so much alike during our courtship; now it was evident that we were as different as a bird and a bulldog. We found we were complete opposites. Things that had attracted us to each other were now pulling us apart.

Leigh is a talkative, sanguine party animal. I am a melancholy choleric who loves quietness and space. In food and fantasies, clothes and calendars, habits and housekeeping, music and moods, we are as opposite as night and day. We came from different backgrounds and entered marriage with different needs and different expectations. Our temperaments clashed. Our expectations went unrealized.

Welcome to the real world of matrimony!

As a thirty-year-old man, I was accustomed to having lots of freedom, and now I couldn't walk down the hall to the bathroom without being asked, "Where are you going?" Close friends who had taken care of me as a bachelor now seemed, in Leigh's mind, to be threats, and I didn't know how to convince her otherwise. For years I had looked forward to marriage as the ultimate experience in happiness and fulfillment, and now, after only six months, I was reeling with anxiety. *What if this is as good as it gets?* I thought to myself. Little did I know Leigh was having similar thoughts and feelings.

I found myself analyzing and attacking my wife. There were things about her I needed to change. I could fix her. Foolishly, I attempted to mess with her uniqueness and make her into another version of me.

Looking back, I think the "angel of duh" must have been hovering over my head. I was so wrong and so clueless.

Fortunately, we knew just enough to get honest with each other and deal with our feelings as well as our fears. With buckets of tears, we peeled back the layers and cautiously revealed ourselves to each other. During our moment of crisis, I began to realize that my wife is a part of me and cannot be separated from me. When she hurts, I hurt. When I hurt her, I hurt myself. If we are one, then our goal must be to make that one as good as it can be.

As a father of two daughters, Shelby and Christy, I know a lot about baggage. Whenever Leigh, the girls, and I would go on a trip together, our car could not hold all the luggage that showed up mysteriously in the hall-way. We would have to ask someone who owned a Suburban to take us to the airport. When Shelby enrolled at Baylor University, she got a room on the fourth floor of the dormitory, and guess who got to carry all the luggage up four flights of stairs?

Yes, I know a lot about baggage.

If a weeklong trip requires a truckload of baggage, how much emotional baggage do you think we collect during the years of our lives? How about tons and tons? Each partner in a marriage brings into that relationship years of mental, emotional, and spiritual baggage. The adjustments required when two unique individuals begin living together as one in marriage present all kinds of opportunities for emotional suitcases to pop open, revealing the good, the bad, and the ugly of our lives. This is seldom a pretty sight.

Leigh and I brought plenty of personal baggage into our marriage. As a result, we have spent nearly thirty years sorting through that baggage and dealing with issues in order to build a solid relationship that is founded on truth and transparency, not fluff and fantasy. After all these years, we still get surprised when a suitcase pops open that neither one of us knew was there. We have not arrived. Our marriage is still a work in progress.

Leigh grew up in a home with an alcoholic father. As you know, the disease of alcoholism poisons the atmosphere in a family and infects every member, coloring every relationship and influencing every action. Life in a home dominated by alcoholism is one of extremes, polarization, and secrecy. Indeed, as someone has said, we are only as sick as our secrets.

Leigh's dad, whom she loved dearly, had littered her entire life with a litany of broken promises, crushing her heart and shattering her dreams. Leigh looked great on the outside, and her happy, bubbling personality fooled everyone around her; but she was sparkle on the outside and sadness on the inside. The tension and trials of marriage brought her feelings of insecurity and insignificance rushing to the surface. The result was "tear city."

I, on the other hand, grew up in a preacher's home, where I felt secure but not significant. My father, a godly man, had grown up in the home of an alcoholic and battled insecurity all his life. He did not know how to express love. I waited nearly fifty years to hear him tell me that he loved me. Oh, he always loved me; but he could not say it, and I desperately needed to hear it. Everyone does. Adding to my feeling of insignificance was my dad's embrace of a common lie among preachers in his day that said, "If a preacher will take care of the church, God will take care of the preacher's children." Consequently, I grew up believing that Dad's job was more important to him than his family.

Please hear what I am saying. I grew up in a wonderful Christian home with wonderful parents. My father was my mentor and my friend. But I still came into my marriage with enough baggage to ruin our relationship if I could not deal honestly with my own insecurities and hang-ups.

That night, in the bedroom of our first home on Madrid Street in Hurst, Texas, Leigh and I made the greatest decision we've made in twenty-seven years of marriage. We acknowledged our baggage—our fears, our insecurities, and our hang-ups, as well as our hopes and dreams—and decided to work on our marriage every day for the rest of our lives. We agreed to do whatever it would take to make our marriage everything we had dreamed it could be. We began the process of building a body-to-body, heart-to-heart, mind-to-mind, soul-to-soul, covenant marriage. After all, we had said our vows before God, family, and friends, and we meant them. We both believed that if we would keep our vows, our vows would keep us over the long term.

It has not been easy, but it has been very rewarding. And we're still working on it.

BEYOND THE FAIRY TALE

Remember the line that always seemed to end the stories we read as children: "And they lived happily ever after"? Well, we didn't! You won't! Outside of fairy tales, nobody lives happily ever after. The best of marriages requires hard work—no short cuts, no exceptions. Marriage is a 24/7 commitment. To live happily with another person is a daily process that demands unselfishness and calls for unconditional love. Granted, some marriages require more work than others, but every marriage is intended to be a continual work in progress.

The good news is that God designed marriage to be both happy and holy—to be the deepest and most fulfilling relationship on earth. And it can be. But how? What's the secret?

In his explanation of Christian marriage in Ephesians chapter 5, the apostle Paul concludes that marriage is a "profound mystery" (v. 32). He implies that there is a secret to marriage that is unavailable to the natural mind but comes only through divine revelation. I believe that "mystery" or secret is covenant. When two people join hands and hearts in holy matrimony at God's altar, they become one in a way that is as mysterious as it is majestic. It is beyond human explanation. It is something that God does. Then we as couples spend the rest of our lives working out the practical application of that mysterious oneness.

There are some things you need to know about your spouse that you cannot know without God's help. God wants to show you what your spouse really needs and help you understand how your spouse really feels. He desires to enlighten and empower you in the process of building a covenant relationship. He is, and always will be, your greatest source of covenant truth. The secret to the marriage of your dreams is in the heart of God and revealed through his word to you.

God designed marriage as a covenant relationship patterned after his covenant with Israel and Christ's covenant with his bride, the church. It is his desire that the home of covenant marriage partners be a foretaste of heaven. For covenant breakers, however, home can quickly become more like hell than heaven. Oftentimes a husband or wife will say to me, "My marriage is a living hell." I'm sure they mean it. There is no relationship on earth that can bring you more grief or more joy than the relationship with your spouse! Marriage is never neutral. It has the potential to bring you your greatest hurt or your greatest happiness.

America is a contract-oriented society. We like contracts because they allow us to bail out of a business deal or a relationship if things turn sour. Well, it may be fine to live by contract, but we must love by covenant. (I discuss the difference between contract and covenant relationships in greater detail in chapter 6.) Covenant is the way God has chosen to work in our lives and operate his kingdom. It is by covenant, and only by covenant, that you and I are found worthy to be a part of God's eternal kingdom. And it is by divine design that life's two most intimate and sacred relationships—the one with our heavenly Father and the one with an earthly spouse—are entered into and maintained on the basis of covenant. Covenant is the skeleton on which marriage is fleshed out. It is unbreakable. Unshakable.

Based on an oath spoken between two parties, covenant is a blood bond for life. It says that no matter what happens, for better or for worse, nobody leaves the relationship. When we enter a covenant marriage, we say, "I am yours by covenant, and you are mine by covenant, and that means neither one of us is going anywhere. Nobody leaves. We belong to each other."

Being a Promise Keeper

My daughters are forever wrapped around my heart. It would be easy to die for them, but it has been a great deal harder to live a godly life before them at all times and in all ways. I'm certainly not perfect. I've made many mistakes. But I've never stopped working at trying to be a good dad. My girls know that I love them and that they, along with their mom, are my number-one priority.

One very important thing I've always tried to do with my wife and girls is to keep my promises to them. The psalmist says this about a good man: He "keeps his oath even when it hurts" (Psalm 15:4). In other words, what he says he will do, he will do, even when it's inconvenient or painful. He keeps his commitments. To be such a man is a worthy goal that I strive for, even though I blow it sometimes. What would it profit me if I built the biggest church in the world and lost my own family? Nothing!

In 1993 my father died from cancer. I miss him so much. Even as I write these words, memories flood my mind and my eyes fill with tears. Dad pastored churches for fifty years; and not even cancer, in all its pain and ugliness, could dampen his unabated zeal for God. He prayed and praised God right up until his death. I was with him that final week of his life, and I was able to thank him for always being there for us—for staying faithful to God, to Mom, and to his kids. Dad was a promise keeper, and he finished strong.

On the night before he died, I did one of the hardest things I have ever had to do. I left Dad's side and drove the two-hundred-plus miles from Dallas, Texas, to my home in Louisiana. It was evident that Dad didn't have much longer to live, but I had made a promise to my daughters that whenever they were involved in something and needed me, I would be there. Christy was in a high-school beauty pageant, and I knew she needed her number one cheerleader—even though she told me it would be fine for me to stay in Dallas. I got to the school in time to catch Christy's eye, and when I saw her smile, I knew that I had made the right decision. Oh, the joy of a promise kept!

Immediately following the pageant, I drove back to Dallas and was with Dad when he passed away the next day. He left us with a big smile, signaling that all was well and that he was in the presence of the one who has never broken a promise—Jesus the Christ.

Dad's death so impacted my life that I made a number of deep commitments and lifestyles changes at that time. Leigh and I exchanged our conventional marriage license for a covenant marriage license (I'll explain more about this in the next chapter) and publicly exchanged covenant vows in a beautiful ceremony in our church. We made a decision to devote a significant portion of our time to helping other couples understand the importance of covenant marriage. We deepened our involvement in a restoration ministry for those for whom broken promises have resulted in broken hearts, broken marriages, and broken lives. I know that I can't fill my dad's shoes, but I can walk in his tracks. Like Dad, I want to be a promise keeper and finish well.

Let me suggest to you seven promises I have made to Leigh that you can make to your spouse:

1. I promise that I will always love you.

2. I promise that, after God, you will always be my first priority.

3. I promise that I am forever committed to this relationship and will always work on this marriage.

4. I promise that I will always forgive you and work through conflicts.

5. I promise that I will always be faithful to you.

6. I promise that I will always be truthful with you.

7. I promise that I will always be there for you.

The Importance of Renewal

These seven promises need to be renewed on a consistent basis. Like hugs, genuine covenant promises are hard to overdo! Perhaps someone might object, "I said my marriage vows once. That should be good enough." But regular renewal has always been an important part of the covenant process.

In ancient Israel, the covenant between God and his people was frequently renewed and the vows of covenant were often repeated. In one example, revival occurred in Israel after Athaliah, the idolatrous Judean queen, was dethroned. We read in 2 Kings 11:17 that Jehoiada, the priest, "then made a covenant between the LORD and the king and people that they would be the LORD'S people." Notice the result in verse 18: "All the people of the land went to the temple of Baal and tore it down. They smashed the altars and idols to pieces and killed…the priest of Baal." Israel already had a covenant with God, but that covenant had been violated. Renewing the covenant under Jehoiada brought revival to the nation.

The marriage covenant should be renewed from time to time, just as God and Israel periodically renewed their covenant. The celebration of a wedding anniversary, for example, is a great time for spouses to repeat covenant vows to each other. Covenant renewal will pay rich dividends and go far in helping a marriage last a lifetime.

A couple of years ago, Leigh and I flew to Atlanta, Georgia, where I performed a wedding ceremony for Johnny and Janet Hunt. Johnny, one of America's outstanding pastors, has been married to Janet for twenty-five years, and they have two beautiful, godly daughters. So why another ceremony? Somehow the congregation learned that Janet had always wanted a church wedding. So the people surprised Johnny and Janet with a full-blown wedding that included a couple thousand guests, a wedding gown, flowers, candles, a reception with the biggest wedding cake I've ever seen, a limousine, and a honeymoon trip to a faraway island. It was incredible!

Yet the beauty of that elaborate wedding paled in significance to the beauty of Johnny and Janet's precious renewal of covenant love. It was their hearts' desire to renew their vows and reaffirm their commitment to each other "until death do they part." Now, that is something to celebrate!

THE COVENANT GUARANTEE

As Leigh and I found out long ago, marital happiness doesn't come with a guarantee. Recently I ran across an ad in a magazine for Lipton's Garlic Mushroom Soup Mix. At the top of the page was a recipe for marriage:

1	Lifelong Commitment
16	Toilet Seat Lessons
1	Hour Daily Cuddling
5	Annual Reminders about Anniversary
21,000	Home-cooked Dinners
30,000	Shirts Folded
19	Subtle Hints about Breath
2	Pieces Lingerie
3	Self-Help Books

Blend ingredients, keeping expectations at low. Let simmer fifty-plus years. Bring to a boil when necessary. *Results may vary.*

At the bottom of the page was a second recipe, this one for Grilled Garlic Chicken using Lipton's soup mix. At the end of the directions was the promise: *Results guaranteed.*[1]

Sounds like Lipton is confident about its soup mix—but not as confident as I am about covenant marriage. The closest thing to a lifetime guarantee for love and marriage is a commitment to a long-term covenant that is irrevocable. Within the parameters of covenant, we have our greatest opportunity to find the love and happiness that we long for in a marriage relationship.

Years ago Leigh and I took advantage of that opportunity, and we're glad we did. How about you?

Chapter 3

MAKING "I DO" HARDER TO UNDO

What the caterpillar calls the end of the world,
the Master calls the butterfly.

—Richard Bach

The First Baptist Church in Bossier City, Louisiana, was beautifully decorated with flowers, greenery, and white tulle. In quiet anticipation, the packed church watched as the candles on the altar were lit one by one, marking the beginning of the ceremony. The reverent silence was broken as the organ sounded the first chords of "The Wedding March," and the congregation stood and turned. The bride and groom walked slowly down the long center aisle—followed by 268 other couples.

A new law had been enacted in Louisiana, and now this couple and a few hundred more were exercising their option to enter a "covenant marriage." The church had actually been decorated the evening before for the wedding of my daughter, Christy, and her fiancé, Ky Faciane—a covenant ceremony that I had written for them based upon the new law. Now these previously married couples were using the perfectly prepared setting to "upgrade" their marriages to the same covenant level.

TILTING THE BALANCE

Under present law in most states, marriage is little more than a non-binding contract between two people, sustained by mutual emotional feelings and easily terminated through "no-fault" divorce when those feelings turn sour. Sadly, thousands are taking advantage of this no-fault option every day. Rather than facing their problems together and working to salvage their relationships, couples are taking the easy way out. In the process, hearts are being broken, homes are being destroyed, and the collateral damage is rippling out into society as a whole.

Fortunately my home state of Louisiana, under the leadership of Representative Tony Perkins, has taken the initiative to change the law—to tilt the balance in favor of marriage and family and away from divorce and dysfunction. Rather than accepting a conventional marriage contract, an engaged couple in Louisiana can now choose to enter into a covenant that, by law, makes it harder to wiggle out of marriage down the road. Likewise, already-married couples can choose to upgrade their standard marriage license to a covenant one.

Arizona has passed similar legislation, and at this writing, at least thirty other states are considering ways to make the entrance and exit requirements of marriage more difficult. In Florida, a new law compels high schools to offer classes that teach marriage and relationship skills. And some southern states are hiring psychologists in an effort to lower divorce rates. "Some type of divorce reform will probably exist in almost every state in the next ten to fifteen years," estimates Steven Nock, a University of Virginia sociologist who is studying the effects of Louisiana's new law.[1]

The Louisiana Covenant Marriage Act that went into effect on August 15, 1997, requires this covenant pledge:

> We do solemnly declare that marriage is a covenant between a man and woman who agree to live together as husband and wife for so long as they both may live. We understand the nature, purpose, and responsibilities of marriage. We have read the Covenant Marriage Act, and we understand that a Covenant Marriage is for life. If we experience marital difficulties, we commit ourselves to make all reasonable efforts to preserve our marriage, including marital counseling.
>
> With full knowledge of what this commitment means, we do hereby declare that our marriage will be bound by Louisiana law on

Covenant Marriage, and we renew our promise to love, honor and care for one another as husband and wife for the rest of our lives.

Under the Covenant Marriage Act, a couple can be granted a divorce only if one partner commits adultery, abandons the family for a year, physically or sexually abuses the other spouse or a child, or gets sent to prison for a felony. Divorce can also be granted if the couple has been informally separated for at least one year, or eighteen months if a child is involved.

No Fault? No Way!

The goal of the new law is to strengthen marriage by reversing the no-fault divorce revolution that has swept through America since the late 1960s, resulting in a doubling of the national divorce rate. Psychologist Blaine Fowers explains:

> The central premise of "no fault" divorce is that no grounds are necessary for divorce; all that is required is that one spouse assert the irremediable breakdown of the marriage. Before "no fault" divorce, the marriage contract had force, which meant that one had a "right" to remain married; now spouses have a "right" to be divorced. This change greatly facilitates divorce because it takes power away from the spouse who wants to stay married and shifts it to the spouse who wants to split up. Thus "no fault" law marks the complete triumph of individual liberty in divorce regulation. Divorce has become an entirely personal decision.[2]

The widespread adoption of no-fault divorce has made getting a divorce so easy that Maggie Gallagher calls marriage "the least binding of all legal contracts."[3] And apparently, what God has joined together in holy matrimony, man will separate for less than the price of a good suit of clothes. Today our no-fault laws make divorce so easy that some lawyers advertise complete divorce packages for less than one hundred dollars.

But in reality there is no such thing as no-fault divorce. It's an illusion. It has become a part of the problem of marital breakup rather than a part of the solution, because it promotes a "test drive" approach to marriage; the owner can easily trade in for a different model somewhere down the road. No-fault divorce treats marital unhappiness like a random illness. The flu happens; it's no one's fault. Take two aspirin, drink plenty of fluids, and call your lawyer in the morning. In the book *Surrendering to Marriage,* Iris Krasnow writes, "People make the mistake of thinking divorce is a cure. But marriage isn't a disease. Marriage is a relationship. If you aren't good at relationships, divorce doesn't make you better." Says Krasnow, "Seventy-five percent of those who divorce run out and marry again. These people need to switch behaviors, not partners."[4]

No-fault divorce is an oxymoron. It is just as absurd to promote no-fault divorce as it is to promote no-fault murder or no-fault theft. Divorce is always somebody's fault, and couples must learn to deal with the issue of fault in realistic and healthy ways. Divorce law must include the possibility of objective fault and identify certain kinds of behavior as unacceptable (for example, the four As: adultery, abuse, abandonment, and addiction). But the law must not make divorce an easy option.

In Great Britain, entrepreneur Richard Cohen has created a Web site called Desktop Lawyer that allows a couple to get a divorce with a few clicks of a mouse (and a fee of $150). In the site's first week, more than three hundred Brits clicked their way to a cheap, quick, and easy divorce. Commenting on the potential of "desktop divorce," Christian analyst Chuck Colson nails it when he says:

> What the West needs is not easier divorce but harder divorce. You see, society can't make people be faithful to their spouses; that is a matter of the heart. But what it *can* do is make it harder to be unfaithful. Society can erect legal and social structures that encourage virtue and discourage vice. People who won't be virtuous out of principle may sometimes be induced to do the virtuous thing merely because it is easier and less troublesome. That is why there was wisdom in the old system that made divorce difficult, expensive, and inconvenient.[5]

Sticking It Out

Many counselors acknowledge that "no-fault" laws have, in fact, made it harder to hold couples together, since spouses find it easier to abandon marriage than to work through difficult issues. The easier it is to get out of a marriage, the easier it is to give up on it.

But according to authors Linda Waite and Maggie Gallagher, "while we tend to talk about bad marriages as if they were permanent things, research suggests that marriage is a dynamic relationship: Even the unhappiest of couples who grimly stick it out for the sake of the children can find happiness together a few years down the road." Based on their analysis, 86 percent of unhappily married people who stick it out find that their marriages are happier five years later. Most say they have become very happy indeed. In fact, the survey found that the worst marriages showed the most dramatic turnarounds: Seventy-seven percent of those couples who rated their marriage as "very unhappy" in the late 1980s said that the same marriage five years later was either "very happy" or "quite happy."[6] Permanent marital unhappiness is surprisingly rare among those couples who hang in there!

Take Ted and Tracie for example. The couple had been married for several years, had two small children, and were serving on a church staff when the bottom suddenly fell out of their lives. The secret was revealed that Ted had broken the marriage covenant—not once, but many times and with several women. He was a sex addict. The family was devastated, and Ted lost his job with the church. Sometime later I met Ted at a retreat. He told me his story, and as I listened, I saw two tiny flickers of light in his sea of darkness. The first was that Ted appeared to be broken and wanted help; the second was that Tracie was willing to try to forgive, pick up the pieces, and go forward. After months of counseling and participation in a support group, coupled with Ted's repentance and reconciliation with God and with Tracie, the two are now building a strong covenant marriage. They have chosen to love each other again and to work on their marriage from this point forward. Their prognosis looks good. Thank God that Tracie made the choice to stick it out, keep her part of the covenant, and stand by her man!

We need to find more ways to encourage married couples to stay married. Their own happiness—not to mention the happiness and stability of their children and of society as a whole—depends on it. More and more researchers acknowledge that covenant marriage agreements, along with a wider use of premarital counseling and tighter divorce laws, could very well put the brakes on family breakups. I'm glad that Louisiana's Covenant Marriage Act is helping to lead the way.

BACK TO THE WEDDING

Let's go back to that special Sunday morning after my daughter Christy's wedding, when 268 married couples walked down the aisle of our church to say covenant vows based on Louisiana's covenant marriage law. Many of the couples had been married for years—even decades. Some had grandchildren. They stood in long lines to sign legally binding agreements making it more difficult for them to get out of their marriages. Witnessed by a state notary, they signed a covenant to do whatever it would take to preserve their marriages until death.

After the mass ceremony, we threw a reception. I don't think I have ever seen our church so filled with happiness and love—true, covenant love. To be honest, I had originally expected only a handful of couples to show up that morning. I was pleasantly overwhelmed when hundreds decided to participate.

The huge success of that event made me realize that people want help with their marriages. They want marriage to be harder to exit. They want support. And I'm not just talking about older folks or those who are already married and know how hard marriage can be. Studies show that Generation Xers (people in their twenties) are the most marriage-oriented of all age groups and are the least likely to endorse divorce. According to a study by University of Chicago researchers, they believe in marrying one person for life.[7] Yes! Let the pendulum swing back in the direction of marriage!

Don't Leave God at the Altar

Louisiana's Covenant Marriage Act is an illustration of the legal system working with civil society to establish a standard that confronts a couple with the seriousness and sacredness of their marriage commitment. Such confrontation, says *Policy Review* editor Joe Loconte, "could help rewrite our nation's most troubling cultural tale."[8]

The law has its limits, however. It can only make a marriage relationship harder to enter and exit in a legal sense. What the law cannot legislate is the spiritual aspect of covenant—the aspect that acknowledges God as the inventor of marriage and the power source behind its success. Ultimately a true covenant marriage can occur only between those partners who have a personal relationship with God and who trust in his ability to help them work through their problems, pressures, and pitfalls. In a covenant marriage between Christians, God isn't left at the altar. In the words of Martha Williamson, "If you invite God to your wedding, he'll want to stay for the marriage."[9]

In the state of Louisiana, it is not necessary to be a Christian in order to get a covenant marriage license. As long as the state requirements are met, any couple can get a covenant license and call their marriage a covenant marriage. That simply means that their marriage will have more legal accountability than a traditional one, and that's good; but it is a long way from being a covenant marriage in the biblical sense. A genuine covenant marriage is always a threesome: God, husband, and wife. God is bound by his word to bless, fight for, and protect the marriage that is entered into on the basis of a covenant pledge.

God takes seriously the pledges we make before him. When Nehemiah was rebuilding the wall around Jerusalem, he encountered internal opposition from Jews who were taking advantage of other Jews. He immediately ordered them to stop what they were doing, correct the problem, and make a public vow before God. Nehemiah writes:

> Then I summoned the priests and made the nobles and officials take an oath [or pledge] to do what they had promised. I also shook out the folds of my robe and said, "In this way may God shake out of his house and possessions every man who does not keep this promise. So may such a man be shaken out and emptied!" (Nehemiah 5:12–13)

Would you want to get "shaken out and emptied" by God? I know I wouldn't! But that's a pretty good description of what happens when Christians break the marriage vows they've spoken before God. During my years of marriage counseling, I've heard all kinds of horror stories from spouses who took advantage of one another, ignored their promises, and found themselves being shaken and emptied. If only they would have heeded the advice to stop what they were doing, correct the problem, and publicly reaffirm their marriage vows before the Lord!

A Three-Stranded Cord

Having two daughters, I know about braiding hair. It's difficult. I can't do it; the braid falls apart every time. My girls never mastered it either. My wife, however, can braid hair, and she often did it for our girls and for their friends as they grew up. The kids loved for Leigh to braid their hair because she knew how to weave the three strands together in a tight hold that looked beautiful and actually stayed in place.

I've been told that it is the third strand of the braid that holds the other two strands together. The same is true with rope. In fact, a three-stranded rope is stronger than a rope with two, four, or five strands. Why? Because with three strands, each part is constantly touching the other two, forming the strongest and tightest bond possible. In covenant marriage, God is that critical third strand; and by weaving a husband and wife into a tight relationship with him, the three strands always touch each other, making the bond as strong as it can possibly be.

As Solomon, the wisest man to ever live, said, "A cord of three strands is not quickly broken" (Ecclesiastes 4:12). Covenant marriage, as divinely planned, is a binding together of three persons: a man, a woman, and Almighty God. As long as the couple stays in close contact with each other and with God, they have an unbreakable bond.

"I Won't" until "I Do"

Many young people during the last decade or so have learned the value of making and keeping a covenant pledge. I remember the "True Love Waits" commitment service we held at our church on Valentine's Day, 1993. Along with a large number of students and parents, Leigh and I stood at the altar with our daughter, Shelby. On that night Shelby and the other students made a pledge to save themselves for the one person God had for them to marry by abstaining from sex until their wedding night. We placed a "virginity ring" on our daughter's finger as a symbol of her pledge.

Popular culture embraces promiscuity and exhorts teenagers to abandon their virginity with barely a second thought. Yet hundreds of thousands of teenagers and young adults across the world have held ceremonies and signed covenant cards vowing to stay sexually pure until marriage through the "True Love Waits" program, sponsored by the Southern Baptist Convention. The program continues to be a huge success, spreading into seventy-six nations around the world with no signs of slowing down. As a father of daughters, I cannot say enough good things about this program. Every church and every family should embrace it.

Research has proven the effectiveness of virginity pledges in modifying teen sexual behavior. Some time ago ninety thousand teenagers were surveyed in a federally funded study called "Add Health," the most comprehensive investigation of adolescent health in history. Perhaps the biggest surprise to secular researchers was the finding that an adolescent pledge to "just say no" is three times more effective than any other effort in helping students remain sexually pure until marriage.[10] No secular psychologist, humanistic school counselor, or liberal social worker can ignore such overwhelming data.

On January 24, 2000, our Shelby entered into a marriage covenant with Jon Koch, the young man God had prepared for her and the one for whom she had saved herself. To our great surprise and joy, we learned that Jon had also participated in a "True Love Waits" service on Valentine's Day 1993, making a pledge to save himself for the young lady God would one day bring into his life—Shelby. Imagine, two students who had never met, who lived in different states, made the same vow on the same day, and God brought them together seven years later as husband and wife. Incredible!

Their wedding was beautiful, glorious, and sacred. Happy tears filled the room as those of us in attendance realized we were standing on holy ground. The bride and groom were relaxed. Peaceful. Confident. Joyful. They stood at the altar with no heavy baggage and no regrets. A sweet spirit filled the air as we all felt a part of the miracle of love and marriage as God designed it to be. True love does wait!

Just as a virginity pledge helps students stay pure until marriage, a covenant marriage pledge helps spouses stay faithful throughout marriage. Recent studies show that those couples who enter marriage with the understanding that it is a binding commitment—"until death do us part"—are able to manage inevitable conflicts and successfully handle pit-falls and problems that otherwise would precipitate a divorce. Statistically speaking, couples whose marriages are based on covenant are at least three times less likely to get a divorce than couples whose marriages are based merely on a conventional legal contract.[11]

REVERSING THE REVOLUTION

Many critics have called for a new paradigm for marriage in this coun-try. But marriage has not failed as an institution; we have failed marriage by giving in to the culture and promoting selfishness over sacrifice. Marriage, as God created it, is still the best way to experience love and companion-ship, create a family, and raise children. And understanding marriage in covenant terms is by far the greatest potential deterrent to divorce.

Just ask Sharan and Guy Samuel of Baton Rouge, Louisiana. Sharan and Guy had been married thirteen years when they decided to upgrade to a covenant marriage under the state's Covenant Marriage Act. Up to that point, Sharon says, "I wouldn't say we were happily married. I wouldn't say we were unhappily married. We were just married." They struggled with all the normal pressures you'd expect in a marriage between two unique individuals holding down two jobs and raising two kids. When the stress mounted, they fought—sometimes a lot.

A few years after their covenant marriage ceremony, Guy lost his job; and as the inevitable pressures on the household escalated, so did the fighting. Finally, tired and frustrated and seeing no other way out, Sharan decided to pursue a divorce. There was one problem, however. In Louisiana, a conventional marriage could be dissolved in six months. But hers was a covenant marriage, which meant that she would have to wait three times as long and get counseling during the waiting period.

"I told my pastor I was very angry about signing the covenant marriage," Sharan remembers. "At the time I felt trapped…. Things were hopeless, I felt, and the law was making us needlessly suffer."

Settling in for the long haul, she agreed to start individual counseling. Guy did too. And amazingly, over time, both began to heal, to change, and to get stronger. Ten months later—four months after a conventional divorce would have been granted—they realized they wanted to get back together. Today, Sharan and Guy have a happier marriage then ever before.

Sharan admits that without covenant marriage's stringent requirements, she would be divorced right now, living a very different and much more difficult life. "We would not be in our house, my children would be bouncing back and forth from home to home, and I'm afraid we would still be very angry; we would not have taken the time to resolve that, and I would probably be feeling a lot of regret," she says.[12]

As Sharan and Guy learned, covenant is the secret to discovering the very best that marriage has to offer. Ultimately, covenant marriage does more than make two people happy; it makes them holy. Today's couples don't need an easy out; they need an understanding of covenant, plus the skills to flesh out their commitment over the long term. I'm convinced we can start reversing the divorce revolution in America—and covenant marriage is the key.

Chapter 4

WHAT IS COVENANT?

*More sure than any mountain is the fulfillment
of every covenant promise.*

—Andrew Murray

It was in a dark and dirty prison along the coast of Florida that I saw covenant fleshed out before my very eyes. I admit I felt a little uncomfortable passing through the heavy steel doors that clanged shut and locked behind me. Still I pressed on, knowing that I was there as a messenger for God. As I walked down a long corridor with cells on both sides, I had ample opportunity to look into the empty faces of hardened criminals. The place smelled like sin. It reeked with hopelessness. At times I would smile and say "good morning" to the faces staring out at me, but there was no response. How could any morning be good in this hellish place?

Finally I arrived at the designated room where I was scheduled to speak to about two hundred inmates who were interested enough to come. To my surprise one of the prisoners immediately walked to the front, picked up an electric guitar, and began to sing "Amazing Grace." He sang as if he were totally amazed that God's grace would be offered to him. Tears moistened my eyes as I realized I was standing on holy ground. Seizing the moment, I spoke to the prisoners about God's wonderful grace and unconditional love. Moving quickly to the gospel, I began to talk about Jesus; and every time I said that name, big smiles would break out on the faces of a few men seated to my right. Baffled and blessed by those smiles, I said the name "Jesus" several times—just to see the smiles again. Even now I can't find words to adequately describe the contrast between those beautiful smiles and the unhappy faces of the rest of the inmates who had messed up their minds, bodies, and souls in ways too numerous and too horrible to mention.

Suddenly Calvary came to mind. I could see the criminal hanging on a cross beside Jesus. I could hear him say, "Remember me," to which Jesus replied, "Today you will be with me in paradise." Can you see it? Can you see the smile on the face of that criminal as he engages the unconditional love and acceptance of Jesus, the Savior of the world? It is a smile made possible by covenant—the covenant between Christ and all those who choose to believe in his name.

When the prison service concluded, those inmates who had smiled at the mention of Jesus' name approached me. They shared how they had come to know Jesus Christ in prison. Inside those dark walls, they had discovered a covenant of grace strong enough to break the shackles of their sin and set them free forever. Even though they were in prison, they were free and happy for the first time in their lives. It was covenant that made them smile. Hallelujah! These men had discovered an irrevocable covenant that brought them strength they had never before realized, security they had never before known, satisfaction they had never before experienced, and a significance they had never dreamed possible. It makes me smile just to think of it!

THE SOURCE OF COVENANT

Even though the word *covenant* is used more than three hundred times in the Old Testament, it is not strictly a biblical term. According to *Webster's Dictionary,* a covenant is "an agreement, usually formal, between two or more persons to do or not do something specified." For thousands of years, the practice of making and keeping covenants has been used by civilized societies to promote understanding, resolve conflicts, and provide parameters for relationships.

If we were to trace the concept of covenant back to its source, however, we would eventually come to God. Covenant was in the heart of God from the day he created mankind. It's a term that describes God's unique relationship with his people and carries with it the guarantee of all the benefits and blessings of that relationship. Covenant is how he chose from the beginning of time to demonstrate his love and his desire to fellowship with his creation.

The truth is, our God is a covenant God, the Bible is a covenant book, and we are a covenant people. As Moses told the Israelites in Deuteronomy 7:9: "Know therefore that the LORD your God is God; he is the faithful God, keeping his covenant of love to a thousand generations of those who love him and keep his commands."

Covenant is the foundational concept upon which all Scripture is built. "The concept of covenant, like a crimson thread, is woven throughout God's Word from Genesis to Revelation," says Bible teacher Kay Arthur.[1] The Old and New Testaments are not two separate books but one book telling one story. The Old Testament told us what was going to happen through Christ; the New Testament tells us that it *did* happen exactly as promised—thus proving beyond all doubt that God is the perfect promise keeper who fulfills every covenant he makes.

Indeed, the Bible teaches that God has fashioned a covenant with us that can be summed up in one promise: "I will be your God, and you will be my people" (see Exodus 6:7; Jeremiah 7:23; Ezekiel 36:28). It is an irrevocable covenant; as God says in Psalm 89:34, "I will not violate my covenant or alter what my lips have uttered." God's covenant power toward us is unlimited. His covenant salvation is eternal. God saves us, indwells us by his Holy Spirit, and guarantees us that we are a part of his eternal family—all based on his irrevocable covenant.

An ancient rabbi once said, "If a thousand angels reported to God about you, but only one angel among them had anything good to say, that is the angel God would listen to." What a wonderful illustration of God's covenant love and, as Martha Williamson says in her book *Invite God to the Wedding,* "his eternal desire that we should come to him anytime, no matter how long we've been away."[2] Once we understand and engage the truth that God is a covenant God, we can begin to experience a satisfaction, a security, a significance, and a strength that we have never known before. Our lives can be changed forever.

God takes the covenants he makes with us very seriously. In fact, covenants are so significant to God that the Bible often shows them being inaugurated by blood. The Hebrew word for covenant is *beriyth,* which means "a solemn agreement with binding force." Though its etymology is uncertain, *beriyth* may come from a root word meaning "to cut." The connotation is that of a cutting of the flesh causing blood to flow out; thus, the Hebrew expression speaks of "cutting covenant."

Dannah Gresh, in *And the Bride Wore White,* explains that the Scriptures identify four blood covenants:

> Before Christ came, God was honored and people showed repentance by the blood sacrifice of animals. And when God made his covenant with Abraham, he requested pain and blood through circumcision as an act of good faith on Abraham's part. By cutting away his foreskin, he demonstrated that his heart had gone through a change. Those are the first two blood covenants. The third and most magnificent is the atoning blood of Jesus, which is God's covenant to us that if we are willing to confess our sins, he is willing to erase them.[3]

The first two blood covenants were fulfilled by Jesus in the third, and they are no longer required today (although circumcision is widely practiced for health reasons). But "there is one left that…God still asks that we practice today. My friend, it is your sexuality. Your sexual union is a blood covenant between you, your husband (wife), and God. God asks us to prize our virginity and hold it up as our only blood covenant to him."[4]

Marriage is a blood covenant that we still enter into today. While the "blood" part may be figurative, marriage nevertheless mirrors the other covenants in its call for sacrifice and dying to self. You and I cannot have a covenant marriage—the kind of marriage God designed for us—without willingly taking the "walk of death" that puts the needs and best interests of a spouse above our own.

THE COVENANTS OF GOD

We'll talk more about the sacrificial aspect of marriage in a later chapter. For now I want to take a closer look at the various covenants God has made with his people over time. It is not my intent to present a technical discussion of covenant here; I'll leave that to others more qualified than I. (I've included a recommended reading list at the end of this book.) However, I do think a basic understanding of God's view of covenant is important if we want to have a full appreciation of marriage as he designed it to be.

The Covenant with Noah

As we've noted, God initiated covenants with mankind at creation and continued to establish covenants throughout redemptive history. In the Bible the word *covenant* appears for the first time in Genesis 6:18, when God told Noah to build an ark to save himself and his family from a flood: "But I will establish my covenant with you, and you will enter the ark— you and your sons and your wife and your sons' wives with you." I'm convinced that if we, like Noah, walk in covenant with God, he will give us the information and the resources we need to save our families from the destructive forces of our modern world.

Following the flood God made another covenant with Noah, promising never again to destroy the earth by a flood and giving Noah and his descendants the covenant sign of a rainbow (see Genesis 9:8–17). Every rainbow reminds us of God's covenant with Noah and the fact that God's promises are always true. Interestingly, astronauts who've flown in space tell us that from high in the sky, a rainbow can be seen as a complete circle. We shouldn't be surprised; after all, the circle of God's love and faithfulness never ends.

The Covenant with Abraham

Noah kept the covenant he'd made with God, but his sons and grandsons did not. So after the passing of many generations, God established a new covenant with a man named Abram, later known as Abraham. God told him, "Leave your country, your people and your father's household and go to the land I will show you. I will make you into a great nation and I will bless you; I will make your name great, and you will be a blessing. I will bless those who bless you, and whoever curses you I will curse; and all peoples on earth will be blessed through you" (Genesis 12:1–3). What an awesome promise! But it was more than a promise: It was a call to absolute obedience and total trust on the part of Abram, who didn't have the faintest idea where God intended to lead him or how long the journey would take.

The details didn't matter to Abram, however; he chose to believe that what God said he would do, he would do. So at age seventy-five, Abram took his sixty-five-year-old wife, Sarah, and began a one-thousand-mile walk with God.

You know the story: Ten years passed, and no children were born to the aging couple. Abram decided to help God along by fathering a son by Sarah's handmaiden, Hagar. Afterward, however, God reminded him that the promise of a great nation was intended to come through his legitimate offspring:

> Then the word of the LORD came to him: "This man [the son born to Hagar] will not be your heir, but a son coming from your own body will be your heir." He took him outside and said, "Look up at the heavens and count the stars—if indeed you can count them." Then he said to him, "So shall your offspring be." Abram believed the LORD, and he credited it to him as righteousness. (Genesis 15:4–6)

At that point God confirmed his promise by obligating himself to Abram through a covenant:

So the LORD said to him, "Bring me a heifer, a goat and a ram, each three years old, along with a dove and a young pigeon." Abram brought all these to him, cut them in two and arranged the halves opposite each other....

When the sun had set and darkness had fallen, a smoking firepot with a blazing torch appeared and passed between the pieces. On that day the LORD made a covenant with Abram and said, "To your descendants I give this land...." (Genesis 15:9–10, 17–18)

In the Old Testament, a covenant was a blood bond of life and death, an all-or-nothing agreement. At its core was the "walk of death" depicted literally in Genesis 15, whereby the one walking through the pieces of dead flesh pledged his unconditional faithfulness to the covenant—even to the point of calling death upon himself if he were to break it. Nothing could be more serious or more binding.

That's why it's so amazing to see our awesome, almighty God— represented by the flaming torch and the firepot—obligating himself to Abram by walking through the prepared sacrifices. And what did Abram do? Nothing. In fact, God paralyzed him by sleep, perhaps to make sure he wouldn't try to do anything. The blood covenant God cut with Abram was unconditional. God promised to do for Abram what Abram could never do for himself. Abram's part was simply to believe God. That was it!

Why was God represented by two objects in this covenant ceremony? We don't know, but my friend Kay Arthur makes a beautiful suggestion. Here is what she says:

Could it be that, when the flaming torch and smoking oven [firepot] passed through the pieces of those animals cut down the middle, it was a picture for us of the role of the Father and the Spirit in covenant? Did those pieces foreshadow the Lamb of God, who would be slain to take away our sins, as once again God the Father obligated himself unconditionally to cut a covenant on behalf of you and me that could be sealed by the indwelling of the Holy Spirit?[5]

This is exactly what happened two thousand years ago when Jesus, who was God in human flesh, came to earth to die on a cross for your sins and mine. We were not there; we were not even born. We couldn't promise God anything. God did it all. It was God's unconditional love and grace that nailed our sins to the Cross. God obligated himself to you and me and cut covenant with us, spilling royal blood in order to offer us salvation as a free gift.

Many years after God cut covenant with Abram, that covenant was severely tested. Remember, God had originally asked for Abram's absolute obedience and complete trust. The question was, Did Abram still believe God to that extent?

After an excruciatingly long wait, Abram and Sarah had finally given birth to a son, Isaac, through whom all the covenant promises would eventually be realized. But as Genesis 22 narrates, God told Abram to take Isaac, now a teenager, to an altar on Mount Moriah and sacrifice him. In total submission, Abram began the trek up the mountain with his only son, saying by his obedience, "God, I trust you because you have already given me your word. We are in covenant, and that covenant includes my offspring. If Isaac dies, I know you can raise him from the dead." You know what happened next. God stopped Abram from sacrificing his son and provided a ram in Isaac's place.

Abram passed the test. He knew beyond a shadow of a doubt that God's covenant promise to him was unbreakable and irrevocable. The Bible tells us:

> Abram fell facedown, and God said to him, "As for me, this is my covenant with you: You will be the father of many nations. No longer will you be called Abram; your name will be Abraham, for I have made you a father of many nations. I will make you very fruitful; I will make nations of you, and kings will come from you. I will establish my covenant as an everlasting covenant between me and you and your descendants after you for the generations to come, to be your God and the God of your descendants after you. The whole land of Canaan, where you are now an alien, I will give as an everlasting possession to you and your descendants after you; and I will be their God." (Genesis 17:3–8)

The covenant that God cut with Abraham and later reaffirmed

through Isaac included all of Abraham's spiritual descendants—all those who are made righteous through their faith in God through Jesus Christ (see Romans 4:16–17). And that means you and me!

The Mosaic Covenant

Many centuries after Abraham, God made a covenant with Israel through a man named Moses. Called the Mosaic Covenant or simply the Law, it was divided into three parts: the moral law (summed up in the Ten Commandments), the civil law (governing daily life), and the ceremonial law (dealing with relationships). By keeping the Law, Israel could indicate its acceptance of its covenant relationship with God. However, the covenant itself was freely offered by God and could not be earned.

> Then Moses went up to God, and the LORD called to him from the mountain and said, "This is what you are to say to the house of Jacob and what you are to tell the people of Israel: 'You yourselves have seen what I did to Egypt, and how I carried you on eagles' wings and brought you to myself. Now if you obey me fully and keep my covenant, then out of all nations you will be my treasured possession. Although the whole earth is mine, you will be for me a kingdom of priests and a holy nation.' These are the words you are to speak to the Israelites." (Exodus 19:3–6)

The Law remained in place until Jesus came and instituted the new covenant of grace. The seal of the Mosaic covenant was the Sabbath, which means "rest." Its purpose is fulfilled in the new covenant as believers now find eternal "rest" in Jesus Christ.

Covenants through the Prophets

The Book of Hosea tells one of the great love stories in the Bible. Seven hundred years before the birth of Christ, God commanded the prophet Hosea to marry a prostitute named Gomer. (Imagine a church having *that* to talk about!) Following the marriage, Gomer gave birth to three children, but Hosea was painfully aware that he was not the father of any of them. As if that wasn't humiliating enough, Gomer left Hosea and continued her lifestyle of drifting from one lover (or client) to the next. Secretly Hosea took care of her by providing her with grain, oil, wine, and money, but she wasted it all on the worthless worship of a false god, Baal.

Finally hitting rock bottom, Gomer found herself stripped naked in front of a jeering crowd of foul-mouthed men, waiting to be auctioned off as a slave. As unbelievable as it sounds, somewhere in that crowd of gawkers was Hosea, who was not there to gawk or jeer but to buy and bless. Hosea paid the price for Gomer and bought her back—not as a slave but to be his wife. Hosea could have abandoned Gomer forever, which was all she had a right to expect. But in true covenant fashion, he obeyed God, bought her back, and chose to love her again as his wife. Incredible! Here's his explanation: The LORD said to me, "Go, show your love to your wife again, though she is loved by another and is an adulteress. Love her as the LORD loves the Israelites, though they turn to other gods and love the sacred raisin cakes" (Hosea 3:1).

The relationship between Hosea and Gomer is a mirror of the relationship that God had with his chosen people, Israel. In the same way Hosea continued to love Gomer, God continued to love Israel, despite the number of times the nation rejected him and violated his trust. Why? You know the answer: covenant love and grace.

Hosea was the first prophet to proclaim God's covenant by comparing it to the human covenant of marriage. Other prophets such as Jeremiah, Ezekiel, and Isaiah also used images of marriage and infidelity to describe God's covenant of grace and the sin of covenant breaking. In their writings, Israel's apostasy was often expressed in the language of divorce. But the final word through the prophets was always one of grace and eternal love, not abandonment. Although separation was often a part of God's punishment, it was never permanent. Time after time the prophets described God's covenant relationship with Israel in terms of an ever-loving, forgiving, faithful husband who never tires of wooing and winning back an unfaithful wife:

"The LORD will call you back as if you were a wife deserted and distressed in spirit—a wife who married young, only to be rejected," says your God. "For a brief moment I abandoned you, but with deep compassion I will bring you back. In a surge of anger I hid my face from you for a moment, but with everlasting kindness I will have compassion on you," says the LORD your Redeemer. (Isaiah 54:6–8)

The Davidic Covenant

Another covenant we read about in the Old Testament is the one God made with David, the Hebrew shepherd who defeated Goliath and went on to become Israel's greatest king. Psalm 89 describes God's promises to David:

I will maintain my love to him forever, and my covenant with him will never fail. I will establish his love forever, his throne as long as the heavens endure.... But I will not take my love from him, nor will I ever betray my faithfulness. I will not violate my covenant or alter what my lips have uttered. (Psalm 89:28–29, 33–34)

God's covenant with David promised a kingdom that would never end. "Your house and your kingdom will endure forever before me; your throne will be established forever," he told David in 2 Samuel 7:16. And in fact, God has kept his promise. Jesus, the Messiah, came through the lineage of David; therefore, the throne of David even now continues into eternity through the kingdom of Christ.

The Covenant with Israel

God never forgets the covenants he makes. We have proof of this from recent history. Consider the modern state of Israel. Scattered to the four winds for two thousand years, Israel returned home to be reborn as a nation in the late 1940s. Before that time, such an occurrence seemed impossible. How did it happen? Covenant! God blesses those people who choose to live in covenant with him. He will not go back on his word, and his promises never fail. God gave the nation Israel to Abraham, Isaac,

Jacob, and their descendants. The only reason Israel is living on that land today is because God is a covenant God. In 1948, when Israel became a nation, the world witnessed the power and majesty of God as a covenant keeper. Let no one think that God is finished with Israel!

The Old and New Covenants

As you know, the Bible is divided into two sections called the Old Testament and the New Testament. Since the word *testament* is interchangeable with the word *covenant,* we could just as accurately call these sections the Old Covenant and the New Covenant. Hundreds of years before Christ, the Old Testament foretold the coming of the New: "This is the covenant I will make with the house of Israel after that time," declares the LORD. "I will put my law in their minds and write it on their hearts. I will be their God, and they will be my people" (Jeremiah 31:33).

The old covenant was based on legalism and a sacrificial system that required the blood of animals to atone for sin. Its rituals were shadows and types pointing to the coming of a new covenant—one through which Jesus Christ, the Lamb of God, would shed his own blood to pay the ultimate price for the sins of mankind.

Perhaps the difference between the old and new covenants can best be described this way: The old covenant was about Jesus; the new covenant is Jesus. Jesus himself gave his disciples the master key for unlocking the mysteries of the old covenant by telling them that the Old Testament authors were writing prophetically about his crucifixion and resurrection. "This is my blood of the covenant, which is poured out for many," he said in Mark 14:24. The apostle Paul quotes Jesus in 1 Corinthians 11:25: "This cup is the new covenant in my blood."

In Hebrews 7:22 we read that "Jesus has become the guarantee of a better covenant." How is the new covenant better than the old? For one thing, under the old covenant, sins were *covered,* and people had to continually offer sacrifices for sin. Under the new covenant, sins are *removed,* and the debt of sin is paid in full by the blood of the Lamb.

Furthermore, the old covenant was conditional upon behavior, requiring Israel to live up to the demands of the Law; it was only good if Israel was good. In contrast, the new covenant is unconditional and unlimited. When we accept Jesus as Savior, we enter into an eternal covenant with God that is not dependent upon anything we do. The Holy Spirit within us is the sign and seal that bears witness to this (see John 20:22).

As a result of the new covenant, we receive forgiveness, salvation, and eternal life as free gifts. We access these benefits and blessings solely on the basis of what God has already done for us redemptively in Christ. As believers, our faith is not in what *we* do but in what *God has done* for us. This is the miracle of grace: that God has "cut covenant" on our behalf:

> When you were dead in your sins and in the uncircumcision of your sinful nature, God made you alive with Christ. He forgave us all our sins, having canceled the written code, with its regulations, that was against us and that stood opposed to us; he took it away, nailing it to the cross. (Colossians 2:13–14)

> He redeemed us in order that the blessing given to Abraham might come to the Gentiles through Christ Jesus, so that by faith we might receive the promise of the Spirit. (Galatians 3:14)

> For this reason Christ is the mediator of a new covenant, that those who are called may receive the promised eternal inheritance—now that he has died as a ransom to set them free from the sins committed under the first covenant. (Hebrews 9:15)

Ultimately the Bible—Old Testament and New—is the story of the blood covenant God has made with mankind through Jesus Christ. Included in this covenant are the wonderful benefits of:

- *covenant blood* that forgives and erases our sins

- *covenant grace* that provides inner strength to handle our hurts and hassles

- *covenant love* that is unconditional and never ending

- *covenant power* that energizes us to cope and to change our lives for the good

- *covenant hope* that guarantees us a future, now and forever

We enjoy these blessings because of the relationship with have with God through covenant. God is a relational being. He is our heavenly Father. And to be a father involves connection; it implies relationship. God was connected to us by creation, separated from us by sin, and reconnected to us by our redemption through the death of Jesus on the Cross. His covenant with us today through Christ is the ultimate relationship.

THE KEY TO LIFE

In fact, the concept of covenant is the key to understanding all relationships—with God, our families, our friends, and especially our mates. God loves us by covenant. He provides for us by covenant. He blesses us by covenant. He operates in our lives by covenant. In reality, every truly valuable thing in life is ours because of covenant.

For forty years I have walked with people down the corridor of crisis and chaos. Often I refer to myself as the "Minister of Crisis," because it is when the bottom falls out of a person's life that I am called. Interestingly, it is through crises that I have gotten to really know the people of our church. These experiences have taught me that life's bottom line is not fame, fortune, and fooling around; rather, it's faith, family, and friendship, in that order. The depth of our relationships with God and others determines the quality of our lives. Sooner or later the only things that will matter in our lives will be our relationships. Only relationships last; everything else will eventually fade into insignificance.

In *The Joy of Feeling Good*, William Miller tells the story of Peter Niewick, who was on a hiking trip with his wife and another couple around beautiful Spirit Lake in Washington State. The surroundings were beautiful, and everything about the trip was wonderful—except Peter, who was carrying the awful burden of knowing he had an active malignant tumor. Literally, his life was in jeopardy. As the foursome walked through the fir trees to the far side of the lake, they came upon a rustic rental cottage at the foot of a waterfall, with a majestic mountain rising in the background. The scene was so breathtaking that it looked like a picture on a postcard. Peter's wife hurried up to the cottage to see if she could make reservations for sometime in the coming weeks, but the concierge told her all the rooms were booked for a year. Undaunted, she made reservations for one year from that date.

Outside the cottage, Peter was visibly shaking and had tears in his eyes. His friends asked compassionately, "Peter, what is wrong?"

"Everything is wrong—the mountain, the fir trees, the lake," he said. "Everything here seems so solid, and my life is hanging by a hair. My wife is inside making reservations for next year, and I may not even be alive next year. I may be dead."

But Peter, it turns out, had it backward. The next year he was still alive, but the lake was gone. The rustic cottage was gone. The fir trees were gone. And even the mountain as it had been known for centuries was gone. Mount St. Helens had erupted, and the volcano had devastated the entire area. That which had seemed so strong, so secure, so permanent, had vanished. And that which had seemed so weak and frail was still standing.[6]

Stuff—cars, houses, and even mountains—can be blown away like leaves on a fall day. They're all temporary. In all my years of ministry, I have never heard a dying person say, "I wish I had spent more time at the office" or "I wish I had spent more time on the golf course" or "I wish I had spent more time accumulating things." Never! What I *have* heard, however, is tearful lamenting over neglected relationships and years wasted on trivialities. One of mankind's greatest sins is that we often give ourselves to those things that do not ultimately matter while neglecting those things that do. That was the case with a multimillionaire I met for lunch some time ago. As we talked over the meal about life's bottom line, he said, "I would give everything I own to put my family back together." He had found out too late that relationships are what matter most.

Some time ago I heard pastor and radio broadcaster Steve Brown tell this story on the air. In a particular smoke-filled bar on the edge of town, a rag-tag group of regular patrons were talking loudly and trying to drown away their sorrows. Over in a corner, a nice-looking young man sat at a piano and played background music for the noisy crowd. Night after night he had been playing the same songs for the same group, but the people barely noticed him.

There has to be more to life than this, he mused to himself. *Surely life must have some meaning and purpose.*

Challenged by his thoughts, he began to ask the people in the bar, "What is the meaning of life?" Some of the regulars gave superficial answers, but most did not even venture a clue. Finally he asked a half-zonked man, "Could you tell me the meaning of life?"

"No," the man replied, "but I know someone who can."

"Who is he?" the excited piano player asked.

"He is a guru in India who lives high in the Himalayan Mountains. It is a long way to travel, but if you are willing to go and really want to know the answer, he will tell you."

So the piano player quit his job, sold everything he had, and got on an airplane to India. After the long flight, he rode seven hundred miles across country by train and then four hundred miles up into the Himalayas by bus. He walked the final twenty treacherous miles on foot. Exhausted, his feet bloody and swollen, he found the guru at last.

"Sir," he panted, "I am told that you know the meaning of life. I've come thousands of miles. Please tell me: What is the meaning of life?"

"Life is a fountain," the guru said.

The piano player could hardly believe his ears. "Man, come on," he cried in frustration. "I've traveled for days, and I'm tired and weary. Please tell me the meaning of life."

The guru looked at him quizzically and said, "Life is a fountain... isn't it?"

I have some great news for that piano player, for you as you read this book, and for every person on the face of the earth. Jesus said, "I am the way and the truth and the life" (John 14:6). The meaning of life is found as we enter into and abide in an everlasting covenant relationship with Almighty God through Jesus Christ. And out of that relationship we can build lasting relationships with our spouses, our children, and our friends. Covenant relationships endure.

Do you know that God loves you and has a wonderful plan for your life? He has taken the initiative to reach out to you and to enter into an eternal love relationship with you. He wants you to know him. He wants to be in covenant with you.

I once heard about a man who came forward in a Billy Graham crusade and accepted Christ. "The sermon was just for me," he gushed to a counselor. "It had my name on it." The counselor recalled that Dr. Graham had preached from John 3:16 that night, as he so often does. The man continued, "My name is John. I've been married three times, and I have sixteen children. See? God does love me!"

The Bible is the story of your covenant God loving you so much that he gave his only Son, Jesus, to die on the cross as a sacrifice for your sins. And when you respond to God's love and enter into a covenant relationship with him, he promises that you "shall not perish but have eternal life" (John 3:16). From that moment on, your covenant salvation through Christ provides the foundation for your relationship with your heavenly Father and for all your relationships—and especially your marriage.

The first step to a happy marriage is always Jesus Christ. In fact, the greatest gift you can give your spouse is to be a genuine Christian who reflects Christ in your relationship. Nothing is more important. God, through Jesus, has cut covenant with you. And by the power of his Holy Spirit within you, he can energize and equip you to keep covenant with your spouse.

Chapter 5

THE BLESSING OF COVENANT MARRIAGE

My lover is mine and I am his.

—Song of Songs 2:16

I once heard a speaker tell a story that beautifully describes the essence of the marriage covenant. A man's wife had Alzheimer's and had to be placed in a nursing home. Every day that husband would go to the nursing home and spend time with his wife. He would talk to her, read to her, comb her hair, and try to meet her various needs. Before he left her room, he would tell her he loved her and kiss her goodbye. He did this day after day, week after week, and month after month. He never missed. Often he would bring her fresh flowers.

After one of his daily visits, a group of nurses asked to meet with him. They spoke admiringly and told him that everyone was impressed with his faithfulness and the special way he cared for his wife.

"But we want you to know that you don't need to come every day to see your wife," the head nurse said gently. "She doesn't know that you are here and doesn't even know who you are. Your wife is fine here with us, and you can do other things with your time. There is absolutely no need for you to feel like you have to keep coming day after day."

The husband lifted his head. Tears ran slowly down his cheek. In a quiet voice he said, "I know she doesn't know who I am, but I know who she is, and that's what matters. She is my wife! Fifty years ago I made a covenant with her that I would never leave or forsake her and that I would be with her in sickness and in health. And I intend to keep that covenant."

Two thumbs up for that husband! He knew that marriage is more than a contract. It is a forever covenant made possible by our covenant God, who has vowed to never leave us or forsake us and who promises to empower us, by his grace, to be faithful to our spouses.

Laying the Foundation

Out of all the places I've ever visited, Israel is my favorite. In a strange and peaceful way, I feel at home there. I love the Jewish people and stand in awe of their ability to persevere and prosper against all odds. The story of the Jews is one of brutality, persecution, and torment, even to this present day. Yet they are a people who refuse to give up. They will not quit. They not only survive, they survive with dignity and success. Why didn't this minority people perish? Why didn't they give up? What held them?

Marek Halter, in *The Book of Abraham,* attributes their magnificent survival to an invisible foundation. Says Halter, "These people, regardless of where they were, believed—no, they *knew*—that the God of Abraham specifically chose them to receive the Law. The language and rulers of their land could change, but not the Law. It was eternal."[1] They survived because they were in covenant with God and with each other. They had an invisible foundation based on words from God that could not change. They knew they could trust God to keep his word. Every permanent relationship is built on an invisible foundation. It is called covenant.

Jesus, in the greatest sermon ever preached, had something to say about building on the proper foundation:

> Whoever comes to Me, and hears My sayings and does them, I will show you whom he is like: He is like a man building a house, who dug deep and laid the foundation on the rock. And when the flood arose, the stream beat vehemently against that house, and could not shake it, for it was founded on the rock. But he who heard and did nothing is like a man who built a house on the earth without a foundation,

against which the stream beat vehemently; and immediately it fell. And the ruin of that house was great. (Luke 6:47–49 NKJV)

According to author Samuele Bacchiocchi, "Marriage is like a house. If it is to last, it needs a solid foundation. The bedrock upon which the foundation of marriage must rest is an unconditional, mutual covenant that allows no external or internal circumstances to 'put asunder' the marital union that God himself has established." Covenant is not just an abstract biblical truth; it is the only secure foundation upon which a happy, fulfilling, and permanent marriage can be built. There is no other way to enter into the joy of Christian marriage than by assuming its covenantal obligations. "When we commit ourselves to honor our marriage covenants of mutual faithfulness 'till death do us part," Bacchiocchi writes, "then we experience how God is able to unite two lives into 'one flesh.' I like how the seventeenth-century Puritan Pastor Peter Bulkley put it: 'When a man takes a wife into the covenant of marriage with him, whatever he is, he is wholly hers; he gives himself and that which he has to her.'"[2]

I remember reading about a family in Miami, Florida, that put the finishing touches on their new house—only to discover they had built their dream home on the wrong lot. Oops! Based on recent divorce statistics, I think it's safe to say that many Americans, including many Christians, have built their marriages on the wrong lot. They may be legally married, but they have not based their marriages on the sure foundation of a covenant commitment. Perhaps some were too immature at the time of their wedding to recognize the importance of making a marriage covenant. No doubt some said their vows with their fingers crossed. In today's culture it's not unusual for couples to enter a marriage relationship believing that it is terminal—that is, expecting that the marriage won't last and that divorce is inevitable.

But couples who go into marriage without an understanding of covenant are jeopardizing the relationship before it starts. Covenant commitment is essential for a lasting marriage. As author Paul R. Stevens says, "A covenant marriage is an elastic link between two hearts. When they move apart, a tug reminds them they belong. Or, a covenant is a net beneath two trapeze artists. It is a risky business, this high wire stunt, and they will undoubtedly fall sometime. But the safety net beneath them holds."[3] Samuele Bacchiocchi concludes, "Marriage is too difficult and risky to expect long term success without the security of a covenant foundation."[4]

If you have never made a covenant commitment to your spouse, whatever the reason, don't let the sun go down before you do. Even if you think you have a good marriage, you need to make a covenant today. "A refusal to make a marriage covenant indicates a flaw in your commitment to your spouse," says marriage expert Ed Wheat. "That flaw is like a tiny crack that can be fatally widened by sinister forces working to destroy your marriage. To avoid such a risk, we must recover and reaffirm the biblical understanding of marriage as a lifelong sacred covenant witnessed and guaranteed by God himself."[5] In the words of the French novelist Andre Maurois, "A successful marriage is an edifice that must be rebuilt every day."[6]

WHAT THE BIBLE SAYS

The popular 1999 movie *Message in a Bottle* starring Kevin Costner has a great romantic line in which the lover says to his love, "You are my true north." What a beautiful sentiment—but it's wrong! When it comes to love and marriage (and anything else in life, for that matter) only God is true north.

"Purpose is in the mind of the inventor," a philosopher once said. Since God invented marriage, we must use the compass of his Word, the Bible, to find the original purpose for marriage. Then we must use that understanding to find direction for our own relationships.

Time after time, the Scriptures describe marriage as a covenant. In Proverbs 2:16–17 we read, "[Wisdom] will save you also from the adulteress, from the wayward wife with her seductive words, who has left the partner of her youth and ignored the covenant she made before God." These verses indicate that the wife, in marriage, enters into a sacred covenant with God and her husband. In Malachi 2:14 we read that the husband, in marriage, also enters into a covenant with God and his wife: "She is your partner, the wife of your marriage covenant."

In the Old Testament, the marriage covenant ideal was rooted in the "marriage" of God to his frequently rebellious children, the Israelites, whom he promised to always love and never abandon. In the New Testament, Jesus models the marriage covenant through his role as the Bridegroom who ever loves and always keeps his promises to his bride, the church. In both cases the covenant is unconditional and permanent; otherwise it could not accurately represent the relationship between God and Israel and Christ and the church.

As British counselor David Atkinson says:

> The fundamental biblical description of marriage is given in covenant terms, and the interchange of analogies by which human marriage is used to describe God's covenant relationship with his people, and by which God's relationship with his people, or Christ's with his church, is used to provide a pattern for human marriage, can be traced through both the Old and New Testaments.[7]

It was through the lens of human marriage that the Old Testament prophets pictured the "saving covenant of God with his people," Atkinson says. Therefore, "human marriage became the means of revealing the meaning of covenant…. By revealing his covenant through the medium of human marriage, God simultaneously revealed a meaning in human marriage which the people had hitherto not fully apprehended."

Atkinson calls this "reciprocal illumination." He explains: "God uses marriage to illustrate his unconditional grace and eternal salvation. By understanding marriage, we understand God's covenant of grace; by understanding God's covenant of grace, we understand marriage as a sacred and permanent covenant."[8]

That understanding, as we've said, is critical for a marriage to succeed. "When a man and woman covenant with one another," Les and Leslie Parrott write in *Saving Your Marriage Before It Starts,*

> God promises faithfulness to them. And that helps couples keep the faith. God's covenantal faithfulness embodied in our partner makes a home for our restless hearts. It accepts our whole soul by saying, "I

believe in you and commit myself to you through thick and thin." Without faithfulness and the trust it engenders, marriage would have no hope of enduring. For no couple can achieve deep confidence in the fidelity of themselves and each other until they first recognize God's faithfulness to them.[9]

Where It All Started

Genesis is often called "the book of firsts," so it makes sense for us to turn to Genesis to see what God had in mind when he invented marriage. In doing so, we're in good company; the Genesis account is quoted by both Jesus and the apostle Paul as the foundation for an understanding of Christian marriage.

In Genesis chapters 1 and 2 we read the account of Creation. God created all matter, light, and life and declared that everything he made was "very good." Then God made man in his own image, and we discover the first "not good" in Scripture: "The LORD God said, 'It is not good for man to be alone. I will make a helper suitable for him'" (Genesis 2:18).

Commenting on this passage, Scott Stanley, in his book *A Lasting Promise,* makes a very interesting point. He notes that this "not good" in God's eyes "came before sin and even prior to the relationship of Adam and Eve." Says Stanley, "There was no sin, no fall, and there were no consequences of these. Still, it was not good for man to be alone. Why? Simply because God created us for relationships—with him, in marriage, and with others."[10]

The Bible tells us that God paraded all the beasts and the birds before Adam to see what he would name them. But Adam was not impressed. Genesis 2:20 strikes me as funny: "So the man gave names to all the livestock, the birds of the air and all the beasts of the field. But for Adam no suitable helper was found." Perhaps lonely Adam blushed at that point and said, "No thanks, that's not what I had in mind!"

I can imagine Adam chatting with God about his situation. "It's not that I'm ungrateful or have anything against animals," he says. "I just need someone who is like me but different. Someone who is sexy, sweet, submissive, and sensitive to all my needs. Someone who is beautiful but not bossy."

"You know, Adam," God responds, "something like that will cost you an arm and a leg."

To which Adam replies, "What could I get for a rib?"

Well, maybe that conversation never took place. But Doctor God did put Adam to sleep, took out one of his ribs, and closed him back up. Then God made a woman from the rib he had taken out of man and presented her to Adam. And in Eve—not anywhere else in creation—Adam found the fulfillment of his unmet needs.

Since God made Adam from the dust of the earth, it might seem logical that Eve would have been made from dust too. But God had a better plan. By deciding to create Eve out of Adam's rib, he demonstrated two critical things: First, the woman is to walk beside the man, not in back of him or in front of him. This means that on the first day of marriage for the first couple, God debunked male chauvinism and liberal feminism in one swoop. These should be non-issues for Christians in covenant.

Second, by making Eve from Adam, God emphasized the closeness of the special relationship between husband and wife. Man completes woman and woman completes man. As Benjamin Franklin once said, "It is the man and woman united that makes the complete human being…together they are more likely to succeed in the world." The two are part of each other and belong to each other in an intimate companionship that is infinitely closer than all other relationships. I like the poetic description Robin Williams's character gives in the movie *Patch Adams:* "So close that when your hand is on my chest, it is my hand. So close that when you close your eyes, I fall asleep."

As an old rabbi once said, "God chose a rib from Adam's side, not a bone from Adam's head that she would be over him, or a bone from his foot that she would be under him, but from his side that she would be next to him, from under his arm that he might protect her, and from next to his heart that he might love her." Pastor and author David Jeremiah sums it up this way: "The man is restless while he misses the rib that was taken out of his side. The woman is restless until she gets under man's arm from where she was taken. It is humbling to the woman to know that she was created for the man, but it is to her glory to know that she alone can complete him. Likewise it is humbling to the man to know that he is incomplete without the woman, but it is to his glory to know that the woman was created for him."[11]

Clearly, the Genesis account shows us that marriage, as designed by God, is a covenant of companionship in which two people become linked in body, soul, and mind. They become, as Genesis 2:24 says, "one flesh." They complete each other and give themselves to each other in a companionship that fills the void in their lives and provides for ultimate happiness and fulfillment. It is the ultimate friendship.

The First Wedding

Last spring I had the privilege of walking my oldest daughter, Christy, down the church aisle and presenting her to the young man who had chosen her for his bride. To be honest, I felt like Steve Martin in the movie *Father of the Bride.* Even though I loved Ky, I remembered what my father-in-law said to me on my own wedding day: "I feel like I'm giving my Stradivarius violin to a gorilla." Twenty-five years later I could finally appreciate those words. With watery eyes, sweaty palms, and a cotton-dry mouth, I responded to the question, "Who presents this beautiful bride on her wedding day?" with the words, "Her mother and I do." My daughter's smile of contentment and the look of joy and excitement on her face were the only things that got me through that experience. She knew that she had found her covenant partner in Ky and that this marriage was God's will for her life. What more could a father ask?

Genesis 2:22 says, "Then the LORD God made a woman from the rib he had taken out of the man, and he brought her to the man." This is a description of the very first wedding, with the Father of the bride presenting the bride to her groom on her wedding day. In verse 23, the groom speaks and describes their unique relationship: "This is now bone of my bones and flesh of my flesh; she shall be called 'woman,' for she was taken out of man."

The next verse describes the nature of their marriage and every marriage relationship that was to follow: "For this reason a man will leave his father and mother and be united to his wife and they will become one flesh" (v. 24). This is the verse quoted by both Jesus and Paul in the New Testament as the foundational verse for covenant marriage. It indicates that the components of covenant marriage are leaving, uniting (or "cleaving," as some Bible translations say), and becoming one flesh. Let's look at each of these components individually.

Leaving

A unique wedding custom on the Indonesian island of Java illustrates well the principle of "leaving." On the day before her wedding, the bride calls together all of her friends. In their presence she burns the things associated with her past life, including dolls, toys, and other cherished items of her childhood. At that point her friends console her over the loss of these past treasures by giving her presents—things identified with maturity and representing her new life. Marriage is the time to leave behind childish things, childlike behavior, and childlike attitudes, as well as childlike dependency on parents. It is only by leaving the past behind that we best walk into the future.

Leaving means that the marriage relationship becomes primary, and all lesser relationships, including the relationship with parents, become secondary. Keith Intrator, in his book *Covenant Relationships,* talks about the primacy of marriage this way: "Of all the interpersonal covenants, the one of highest priority is marriage. Family has the highest priority because one spends more time with his family than with anyone else. There must be corresponding commitment with every degree of intimacy. Since a husband and wife have absolute intimacy, they must have absolute covenant."[12]

Even children who are born into a marriage must take a secondary position. The parent-child relationship cannot be allowed to take precedence over the marriage relationship. We rear children to leave us—but we mate for life. One of the worst mistakes a parent can make is to put the children before the spouse. Children must never be allowed to come between a husband and wife in matters of affection, communication, and discipline.

Uniting

The Hebrew word for "unite" presents the idea of two things being glued together permanently. This stick-like-glue fidelity is a core concept of covenant. It means wholehearted commitment and absolute loyalty. If a husband and wife are permanently glued to each other, marital unfaithfulness is virtually impossible. To unite in covenant is to form a blood bond for life. The husband is to remain a one-woman man for the rest of his life, and the wife is to remain a one-man woman for the rest of her life. Covenant takes the husband and wife out of circulation—permanently. And as the nineteenth-century English novelist George Elliot said, "What greater thing is there for two human souls than to feel they are joined for life?"

Becoming One Flesh

After the first wedding, Genesis 2:25 says, "The man and his wife were both naked, and they felt no shame." It is only in the safety and security of a marriage covenant that we feel free to reveal our nakedness—physically, emotionally, and spiritually. Keith Intrator explains it well: "To every degree of intimacy, there must be a corresponding degree of commitment. If a man brings a woman to a level of intimacy beyond what he is really committed to, he has violated her as a person."[13]

Theologian G. R. Dunstan writes:

> The great word of Genesis that a man shall cleave to his wife and they shall become one flesh, is at once command and promise. It is a com-

mand: Press on to that unity…see that you fall not out by the way; do not forsake the covenant yourself; and if the other does, remember God in Christ, faithful to his bride the church, and so forgive to the uttermost. And the promise is that this, the impossible, is possible. The two do become one, and "signify" or exemplify to the world "the mystical union that is betwixt Christ and his church." What God commands, he also gives," or, to put it another way, "What God commands, he enables." God will never ask a couple do something they cannot do.[14]

Leaving, uniting, and becoming one flesh are the foundational principles of the marriage covenant. Two become one. "I" becomes "we." "Me and mine" are replaced by "us and ours." As Mark Twain said, "Marriage makes of two fractional lives a whole."

Divorce, on the other hand, is the opposite of covenant and reverses the plan of God. In covenant, two become one; in divorce, one becomes two. Covenant binds together; divorce breaks apart. Jesus said, "What God has joined together, let man not separate" (Matthew 19:6). Why? Because marriage is a covenant relationship. By an act of their wills, two people exchange their lives and intermingle their natures. That which is miraculously blended together cannot be pulled apart without leaving gaping holes and horrendous hurts that never totally heal.

COVENANT VOWS

There is a wonderful quote from Thornton Wilder's play *The Skin of Our Teeth* that should be given to every couple on their wedding day:

I didn't marry you because you were perfect. I didn't even marry you because I loved you. I married you because you gave me a promise.

That promise made up for your faults. And the promise I gave you made up for mine. Two imperfect people got married and it was the promise that made the marriage. And when our children were growing up, it wasn't a house that protected them; and it wasn't our love that protected them—it was that promise.[15]

Change the word *promise* to *covenant,* add God, and you have the thesis for this book. The success of a marriage is based on the strength of the promise. God calls that promise a covenant. As Dennis Rainey says in *One Home at a Time,* "Keeping a marriage covenant is more than just pledging to remain married. It also involves making a holy promise to God and your spouse to care for, love, and remain faithful to your spouse for life. It means making your marriage all that God intended it to be."[16]

The words *steadfast love* and *faithfulness* often used to describe God's covenant relationship with his people are also words that describe the kind of self-sacrificing love expressed between marriage partners. The Old English word for this kind of loving faithfulness is *troth*. David Atkinson writes:

> The center of the meaning of marriage is the expression of a bond of moral troth (that is covenant faithfulness) in which two people marry each other before God and pledge to each other loyalty, trust, devotion, and reliability. The model of creative covenant faithfulness seen in the steadfast love and faithfulness of God indicates that faithfulness in marriage should be something positive, creative, and dynamic: much more than the avoidance of adultery within a marriage, covenant faithfulness will mean at least the following four things: faithfulness to a vow; faithfulness to a calling; faithfulness to a person; and faithfulness to a relationship.[17]

Keith Intrator explains that the specific purpose of any covenant is "to guarantee a given relationship." Says Intrator, "The covenant itself is actually a set of words that are spoken to define the nature of that relationship and set forth the principles of commitment to it." In particular, the marriage covenant is "the words of oath commitment that pass between [spouses] at the marriage ceremony and seal them forever."[18] The marriage covenant puts an unbreakable seal upon the relationship between husband and wife. It declares that the marriage is an indissoluble union and pledges to guarantee its permanence. It is the most binding, most blessed, most serious, and most sacred agreement two people can make.

Dennis Rainey agrees:

Marriage is not a private experiment littered with prenuptial agreements and an attitude of "Try it! If it doesn't work, you can always bail out!" Marriage is not just a convenient relationship based on "What is in it for me?" Marriage is not some kind of social contract— something that you just "do" for as long as you both shall "love." It is none of those. Marriage is a sacred covenant between one man and one woman and their God for a lifetime. It is a public vow of how you will relate to your spouse as you form a new family unit. The traditional wedding vows used by most couples constitute a *covenantal oath*, not a two party contract.[19]

In his book *The Mystery of Marriage,* Mike Mason gives the best description of the wedding vows I have ever read. Look carefully at his words:

The joining of a man and a woman in holy matrimony is a supernatural event, founded upon a mutual exchange of holy pledges. The saying of them requires about thirty seconds. But keeping them is the work of a lifetime…. To keep a vow, however, does not mean to keep from breaking it. If that were the case, marriage vows would be broken the day they were made. It is not like the signing of a contract and not like any other form of human promise. A person cannot promise to love another person: He can only vow to do so. A vow is, per se, a confession of inadequacy and an automatic calling upon the only adequacy there is, which is the mercy and power of God….

In a very real way it is the vow that keeps the man rather than vice versa. The vow is a mystery, an insoluble riddle, which somehow corrects and shames him at the same time as it picks him up and spurs him on to higher things. So a married person is a kept person, kept in the profound protection of vows that have been taken before the Lord…. Adherence to the vows is not a confining so much as a delimiting discipline, a marking of the natural boundaries of our human abilities. Far from being trapped, we are actually set free, set free and consecrated for the performing of a task which turns out to be the most vital work in the world: the work of covenant, of loving relationship.[20]

A clear understanding that marriage is a forever covenant is the most powerful preventative you have to keep you from becoming one more divorce statistic—one more marriage casualty along life's littered highway. The words that define and give parameters to your marriage relationship are to be reiterated over and over again. Hang them on the wall of your heart. Engrave them on your soul. Let them saturate your mind so that they pop to the surface the instant your relationship is threatened in any way. Allow the spoken words of covenant to give stability and security to your marriage.

My friend Kay Arthur has taught me much about the beauty and blessing of covenant vows. In her book *Our Covenant God,* she has this to say:

> We have sworn! A covenant is a covenant is a covenant!
>
> Oh, if only we realized this, what a different nation we would be! Our land would not be riddled with divorce and the awful consequences that come with the shattering of marriage vows. Husbands and wives would stay together. Children would know the security of family. Homes would stand strong through the temptations that work to destroy their foundations. Our people would be healthy, and our nation would prosper in righteousness. For marriage is a covenant—a covenant unto death.[21]

ONENESS IN COVENANT MARRIAGE

As we've noted, the essence of covenant marriage is that two people become one flesh. "I" becomes "we." Two wills die and one is born. I like the way this wedding vow describes oneness:

> Now we feel no rain, for each of us will be shelter to the other.
> Now we will feel no cold,
>   for each of us will be warmth to the other.
> Now there is no loneliness for us.
> Now we are two bodies, but only one life.
> We go now to our dwelling place,
>   to enter into the days of our togetherness.
> May our days be good and long upon the earth.[22]

I wish I could tell you that this kind of oneness happens automatically on your wedding day, but that's not the case. Somebody once joked that when you get married, you become one—and then you live together for a while to find out which one!

Texas pastor and television host John Hagee says that marriage is like making mashed potatoes. You start with two very different, individual potatoes, each with rough exteriors and multiple flaws, and the first thing you do is peel them. (Ouch—that hurts in real life!) After the bumps, knots, and rough spots are peeled off, you throw the potatoes into hot water, and God turns up the heat until the water comes to a boil. (Covenant love can take the heat, but convenient or contractual love screams for a lawyer, claiming irreconcilable differences.) After the potatoes have boiled for some time, you take a metal masher and start smashing the potatoes, pushing, grinding, and stirring them around until all the lumps are gone. Then you spoon them onto a plate—and you can't tell one from the other. (That's covenant oneness!)

It doesn't matter how much a husband and wife think they love each other when they first get married; they still start with two personalities, two minds, two souls, and two backgrounds. The end result of becoming one is wonderful—but getting there is no piece of cake. Becoming one is a process that takes time, hard work, desire, love, and the power of God.

The oneness of covenant is beautifully illustrated in an old wedding tradition called the "covenant of salt." Diane Warner, author of *The Complete Book of Wedding Vows,* explains that when a husband and wife pour individual bags of salt into a single, third bag, they are symbolizing the total meshing of their two lives into one, to the point that separation is virtually impossible:

> This covenant relationship is symbolized through the pouring of these two individual bags of salt—one representing the groom, all that he was, all that he is now, and all that he will ever be, and the other representing the bride, all that she was, all that she is and all that she will ever be. As the bride and groom pour their individual bags into a third bag, the individual bags will no longer exist, but will be joined together as one. Just as the grains of salt can never be separated and poured again into the individual bags, so will the marriage be. Far more important than the individuality of each is the reality that they are no longer two but one, never to be separated one from the other.[23]

Salt is an appropriate symbol for the marriage covenant. A natural pre-servative, it has long symbolized longevity in relationships. According to the *International Standard Bible Encyclopaedia*, "the Arabic expressions 'there is salt between us' and 'he hath eaten my salt' refer to the 'partaking of hospitality which cemented friendship.' Covenants were generally con-firmed by sacrificial meals, and salt was always present…. Salt is emblem-atic of loyalty and friendship. A person who has once joined in a 'salt covenant' with God and then breaks it is fit only to be cast out."[24] The Bible even says that David received his everlasting kingdom from God by a "covenant of salt" (2 Chronicles 13:5). As part of a wedding ceremony, the covenant of salt perfectly illustrates the enduring quality of covenant marriage.

Oneness in Heart and Mind

Paul writes to the church at Philippi: "Make my joy complete by being of the same mind, maintaining the same love, united in spirit, intent on one purpose" (Philippians 2:2 NASB). And in Acts we read, "All the believ-ers were one in heart and mind. No one claimed that any of his possessions was his own, but they shared everything they had" (Acts 4:32). Aren't these beautiful descriptions of how Jesus intends for believers to function within the church? To me, it's a no-brainer to conclude that God intends this same oneness for believers united in marriage. The husband and wife are to be "one" in heart and mind, sharing all things. God wants that oneness for the church; I believe he requires it for the home.

Christian psychologist Larry Crabb says, "The goal of oneness can be almost frightening when we realize that God does not intend [only] that my wife and I find our personal needs met in marriage. He also wants our relationship to validate the claims of Christianity to a watching world as an example of the power of Christ's redeeming love to overcome the divisive effects of sin."[25] Covenant marriage is a divine call to display unity to a bro-ken world and to reflect the character of Christ. It is a call to holiness—not just happiness.

Enhanced Identity, Not Lost Identity

In Romans 12:4–5 and 1 Corinthians 12:12, Paul describes the church, the body of Christ, as one entity made up of many individual parts. It's a union that embraces individual uniqueness—and even thrives because of it. This same concept of diversity in oneness is the divine mystery that brings color, interest, and wonder to Christian marriage. Oneness in marriage does not mean that your identity is forever lost. On the contrary; it is forever enhanced. The coming together of two unique individuals forms a third entity that is more than the sum of the parts. You are what you are; and together with your spouse, you are more than you are. When your "I" becomes "we," you are in a stronger position because your spouse's strengths compensate for your weaknesses, and vice versa. The biblical image of two becoming one is not about a loss of identity; it's about an enhancement of identity through the wonderful richness of diversity combined.

Union without Unity

Some people say that a couple's differing beliefs shouldn't make any difference in marriage. The Greek word for that is *boloney.* As we've said in previous chapters, God's role in covenant marriage is crucial. We are spiritual beings, and God has set up marriage as a divine institution. You cannot experience the fullness of spiritual oneness and supernatural love without God as your third partner. For the closest bonding, you need a personal relationship with God through Jesus Christ, and you need to be married to someone who has a personal relationship with God through Jesus Christ. Your spouse needs to share your compassion and conviction about the things of God.

The Bible clearly states that a believer and an unbeliever should not be united in marriage. In 1 Corinthians 7:39 Paul writes: "A woman is bound to her husband as long as he lives. But if her husband dies, she is free to marry anyone she wishes, *but he must belong to the Lord"* (emphasis added). In other words, a widow is free to marry anyone she wants, as long as the one she wants is also a believer. Paul goes on to say explicitly in 2 Corinthians 6:14: "Do not be yoked together with unbelievers. For what do righteousness and wickedness have in common? Or what fellowship can light have with darkness?"

In marriage you become one with another person. If that person is an unbeliever, you have *union* but no *unity*. There is no agreement at the deepest level of the spirit. Genuine openness, intimate companionship, and sweet communion will be difficult, if not impossible, to pull off. To get the full benefits and blessings of covenant marriage as designed by God—and to avoid endless and unnecessary conflict—both you and your spouse should be believers who are committed to God first and then to each other.

Marriage is often described as a triangle with God at the top point and two believers at the bottom points, bowing in submission to him. As you and your spouse move up the lines of the triangle, you get closer to God, and you also get closer to each other. That's because there are at least three things you and your spouse need that you cannot give each other consistently apart from God's grace and power:

- A love that is unconditional

- A forgiveness that is unending

- An attitude that is unselfish

In a later chapter we'll talk more about the unselfish, sacrificial nature of covenant marriage. For now, suffice it to say that true fulfillment in marriage comes only through the oneness created by the power of God in the lives of two believing spouses. The Psalmist says, "Unless the LORD builds the house, its builders labor in vain" (Psalm 127:1). In other words, if God is not first in your life and in your relationship with your spouse, you cannot expect to experience the fullness and blessing of true covenant marriage. Your own efforts to achieve happiness will fail every time. However, if you make knowing and obeying God your priority, God himself will help you to build a marriage that is both happy and holy.

No wonder sociologist Andrew Greeley, reviewing the results of a survey of married people, found that the happiest couples were those who pray together. "Couples who frequently pray together are twice as likely as those who pray less often to describe their marriages as being highly romantic," Greeley reports. "They also report considerably higher sexual satisfaction and more sexual ecstasy." In fact, Greeley says, "Married couples who pray together are 90 percent more likely to report higher satisfaction with their sex life than couples who do not pray together."[26]

Is It Too Late?

What if you are already married to an unbeliever? No doubt you have experienced the kind of conflict and confusion we've alluded to, and you know that what God says is absolutely true. You probably long for that deepest kind of love and companionship available within the context of Christian covenant marriage. The good news is there is always hope. I have known both men and women who have won their mates to Christ, and the Bible tells us how to do it: "Wives, in the same way be submissive to your husbands so that, if any of them do not believe the word, they may be won over without words by the behavior of their wives, when they see the purity and reverence of your lives" (1 Peter 3:1–2).

This passage says that it is possible for a wife to win her spouse to Christ by living before him with Christlike behavior characterized by submissiveness, inner beauty, and "a gentle and quiet spirit" (v. 4). She will not win him by preaching or pouting. Pinning a note to his pillow that says "turn or burn" won't do it. What will work is for her husband to see Christ's character clearly and consistently displayed in his wife. The same is true for a non-Christian wife who sees Jesus in her husband.

With God Nothing Is Impossible

Several years ago a prominent doctor and his wife came to me for marriage counseling. It seems that the handsome doctor had gone to bed with half the nurses in town. Now he wanted not only to keep his marriage and his mate, but his mistresses as well. His solution was simple: "I'll stay in this marriage and continue to provide my wife with the finer things in life," he told me, "but I must have the freedom to date other women!" At that point I had to silently beseech God to keep me from informing this man that he was the new poster child for "Jerks Anonymous." *This marriage is toast,* I thought to myself. *Over. Done. Finished. Curtains.* But God had other plans. The doctor and his wife both entered into personal relationships with Christ and became involved in the church. The doctor willingly gave up his extracurricular activities and began to work on building a good marriage.

When another couple, Bill and Nancy, came to see me, they were so filled with anger that they didn't want to be in the same room together. Bill turned to Nancy and hissed, "I hate you, and I never want to see you again as long as I live." The air in the room was so thick you couldn't cut it with a knife! As I listened to the litany of complaints they rattled off against the other, I thought, *There is absolutely no hope for this marriage. It's too late. The bridges are burned. The damage is done.* But once again God had other plans! Nancy knew God, and she knew how to pray. With some encouragement, she refused to give up on her marriage and kept loving her unlovable spouse. Bill became a Christian, and the two have a great marriage today.

Why do I tell you these stories? Because God used these two couples to change my whole attitude toward marriage counseling. I know now that as long as God is alive, there is no such thing as a "hopeless" marriage. Believe me, I have seen many miracles over the years. God has taught me that I must never give up on a couple if he hasn't. The Bible says, "Nothing is impossible with God" (Luke 1:37), and that includes transforming a bad marriage into a good one. God can and does resurrect dead marriages!

I'm convinced that the major reason Christian marriages are falling apart in epidemic proportion is that couples give up too soon. Persistence is one of the keys to achieving oneness in marriage. We all get tired, run down, and stressed out at times, and the future never looks very promising from that perspective. Those are the times when we have to rely upon knowledge rather than feelings, covenant rather than contract, and refuse to give up.

Whether your marriage is average or awful, it has the potential to be awesome. Don't quit too soon. Don't bail out! And since you brought it up, don't let some secular counselor talk you into throwing in the towel. As long as God is alive, there is hope. "Is anything too hard for the LORD?" (Genesis 18:14). Never!

The story is told of the aging British statesman Winston Churchill returning to speak to the students at the boarding school where he had grown up. Years before this courageous leader had successfully led his countrymen through the worst period in England's history—the Battle of Britain during World War II. Nazi bombs had fallen on London day and night for weeks on end. Yet Churchill had stood firm, and Hitler was eventually turned back. Now as the imposing leader struggled to get up from his seat, silence fell across the schoolroom. What would this great statesman, leader, and orator say to the students of his alma mater? Finally reaching the podium, Churchill studied the fresh faces of the anxious students. Then he bellowed, "Never give up. Never give up. Never, never give up." And with that he sat down.[27]

Think about the state of your marriage at this moment. Does it seem hopeless? Don't give up! Does the road seem long? Don't stop! Does the task seem difficult? Don't quit! Somewhere I read this little gem: "A diamond is a piece of coal that stayed on the job." If you quit now, you may miss the answer to your prayers. You may miss the best that God has for you. You may miss the incredible blessing of covenant oneness with your mate. You may miss that diamond.

Very few—if any—great things happen instantly. Be patient. Keep praying. Keep polishing. Stay on the job. For all you know, three words are all that stand between you and success in your marriage: *Don't give up!* I love these words of Harriet Beecher Stowe: "When you get into a tight place and everything goes against you, till it seems as though you could not hang on a minute longer, never give up then, for that is just the place and time that the tide will turn."[28]

Radio preacher Steve Brown tells the story of a British soldier in the first World War who became discouraged and disenchanted to the point that he decided to desert. Slipping away into the darkness, he walked for miles hoping to find water and a boat back to England. Suddenly, he came to what he thought was a signpost, but it was too dark to read it. Climbing up the post to get a closer look, he struck a match and found himself looking squarely into the face of Jesus Christ. Instead of a signpost, he had climbed a crucifix that had been placed on the side of a road. His mind raced back to the Christ who had died for him, enduring the cross—the Christ who refused to give up. Inspired by what he saw, the man returned to the trenches and continued to fight.

Now let's apply that to marriage: When darkness covers your marriage—and it surely will—strike the match of hope by looking into the face of Jesus Christ. Remember that because he didn't give up, you, too, can find the strength to continue on.

Remember, marriage is ultimately a covenant between you, your spouse, and God. And God promises to bless your marriage as you honor that covenant—even through the hard times. In a covenant marriage, it's always too soon to give up. Never give up.

Chapter 6

Is Your Marriage a Contract or a Covenant?

*A contract is an agreement made in suspicion. The parties
do not trust each other, and they set limits to their own responsibility. A covenant is an agreement made in trust. The parties
love each other and put no limits on their own responsibility.*

—*Wambdi Wicasa*

"But I have a signed contract in my hand! Doesn't that mean anything? How can a person, especially a Christian, just walk away from a contract?" Those questions came at me like machine-gun fire. My daughter was selling a house, and this was her first experience with business contracts. Two different times she and her husband had signed contracts with buyers, and both times the buyers had backed out and walked away from the deal without even an "I'm sorry."

Obviously those buyers didn't see anything wrong with their actions. In their minds the time-honored phrase, "Your word is your bond," had long been replaced by the new mantra of modern culture: "Contracts are made to be broken." Being more familiar with the world's ways, I consoled my daughter and told her to take the "high road" and move on. She did—at least until a third contract fell through.

Not surprisingly, she's now convinced that she can't put her hope and trust in a contract that may or may not turn out to be binding. That revelation has helped her appreciate why it's so important to base marriage on a covenant rather than a contract.

Today on my morning walk, I was thinking about the differences between a covenant and a contract. I asked God to help me explain those differences in a way that would be eye-opening and life-changing for everyone reading this book. As I mentioned in an earlier chapter, America has become a contract-oriented culture, and we as Christians have bought into the mentality that all binding agreements, including marriage, are contractual in nature. We tend to think of marriage—life's most serious and sacred relationship—in terms of conditions, limits, rights, and even "outs." To our modern way of thinking, marriage is a social contract governed by the state and negotiated between two sovereigns who share the same bed.

But biblical marriage, as God designed it, is radically different. It's not a contract; it's a sacred blood covenant witnessed and guaranteed by God himself. It is unconditional, unlimited, and unending. A covenant marriage is more about trust than terms, more about character than convenience, more about giving than receiving. It is intended to be a reflection to the world of the very character of God.

Perhaps you've heard the word *earnest* used in the context of a business deal. Generally speaking, to be "earnest" about something means to be serious about it, but not necessarily sold out to it. A buyer wanting to purchase a house will give a small amount of money to the seller as an indication of his or her seriousness in binding the sale. This is called "earnest money," and the fact that it has to be put up at all indicates that the contract is born out of suspicion and distrust. The parties don't know each other or trust each other, so they set limits on their liability and responsibility. It's no surprise that contracts bound by *cash* are easily broken and walked away from. A covenant, on the other hand, is bound by *character*. It is both serious and sacred and calls for a sold-out commitment. No "earnest money" is necessary. When you are bound by covenant, you refuse to walk away.

Contract says, "Let's make a deal." You agree to do certain things over a specified period. For instance, you purchase a car and sign a contract that obligates you to pay a specific amount of money each month for a certain number of years. If you fail to keep up your end of the bargain, your car can be repossessed. A covenant, by contrast, says, "Here is your gift." You give freely, without conditions and without expecting anything in return. What is given cannot be taken back. It stays in place regardless of the performance of the person on the receiving end.

God's covenant of salvation is the perfect example. We receive forgiveness of sin through Jesus Christ as a free gift. It is not earned, and it cannot be unearned. And thank God for that! If God operated in our lives on the basis of contract, we would all be doomed. Personally, I have broken many promises to God. I have defaulted hundreds, if not thousands, of times. I have not kept up my end of the bargain. If God were a contractual God, I would have no hope and no future. What about you?

A marriage may begin by contract, but if it's going to have the best chance of succeeding, it must be sustained by covenant. A contract is about legalities and leverage; a covenant is about love and loyalty. The vowed love of covenant is not dependent upon circumstances or responses and remains in effect until death. As Samuele Bacchiocchi notes in *The Marriage Covenant,* "It is this covenant foundation that will motivate us to seek God's help in trying again to make successes out of our marriages—even when our needs are unfulfilled and our relationships seem to be sterile or sour."[1] No other commitment runs so deeply or binds more permanently.

THE BIG "I"

The modern approach to marriage is to focus on personal rights and needs. Questions like, "Am I getting what I deserve from this relationship? Am I getting my needs met?" are the telltale signs of a marriage that is based on contract rather than covenant. Spouses tell themselves, "I deserve to be happy"—and as long as they're happy, they think it doesn't matter if they forsake their vows and break their promises. Marriage today is all about the big "I." No-fault divorce, a sex-obsessed media, liberal courts, and an idolized youth culture all send the same message: "If the relationship ceases to give me what I want, if it gets tough, or even if it just gets boring, I can walk away and start over." After all, marriage is a contract, and contracts are made to be broken, right?

Prenups and Postnups

Perhaps the most significant evidence that marriage is largely viewed as a contract is the increasing prevalence of prenuptial and postnuptial agreements. These are full-blown contracts that, along with no-fault divorce, stand as the blatant legal enemies of covenant marriage. Prenups and postnups say in effect, "We know this marriage won't go the distance, so let's spell out right now who will get what when it ends." What bride or groom could feel secure going into marriage with such a pessimistic prognosis?

According to a recent *20/20* television special, today's prenuptial agreements address much more than money matters. Increasingly they include such things as how often a couple will be expected to have sex, what time spouses will get up in the morning, and what time they will go to bed at night. No doubt many prenups will soon answer the burning questions:

- Is the toilet seat to be left up or down?
- Will toothpaste be squeezed from the top, middle, or bottom of the tube?
- How many pillows will be allowed on the bed in the master bedroom?
- Who will take out the garbage?
- Which specific Jones family will we keep up with?
- How often will meals be cooked and served at home?
- How long will in-laws be allowed to stay, and who will tell them to leave?

The truth is, nuptial agreements and covenant marriage are mutually exclusive concepts. If you base your relationship with your spouse on a prenup or a postnup, you do not have a covenant marriage. You have a legal contract—that's all. And a legal contract will do little to help your marriage survive in the long run.

Watch Out!

Recently a man told me of his plans to divorce his wife of thirty years. "My wife is a good woman and has always worked hard at making me happy, but she just can't do it anymore," he said. "It's time for me to move on and find somebody who can make me happy. I know God wants me to be happy."

At that moment I wanted to kick the guy in the seat of the pants and say, "Do you know what an egomaniac you are? Grow up!" Instead I told him, "Your wife is not responsible for your happiness. You are. Divorcing your wife and finding someone else isn't the answer—and it certainly isn't God's answer."

Clearly this man viewed his marriage as a contract, not a covenant. But before we think too harshly of him, we need to recognize that every marriage—even one that begins in covenant—faces the subtle danger of degenerating into contract over time. If we are not vigilant, we may begin to frame our own marriages in contractual rather than covenantal terms. Have you ever said one of these things to your spouse?

- I'll do my part if you'll do yours.

- I'll meet you in the middle.

- If you'll do this, then I'll do that.

- Marriage is a fifty-fifty proposition.

- That's not my role.

These phrases relate to terms and conditions; they're contractual in nature. And the problem is that what we think and how we talk will eventually show up in our actions. A contract mentality can easily creep into any marriage—including yours and mine.

HOW COVENANT IS DIFFERENT

Theologian Paul E. Palmer offers the following explanation of the difference between covenants and contracts:

> Contracts engage the services of people; covenants engage persons. Contracts can be broken, with material loss to the contracting parties; covenants cannot be broken, but if violated, they result in personal loss and broken hearts.... Contracts are witnessed by people with the state as guarantor; covenants are witnessed by God with God as guarantor.[2]

That's contract versus covenant in a nutshell. Let's take a closer look at some of the radical differences between the two.

Covenant Is Relational

The biggest purchase most people make is a house. Yet Leigh and I signed a contract and bought a house without ever meeting the seller. The deal was consummated and considered legally binding even though we had no relationship with the person selling the house. We had a non-relational contract.

Non-relational contracts are very common in America. I've used the credit card issued to me by Chase Manhattan Bank so many times that the magnetic strip has deteriorated and the numbers have to be manually punched in by a cashier. Although I have contracted to consistently pay the balance due on that card, I have never actually entered Chase Manhattan Bank, nor have I met or talked to anyone at that bank. We have an impersonal relationship based strictly on a contractual agreement.

Covenants are much different. They involve relationships. In fact, they are predicated upon the existence of relationships. That's why God put marriage and covenant together. Marriage is much more than a legally binding contract written on a piece of paper; it's a permanent covenant commitment that is engraved upon two people's hearts. Covenant involves the merging of one life into another. Two become one. It's a mystery—two separate individuals blended into one intimate relationship. It's something supernatural that only God can do.

A contract calls for the signing of names, but a covenant calls for the binding of hearts. A contract is made at arm's length; a covenant is made at arm's embrace. A contract connects two parties until someone defaults or the agreement expires; a covenant commits two people to one another "until death do us part."

Think about it. If marriage were merely a contract, what do you think the divorce rate would be? One hundred percent! After all, no marriage is without broken promises. No spouse is unselfish and loving all the time. Everyone has defaulted on the terms at one time or another. Marriage based on the legalistic score keeping of contract is destined for failure, because grounds can always be found for declaring such a contract null and void. Marriage based on covenant, however, doesn't keep score. As the Bible says, "[Love] keeps no record of wrongs" (1 Corinthians 13:5). What marriage could survive without the wonderful grace of having the slate wiped clean?

Covenant Focuses on Giving

To marry by contract is to say, "Now, that I've signed on the dotted line, what do I get? How are you going to meet my needs—and even my greeds?" The focus is on *receiving*. In contrast, to marry by covenant is to say, "I am giving myself to you unconditionally. What may I bring to this relationship? How may I serve you?" The focus is on *giving*. Because of this difference in focus, covenant and contract bring entirely different attitudes to a marriage relationship, as the following chart shows:

CONTRASTING ATTITUDES

Contract Attitude	**Covenant Attitude**
You had better do it!	How may I serve you?
What do I get?	What can I give?
What will it take?	Whatever it takes!
It's not my responsibility.	I'm happy to do it!
It's not my fault.	I accept responsibility.
I'll meet you halfway.	I'll give 100 percent.

I'll be faithful for now.	I'll be faithful forever.
I am suspicious.	I am trusting.
I have to.	I want to.
It's a deal.	It's a relationship.

Which attitude best describes your own approach to marriage? If you can relate to more statements in the left column than in the right, your marriage may be more contract than covenant.

Covenant Provides Security

As my daughter found out when she was trying to sell her house, a contract is frequently superficial and too often temporary. It provides no real security. It is initiated from a position of distrust and fear of being taken advantage of. In contrast, a covenant is initiated from a position of trust and faith. It's the key to making a marriage secure.

"In marriage, unquestioned trust means giving your heart to each other for safekeeping with absolute confidence that it will not be broken," write Evelyn and Paul Moschetta in *The Marriage Spirit*. It is "a level of trust that is indisputable. It is the same level of trust you have in the sun rising and setting, in your heart beating and lungs breathing. Unquestioned trust is the bridge that carries you from insecurity to security."[3] The Moschettas don't use the word *covenant* in this passage, but they describe it beautifully. Only in the blood bond of covenant is absolute trust realized and maintained. To marry in covenant is to form a bond strong enough that a mate's heart can rely on it; and, later, a child's heart can count on it. Covenant is indeed the bridge that provides the passageway from insecurity to security.

Covenant Goes the Distance

Living with a wife and two daughters in what I lovingly refer to as the "girls' dorm" has validated for me the oft-repeated phrase, "Women are prone to change their minds." I wonder how many men have had to have back surgery because their wives kept changing their minds about where to place the living room furniture? Before I lose half my audience, let me quickly acknowledge that men can be just as guilty of reversing decisions on a frequent basis. Fortunately, the repercussions of most changes of mind are benign. I mean, does it really matter if the couch is against the wall or under the window?

When it comes to covenant marriage, however, neither men nor women have the prerogative to change their minds. Remember the "walk of death" we described in chapter 4? In that Old Testament ceremony, as the two covenant partners walked between the animal sacrifices, they recognized that they could no more change their minds than those dead animals. While a contract always includes an "out" clause or an expiration date, covenant says, "We are in this for life, and we will not change our minds." Regardless of circumstances, feelings, or situations, a covenant binds two people in marriage before God, family, and friends. That means that whatever happens—good or bad, happy or sad, up or down—nobody leaves. Changing your mind is out of the question.

God knows us so well! When he created us, he knew we would have difficulty maintaining deep relationships. He knew we would have trials, troubles, tragedies, and temptations that would try even the closest of couples. He knew we couldn't build marriage on lust, because lust lapses. He knew we couldn't build marriage on feelings, because feelings are fickle. He knew we couldn't build marriage on physical attraction, because beauty fades and gravity takes its toll on the human body. (You think you married Brad Pitt, and you end up with Goofy. Or you think you married Julia Roberts, and you end up with Olive Oyl.) And he knew we couldn't build marriage on circumstances and stuff, because circumstances change and stuff can be lost when the inevitable tornadoes of daily life rip through the orderly structures of our lives.

God also knew that we couldn't build marriage on a private contract that is easily canceled and cast aside on the basis of personal whims and weaknesses. That's why he designed marriage to be built on the foundation of covenant, not contract. He knew that a contract would not sustain the pains, pitfalls, and pressures of marriage between two inherently selfish and imperfect human beings. God realized that the inevitable hurts and hassles, difficulties and disappointments, and storms and struggles of life would constantly tear at the fabric of a contract, causing it to eventually scatter into a thousand pieces along a trail of hurt and horror.

Long-term marriage demands more than a signed piece of paper to go the distance. It required the supernatural merging of lives and the binding of hearts that is possible in covenant alone.

Covenant Leads to Communion

Contracts are formal and cold; covenants are friendly and warm. There is no joy in having to perform marital duties when you are locked into a contract that is legally binding. But covenant marriage transcends civil formalities. It paves the way for individuals to connect with a soul mate, not just a roommate. Listen to the words of Les and Leslie Parrot: "The aching, burning urge that you and your partner have to be connected soul to soul can only be quenched when your spirits are joined by a greater spirit, Jesus Christ. The sacred secret to becoming soul-mates is pursuing a mutual communion with God."[4]

It may take two to tango, but it takes three to triumph in relationships. The single most important difference between contract and covenant is that a contract does not necessarily involve God, but covenant does. Covenant marriage calls for a God-centered relationship in which two hearts beat in mutual agreement because both are focused on the Lord. It is by first submitting to God that we have the desire and power to submit to one another. Likewise, it is by receiving God's love and loving ourselves that we are free to really love each other and experience the joy of communion.

Covenant Promises Power

Recently I stood in a valley in Israel and picked up a handful of smooth stones from the brook of Elah. Centuries earlier the imposing mountains on either side of me had provided the setting for one of the most popular stories in the Old Testament. You know it well: the story of David and Goliath. What you may not know is that this tale is a beautiful illustration of the power of covenant.

The story begins in 1 Samuel 17 with the army of Israel camped on one mountain and the army of its enemy, the Philistines, camped across the valley on the opposite mountain. One day a ten-foot giant named Goliath emerged from among the Philistine ranks and challenged the Israelites to send out a man to meet him in the valley for a one-on-one fight. Whoever won the fight would win the battle for his entire army. But out of all of Israel's soldiers, no one stepped forward. For forty days the soldiers of Israel quaked and cowered at the sight of this imposing Philistine warrior.

That's when David, a teenage shepherd boy, arrived to deliver food to his brothers on the battlefield. He heard the giant's challenge and immediately decided to volunteer for the fight. "Who is this *uncircumcised* Philistine that he should defy the armies of the living God?" David cried (1 Samuel 17:26, emphasis added). You see, circumcision was a sign of Israel's covenant with God. David knew that God had covenanted with Israel to protect them and give them victory over their enemies. Goliath, on the other hand, was uncircumcised; he had no covenant promise from the Lord. David summed up his covenant theology and explained the source of his confidence in verse 47: "All those gathered here will know that it is not by sword or spear that the LORD saves; for *the battle is the LORD's,* and he will give all of you into our hands" (emphasis added).

Simply put, David's reasoning went like this: "I am in a binding covenant, and God is my covenant partner. It is not how big I am that matters, but how big God is. As a shepherd I had to fight a bear that was too big for me, but that bear was not too big for my partner. I had to fight a lion that was too powerful for me, but that lion was no match for God. Now this pea-brained giant wants to fight. He is not in covenant; but I am. He has no covenant partner, but I do. So let's go, God! I'm ready to kick some giant!" And he did—or, as we both know, *God* did.

Are you facing a giant in your marriage? Is it the giant of unresolved conflict? Of misunderstanding? Of broken promises or betrayal? Of possible divorce? Yes, that giant is too big for you to handle. But it's not too big for your covenant partner. Listen carefully: If you and your mate will obey God and walk in covenant with him and with one another, you can say, "God, this giant is too big for me. It's too big for my mate. But we know we are not in this alone. You are the third party in this covenant. Engage this battle with us. Fight for this marriage. Work in our hearts."

If your marriage is merely a contract, then the battle is yours and your spouse's alone. There is no third party involved. And let me assure you, spouting legalisms will only get you so far. But if your marriage is a covenant, then the battle is the Lord's. And nothing is too hard for God!

Perhaps you are saying, "I want to keep my marriage covenant, but I'm weak. I don't know if I can do it." Good news—it's not up to you! David knew this in the Old Testament. And in the New Testament, the Cross screams to us that God always keeps his covenant of love with us. That means we can keep our marriage covenant because of Christ. We are weak, but he is strong. Paul says it clearly: "I can do everything through him who gives me strength" (Philippians 4:13). That "everything" includes keeping your marriage covenant.

How does it happen? By God's grace and power. Elsewhere Paul writes, "But he said to me, 'My grace is sufficient for you, for my power is made perfect in weakness'" (2 Corinthians 12:9). Paul goes on to say that he actually delights in weaknesses, hardships, and difficulties: "For when I am weak, then I am strong" (v. 10). By obeying God and living in covenant with him, our weakest times are supernaturally transformed into our strongest times. Our acknowledged weaknesses allow God the opportunity to show himself strong. Because he is able, we are!

The truth is, the devil and all his demons are powerless against covenant. There is not a situation, circumstance, or power on earth that can break the bond between a husband and wife who continue to walk in covenant with God and each other. Success in marriage, as in all of life, lies in obedience to God's Word and total reliance on God's power.

How About You?

Now I want to ask you a personal question: Is your marriage based on covenant or contract? Your answer will determine how you approach your marriage and how hard you work on your marriage. Whether you view your marriage as a contract or a covenant may well determine the ultimate success or failure of your marriage.

It will also determine how you see your spouse. If you consider your marriage a contract, you will see your spouse as he of she is—flaws, faults, foibles, and all. Little irritations will be huge. On the other hand, if you consider your marriage a covenant, you will see your spouse not as he or she is, but as he or she can become. You will assume the best and willingly overlook the imperfections. A contract magnifies faults. A covenant covers faults with love.

Let me tell you a beautiful story. Long ago in the Hawaiian Islands, it was customary to give cows as a dowry for a bride. Essentially, the groom would buy the bride by giving her father a certain number of cows—five being the most anyone had ever heard of. (I thought that seemed like a strange custom until, on a recent trip to Israel, I was offered camels for one of the women in our group!)

In those days a man with two daughters lived on the big island. The younger daughter was quite beautiful, and it was wagered that she would bring five cows when she married. Her older sister, on the other hand, was so homely that someone overheard her father saying, "If a man offered me one cow for my Mary, I would take it with no questions asked." Unfortunately, Mary was aware of how her father and the other villagers thought of her, so she stopped hoping that she would ever find a husband.

Then one day a rich and handsome farmer named Johnny Lingo came to the island. To everyone's surprise he asked for Mary's hand in marriage and offered her father an incredible ten cows for the dowry. Everyone was flabbergasted! Before Johnny had time to change his mind, the father took the cows. The couple was married and left for an extended honeymoon.

Many months later, Johnny and a strange but somewhat familiar woman came back to the island for a visit. The villagers quickly recognized Johnny, but where was Mary? And who was this beautiful lady by his side? She was poised, dignified, and exquisitely dressed. You can imagine their shock when the villagers realized that the once homely Mary had been dramatically transformed into the drop-dead gorgeous lady by Johnny's side.

What happened? The answer is simple: Because Johnny had treated Mary like a ten-cow wife, she had become one.[5] The German philosopher Goethe put it this way: "If you treat a man as he is, he will stay as he is. If you treat him as if he were what he ought to be and could be, he will become that bigger and better man." That's what covenant partners do for one another. By treating each other as "tens," they help one another become all that God designed them to be.

So back to the question on the table: Is your marriage based on covenant or contract? Before you answer, let's review a list of the major differences between the two:

A contract is an agreement made in distrust.
A covenant is an agreement made in trust.

A contract is based on limited liability.
A covenant is based on unlimited responsibility.

In contract you sign on the dotted line.
In covenant you tow the line.

A contract is conditional in nature.
A covenant is unconditional in nature.

A contract focuses on the growth of self.
A covenant focuses on the giving of self.

A contract is predicated on results.
A covenant is predicated on relationships.

A contract is made at arm's length.
A covenant is made at arm's embrace.

A contract asks, "What am I getting from this marriage?"
A covenant asks, "What am I bringing to this marriage?"

A contract is enforced by a court.
A covenant is enforced by character.

A contract is bound by legalism and leverage.
A covenant is bound by love and loyalty.

A contract is convenience-based.
A covenant is commitment-based.

A contract is a "have-to" commitment.
A covenant is a "want-to" commitment.

A contract is for a specified period of time.
A covenant is forever.

In contract two are connected until the agreement is broken.
In covenant two are committed "until death do us part."

In contract nobody leaves until the terms are met.
In covenant nobody leaves—period!

I hope you can say that your marriage is a permanent covenant between you, your spouse, and God. If it's not, now is a good time to upgrade! Don't waste another day living as if your marriage were nothing more than a legal contract that can be easily broken. There's no security, no longevity, no communion, and no power in that. Make your marriage a covenant marriage, and begin today to enjoy the blessings and benefits of doing marriage God's way.

Chapter 7

Is "I Do" Your Final Answer?

One of the best wedding gifts God gave you
was a full-length mirror called your spouse.
Had there been a card attached, it would have said,
"Here's to helping you discover what you are really like."

—*Gary and Betsy Ricucci*

Weddings in America are a big deal. The average couple spends more than one thousand hours in preparation for their wedding. Thousands of dollars are spent on frills, flowers, food, and formalities. Over the years, I have dealt with enough upset brides, angry moms, and uptight dads to know that people take weddings *very* seriously. Unfortunately, it is often the *marriage* that isn't taken seriously enough.

I wonder how much better marriages would be if couples spent as much time, energy, and money preparing for the marriage as they do preparing for the wedding. Because the truth is, after every wedding comes a marriage—and that's the main event. The wedding is just one day in one week in one month in one year in hopefully dozens of years of married life. And while I've never presided over a bad wedding, I have watched the demise of hundreds of bad marriages. The wedding gets all the attention, but it's the marriage that demands and deserves the serious work. In a few short hours, the candles are gone, the music has played, the flowers are removed, the cake has been eaten, and the dress is packed away. But one thing remains: the vows that the husband and wife have spoken to each other before family, friends, and Almighty God. Those vows are permanent. Everything else is disposable.

Some time ago a beautiful and bubbly bride-to-be dropped off a set of videotapes at our office. This same set of tapes had been checked out and returned by numerous couples who'd been required to watch them as part of their premarital counseling. There was one problem: The tapes were defective. They had no audio—just my "talking head" minus any sound! Yet none of the couples ever mentioned this flaw when they brought the tapes back. Apparently, none had taken their upcoming marriage seriously enough to actually insert one of the tapes in a video player and discover the trouble!

Given the high rate of divorce in today's world, every engaged couple should be asking themselves one question: "How can we guarantee that our marriage relationship will not be broken?" In other words, will "I do" be our final answer? It should be. It *must* be!

Outside of a personal relationship with Christ, there is nothing in life more serious than a relationship with a mate—not a job, a house, hobbies, a car, friends, or even children. Unfortunately, the couples who come to me for marriage counseling have taken everything seriously except their marriage. By the time they step into my office, they typically have been having serious problems for two to five years but have never sought help. As a last resort, they call me. And despite their huge backlog of unsolved problems, they make three unbelievable requests:

- We need to see you today.

- We need to see you after office hours, because we really don't want to take off from work.

- We want you to fix us in one session because we are very busy and that's all the time we've got.

Hello? Couples need to decide from the start that they will take the time, do the work, spend the money, and do *whatever it takes* to keep their marriage growing and glowing from the wedding day "until death do us part." Their spouse and their marriage must be their absolute first priority. First runner-up is unacceptable. Otherwise, they will be vulnerable to pressures that might lead them to break covenant with their spouse—and nothing could be more serious in the eyes of Almighty God.

As we've said before, the Bible defines marriage as a sacred and permanent covenant witnessed and guaranteed by God. When you make a marriage covenant, you do more than just pledge to remain married. You make a holy promise to God and your spouse to care for, cherish, love, and remain faithful to your mate until death. You accept responsibility for working continuously to make your marriage all that God intended it to be.

Listen to this beautiful description of marriage by Ruth Harms Calkin:

> Marriage means.....
> You are the other part of me
> I am the other part of you.
> We'll work through
> With never a thought of walking out.
>
> Marriage means…
> Two imperfect mates
> Building permanently
> Giving totally
> In partnership with a perfect God.
> Marriage, my love, means us![1]

Our culture has tried hard to strip marriage of its meaning. It has tried to make light of its seriousness as a covenant commitment. Many couples today go into marriage with the attitude, "We'll try it, and if it doesn't work, we'll get a divorce. No big deal!" But they're wrong. It's a huge deal!

In the Old Testament, covenants were taken so seriously that God held accountable any person who violated their terms. The Mosaic covenant, for example, came with both blessings for obedience and curses for disobedience. (See Deuteronomy 28 for a list of blessings and curses.) People who failed to do their part in keeping their covenants with God always paid a huge price. The Bible says in Jeremiah 11:10–11, "Both the house of Israel and the house of Judah have broken the covenant I made with their forefathers. Therefore this is what the LORD says: 'I will bring on them a disaster they cannot escape.'"

The marriage covenant is a commitment you make with your spouse and with God, and God holds you accountable to it. Breaking that covenant is nothing less than an invitation to disaster.

GOD HATES DIVORCE

When the Pharisees came to Jesus, they asked, "Is it lawful for a man to divorce his wife for any and every reason?" In response, Jesus did not deal with legal technicalities but went straight to the covenant foundation of marriage by quoting from Genesis: "'For this reason a man will leave his father and mother and be united to his wife, and the two will become one flesh.' So they are no longer two, but one. Therefore what God has joined together, let man not separate" (Matthew 19:3, 5–6).

Divorce is always less than God's ideal. Not only does it break the most sacred of human vows, but it represents life's greatest betrayal, devastating the mind, heart, and spirit—oneness created supernaturally by God between husband and wife. God is the one who joins two people together in marriage. Neither they nor anyone else can separate that union without experiencing painful consequences.

God takes very seriously the breaking of the marriage covenant. In Malachi 2:13 we read a statement that sounds harsh at first glance: "Another thing you do: You flood the LORD's altar with tears. You weep and wail because he no longer pays attention to your offerings or accepts them with pleasure from your hands." In other words, "you claim to be religious, but God is not moved by your crocodile tears. He is not motivated by what you put in the offering plate. Your worship is a waste of time, and your prayers are a waste of energy."

Why? The next verse provides the answer: "It is because the LORD is acting as the witness between you and the wife of your youth, because you have broken faith with her, though she is your partner, the wife of your marriage covenant" (v. 14). The passage goes on to tell us exactly what God thinks of divorce: "'I hate divorce,' says the LORD God of Israel.... So guard yourself in your spirit, and do not break faith" (v. 16).

As Gary Thomas writes in *Sacred Marriage,* "What most divorces mean is that at least one party, and possibly both, have ceased to put the gospel first in their lives. They no longer live by Paul's guiding principle: 'I make it my goal to please him.'" I think Thomas's personal statement on marriage is a must-read for every Christian:

> One of the reasons I am determined to keep my marriage together is not because doing so will make me happier (although I believe it will); not because I want my kids to have a secure home (although I do desire that); not because it would tear me up to see my wife have to "start over" (although it would). The first reason I keep my marriage together is because it is my Christian duty. If my life is based on proclaiming God's message to the world, I don't want to do anything that would challenge that message. And how can I proclaim reconciliation when I seek dissolution?[2]

God Sees the Big Picture

Why does God hate divorce so much? Because he *loves us* so much! He sees the big picture when we cannot. He knows that divorce shatters covenant, and people on both sides get hit with the flying debris—especially the children involved. A dissatisfied spouse may think there are ten thousand reasons to end his or her marriage, but the emotional and spiritual needs of children to have a mom and a dad at home refute them all. An old Chinese proverb says it well: "In the broken nest there are no whole eggs." The headaches of marriage pale into insignificance when compared to the consequences of divorce on both partners and the people around them.

God also hates divorce because he knows that the "greener grass" we think we see on the other side of marriage is an illusion. It's Astroturf! The truth is, a second marriage is almost always more difficult than the first one. Unsolved problems accompany a divorced person into the next marriage (and the next) and compound. The failure rate goes up with each subsequent marriage.

And finally, God hates divorce because he knows that sins are forgivable and marriages are repairable. He knows that adultery, the ultimate betrayal, does not automatically end a marriage. It is not the unpardonable sin. Personally, I know of marriages that have survived an affair—even multiple affairs—and have gone on to soar again. With God nothing is impossible, and that includes the reviving of a seemingly dead marriage.

God Is Our Witness

If we insist on divorce anyway, the passage in Malachi says that God comes into the courtroom as a witness against us for divorcing the "[spouse] of your youth." This is one decision we must not make lightly. God is unequivocally clear that no man should separate what God has joined in covenant. According to the Bible, God only allows the dissolution of a marriage covenant for two reasons: adultery (see Matthew 19:9) and death (see 1 Corinthians 7:39). The apostle Paul says that divorce is also possible for someone married to an unbeliever, if that unbeliever wants to leave (see 1 Corinthians 7:12–16).

What about spousal abuse or serious addiction problems—a sad reality in many marriages these days? In such cases, a husband and wife may need to physically separate for a time. But even then (and certainly, there are exceptions), the prayerful goal should not be divorce but rather the pursuit of professional help, healing, and reconciliation if at all possible.

Have I been too hard on divorce? I don't think so. I want anyone reading these words who happens to be in a bad marriage to know there is hope. God specializes in the impossible. If you're in a terrible marriage, please know that with hard work and God's help, it can become a triumphant marriage. Divorce will only serve to bring you and your family more pain—pain you can't see right now. But God sees it, and he wants to save you from it. He wants to help you make your marriage soar again.

Have I been too hard on you, my divorced friend? Oh, I hope not! My message to you is one of love and grace. God hates divorce, but he loves divorcees. It is never you that he is displeased with, but the sin you have committed. If you repent, God will forgive you and remove your sin as far as the east is from the west. He will mend and heal your broken heart. But I must be honest with you: He cannot take away the consequences. No matter how good life gets after divorce, you will always have scars. There will always be pain. Still, the best thing you can do is to seek God's plan for your life consistently and persistently from this point forward.

God does not love you less because you are divorced, and neither should anyone else. The truth is, our covenant God loves us unconditionally, and there is nothing we have done in the past or could do in the future to cause him to break covenant and stop loving us. His grace will always reach lower than our worst mistakes. He loves us in spite of what we do, because of *who he is.* As the Bible promises, "If we are faithless, he will remain faithful, for he cannot disown himself" (2 Timothy 2:13). I have not been divorced. But as a fellow sinner, I have failed God enough to know that he always will do whatever it takes to love us back to wherever we need to be.

A Sacred Commitment

As we've well documented in previous chapters, our modern culture is friendly to divorce and hostile to the idea of marriage as an irrevocable covenant. If we want marriages to survive in this environment, we must be willing to go against society's grain and embrace marriage as the sacred institution God created it to be. In his article "Bonds of Steel," Donald Harvey is right on target when he says marriages that survive share at least three characteristics:

- They are "committed to marriage as a sacred institution."
- They are "committed to marriage as a relationship."
- They have "a vital faith and commitment to God."[3]

These characteristics not only enable couples to survive the storms of life but to soar because of them. Adversity puts steel into our souls. Believing that marriage is sacred and God is sovereign will get couples through the deepest troubles and darkest nights.

As a minister I always conclude a wedding ceremony with these words to the bride and groom: "In the presence of God, and with your family and friends as witnesses, I pronounce you 'one'—together in the Lord. You are now husband and wife. What God has joined together let no one separate." Why do I say this? Because I want the newly married couple to understand that what they've just done is sacred. It's forever. Deuteronomy 23:23 says that God will hold them accountable for their vows: "Whatever your lips utter you must be sure to do, because you made your vow freely to the LORD your God with your own mouth." And they not only made their vows before God. They also spoke them publicly. Their fundamental integrity in the eyes of friends and family is also at stake.

How much better would marriages fare if wedding parties met on an annual basis to hold couples accountable for the promises made on their wedding day? Just a thought!

SACRIFICE: THE HEART OF COVENANT

Once a little boy asked his dad, "How much does it cost to get married?"

"I don't know yet," the father replied. "I'm still paying."

Let's face it: Marriage costs. In fact, marriage is the most expensive and sacrificial of all earthly relationships. It demands total sacrifice and complete death to self—and self never dies easily. That may be why someone has said, "Marriage involves three rings: an engagement ring, a wedding ring, and suffering!"

In an article called "Love and Its Counterfeits," social commentator Douglas Minson says that he is suspicious of any universal formula promoted for making marriage work. (Aren't we all!) "But if there is a formula," Minson continues, "I suspect it can be boiled down to a mutual confidence in the selfless, even sacrificial, commitment of each spouse to the other." Minson's suspicions are correct. The Bible gives us God's guaranteed formula for making marriage work: covenant. And at the heart of covenant is exactly what Minson described: "the selfless, even sacrificial, commitment of each spouse to the other."

Covenant is the singularly spectacular gift of giving yourself totally to another person. "Marriage is not a joining of two worlds," says Minson, "but an abandoning of two worlds in order that one new one might be formed."[4] Upon entering covenant, each individual surrenders completely in loving trust to the other person. Two become one. Both spouses sacrifice their own desires in order to fulfill the desires of their mate. Sexual relationships and even emotional affairs with people outside of marriage are ruled out. In fact, all narcissistic selfishness is put on the chopping block. When you're in covenant, you have to talk when you don't want to talk, listen when you don't want to listen, love when you don't want to love, even stay when you want to leave. The price is high—but that's the cost of covenant. And the return on the investment is well worth it.

Recently a pastor friend of mine told me about a lady in his church who turned in an envelope marked "Building Fund." Inside the envelope was a beautiful diamond ring along with an unsigned letter that read:

> My husband and I are well blessed financially, and we give regularly to the church. We have given liberally to the building fund. However, after reading the words of David, "I will not sacrifice to the Lord my God burnt offerings that cost me nothing," I realized that I had not yet sacrificed anything. So I have enclosed my diamond ring, which is my most treasured material possession. My husband worked two jobs for several years in order to buy me this ring. This is my sacrifice to one who loves me even more than my husband.

Beautiful! This woman understood something that few people ever grasp: Covenant requires sacrifice—and sacrifice isn't sacrifice unless it actually costs something. Her letter referred to an Old Testament story in which God told King David to build an altar on a certain threshing floor so that a plague on Israel might end. David went out immediately and offered to buy the threshing floor from its owner. When the owner said that he would give the threshing floor to the king at no charge, David replied, "No,

I insist on paying you for it. I will not sacrifice to the LORD my God burnt offerings that cost me nothing" (2 Samuel 24:24).

In his book *The Marriage Covenant,* Derek Prince writes: "Two things are essential for entering into a permanent relationship with God: a covenant and a sacrifice. Without a covenant there can be no relationship with God; without a sacrifice there can be no covenant."[5]

Marriage, as a forever covenant between a husband, wife, and Almighty God, requires continual, daily sacrifice. That being true, let me ask you a personal question: What do you do daily for your spouse that costs you something?

Sacrifice Requires Humility

Surfing the Internet one day, I ran across an interesting article entitled "The Essential Humility of Marriage." It was based on a presentation made by Dr. Terry Hargrove at a Smart Marriages conference in July 2000. In closing his keynote address, Hargrove gave this description of the essential humility that is needed for sacrifice in a long-term marriage:

> This is the essential humility of marriage: partners committing themselves to the enormous task of creating a new person—a relationship—an "us-ness." Then these partners growing that marital "us" by the humiliating process of realizing that many of the issues that cause conflict are about their own backgrounds and destructive patterns; by being humble enough to embrace marital work responsibly and reliably so as to not take advantage of each other; and finally, by subjugating [themselves] to the tough training of sacrifice and teachability—giving up old habits and defenses that prevent us from growing.
>
> Is subjugation, humility and humiliation painful? In the long run, not really.... When we lose control of ourselves and totally give to our spouses and the relationship, we get a sense of peace of who we are as individuals, and a sense of satisfaction that we are truly connected. And if that kind of humility can take place in creating a stable, secure, and sincere "us," then we will have long and loving marriages.[6]

I think Mike Mason nails it: "There is nothing like the experience of being humbled by another person, and by the same person day in and day out. It can be exhausting, unnerving, infuriating, disintegrating. There is no suffering like the suffering involved in being (intimately) close to another person." Mason goes on to say that there is no joy or comfort like "the joy and comfort wrung out like wine from the crush and ferment of two lives being pressed together."[7]

The Sweetness of Surrender

As a guest on Oprah Winfrey's talk show, respected journalist Iris Krasnow said that four things about marriage are certain:

- At times it can be hell.

- The grass is never greener on the other side.

- Nobody is perfect, including you, so you may as well love the one you are with.

- You should savor the highs, because the dips are just around the corner.

Krasnow admits to going through times when she and her husband were ready to quit their marriage. What married person hasn't felt that way at some point? I know I have. But the Krasnows' marriage took a dramatic turn for the better when they decided to let go of Hollywood's "happily-ever-after" myth and accept the fact that their marriage was imperfect. Every marriage is! They surrendered to the reality that marriage can be a pain, and they went on. This change of expectations brought immediate positive results and led to the writing of her book *Surrendering to Marriage*.

Krasnow defines surrender not as subjection but freedom. She says that surrendering to marriage means "surrendering to the promise of 'I do' that you made on your wedding day, and working as hard as you can to fulfill it." It means letting go of the common fantasy that says the quality of your happiness will dramatically improve once you walk down that aisle. The truth is that no person can make you happy. Happiness is an inside job, and only you can make it happen. Marriages that are headed for divorce can be salvaged if couples would only change their expectations and let go of the idea that their spouse is responsible for their happiness.

To Krasnow, surrendering means that you "push through waves of sadness and rage and accept them as part of the whole marriage organism that also includes the profound joy of being in a committed union and of giving your kids a rock to hold onto." It means "we must be forgiving and flexible. We must keep our marriages alive, and revive them when they are dying. We must surrender to reality and let go of fantasy."[8]

On the back page of Iris's book, her husband, Chuck, gives his take on the key ingredients of marriage: "Love is the attraction, even lust, for your partner. That is how it starts. Devotion is a commitment to the other, even when it's not easy or fun. Surrender is the pleasure of understanding the first two." Both Krasnows believe that "staying married and staying humble is a path to psychic and spiritual wholeness."[9] Is the fact that *Surrendering to Marriage* has hit the top of the charts a signal that unhappy couples are tired of trying all the things that don't work and desperate enough to take a look at what does: sacrifice and surrender? I hope so.

Taking the "Walk of Death"

Please don't miss what I'm about to say. It's worth the price of this book: *Covenant is the heart of marriage, and sacrifice is the heart of covenant.* Marriage is the closest bond possible between two human beings, and the cost of that extraordinary closeness is nothing less than the sacrifice of your whole self. If you leave sacrifice out of your marriage covenant, you have only the shell of empty ritual. Apply it, however, and you have the potential to revolutionize your marriage.

In covenant marriage you must be willing to take the "walk of death" we described in chapter 4. Every time self raises its ugly head in protest, that's the time for another walk. You must die to yourself again and again. It's a continuous process—a lifetime of minifunerals.

Yes, sacrifice will cost you. As Mike Mason admits, "There is really nothing like this lifelong cauterization of the ego that must take place in marriage."[10] But I guarantee the return on your investment of total self will be worth every sacrifice. Nothing is closer to heaven on earth than a marriage in which a husband and wife rival each other in giving themselves sacrificially to one another. At its best, "marriage is defined by a positive virtue," Gary Thomas says. "It presumes the gift of self."[11]

THE ROOT OF ALL MARRIAGE PROBLEMS

Once a well-built, middle-aged man was questioned about his tremendous physique. "I really owe it all to my wife," he explained. "We got married twenty years ago and began arguing. I decided, however, that I was not going to argue. Every time an argument broke out, I went for a walk. This magnificent body that you see is a result of twenty years of outdoor living."

I want to be gut-level honest with you: Maintaining a loving, intimate relationship between two selfish and imperfect human beings is the most difficult, most complex, and most time-consuming challenge any of us will face in this lifetime. Did I hear a silent amen? Marriage is never neutral. When it's good, it's awesome; when it's bad, it's awful. Marriage has the potential to produce our greatest joy and highest sense of fulfillment. It also has the ability to produce our greatest pain and deepest sense of dissatisfaction. Did I hear another amen?

Which will characterize your marriage—joy or pain? Fulfillment or dissatisfaction? The answers are really up to you. That's because the root cause for every problem in marriage is selfishness. If we could kick the person responsible for most of our marriage problems, we wouldn't be able to sit down for a solid week. We're all selfish—no exceptions. And marriage forces us to confront our selfishness. As the late journalist Helen Rowland said, "Marriage is the operation by which a woman's vanity and a man's egotism are extracted without anesthetic."[12]

In the previous chapter we contrasted covenant and contract. Here is another difference between the two: Contract is an "if you do this, then I'll do that" relationship; covenant is a "whatever it takes" relationship. In contract the focus is on self, and the question is "What are my rights?" or "What do I get out of this?" In covenant the focus is on the other person, and the question is "How can I meet the needs of my partner?" or "How can I put the personal interests of my spouse before my own?" Covenantal unselfishness is critical for a loving, lasting marriage. You can read a hundred books on marriage, but none will tell you anything more important than this one truth.

All Wrapped Up

I grew up in Alabama with honeysuckle vines in the ditch behind our home. Honeysuckle is stubborn; its tendrils twine in one direction only, and nothing can make them coil another way. Selfishness, like a honeysuckle vine, wraps itself around the heart and demands control. And getting a selfish heart to bend the other way is almost impossible.

Did you hear about the husband who was so selfish that when he won a trip for two to Hawaii, he went twice? Or how about the self-centered wife who came into her marriage with a large inheritance? She told her husband, "If it weren't for my money, this house wouldn't be here. If it weren't for my money, the Mercedes wouldn't be in the driveway. In fact, if it weren't for my money, the recliner you're sitting in wouldn't be here."

To which her husband replied, "If it weren't for your money, *I* wouldn't be here!"

Selfishness has to be right, has to win, has to be in control, has to have the final word. In modern culture such selfishness is the norm, and personal gratification is life's highest goal. We have bought into the Burger King philosophy: "I'll have it my way." When another person's goals or desires cross our own, we tell them, "It's my way or the highway!"

For several years a particular insurance company gave its customers the promise of security by offering them "a piece of the rock." The company's newest advertisement has changed for the times, however. It says, "Be your own rock." That's the cry of selfishness: "I want what's best for me in all situations. My good is what's most important. I am my own rock!"

But selfishness makes false promises. It doesn't deliver. I'm told that when Elvis Presley decided to be "king" of his life and began to drift into greater and greater self-indulgence, he ended up self-destructing. The story is told that in his battle with prescription drugs, he would slip off into a stupor and tell his bodyguards, "I'd rather be unconscious than miserable."

You see, selfishness promises freedom and fulfillment, but it delivers misery and devastation. It's even hazardous to our health. Larry Sherlitz of the University of California cites research proving that the degree to which people talk about themselves—how much they say "I," "me," and "mine"—predicts death from heart disease more effectively than cholesterol levels and weight.[13] Amazing, isn't it? Unselfish people not only have longer marriages, they live longer lives!

A "We" Experience

The twentieth-century poet T. S. Eliot said, "Marriage is the greatest test in the world.... It is much more than a test of sweetness of temper, as people sometimes think; it is a test of the whole character and affects every action." When two self-willed people get married, the possibilities of conflict, crisis, and chaos are mind-boggling. There is a constant test of whims and wills. He wants his way. She wants her way. As Katherine Porter says, marriage "is the merciless revealer, the great white searchlight turned on the darkest places of human nature."[14]

The only chance a couple has for passing the test of marriage is to stop insisting on getting their own ways. "Me-ness" must become "we-ness," or it will turn into meanness. Marriage is designed by God to be a "we" experience. And only when your happiness results primarily from the happiness of your mate do you know that you have successfully moved from "me" to "we."

A few years ago, an Alabama couple won a "Happy Marriage" contest with this description of their marriage:

We gave...when we wanted to receive.
We served...when we wanted to feast.

We shared…when we wanted to keep.
We listened…when we wanted to talk.
We submitted…when we wanted to reign.
We forgave…when we wanted to remember.
We stayed…when we wanted to leave.[15]

Wow! I'm thrilled that a description of one couple's "walk of death" won the contest, because that kind of unselfish sacrifice is the only way to have a truly happy marriage. The more unselfish we are, the happier we will be.

Unfortunately, most of us are too self-centered to ever experience the fullness of joy that we long for in marriage. We are the "Jesse James" of our own lives, robbing ourselves of the best that life has to offer. We are our own worst enemy.

Divorce Is an Act of Selfishness

Richard Cohen, *Washington Post* critic-at-large, once defended the divorces of public figures Bob Dole and Newt Gingrich by saying, "These guys were in a dead marriage. To remain in such a marriage would be itself a form of death." Commenting on Cohen's assessment, Diane Sollee writes, "That represents the mood of the majority. Americans believe they can 'have it all' and deserve to have it all…no one, we have come to believe, should have to live in an unhappy marriage. We hold this truth to be self-evident."

Paradoxically, according to research Americans say they value marriage and family above everything—and then divorce over nothing. In explaining why we say one thing and do another, Sollee says, "Social scientists postulate a diminished ability for self sacrifice; a lack of commitment; a loss of a sense of duty; a pervasive narcissism; and an overwhelming sense of entitlement."

But Sollee believes that divorce has little to do with character and much to do with knowledge. She says that people have "an inaccurate understanding of what makes marriages work—or fail." Therefore, she says, "if people knew how to make their marriages work they would keep their vows, raise their children, and no one would have to point fingers and accuse them of being 'entitled narcissists.'" According to Sollee, the solution lies in skills-based education.[16]

That reminds me of the story of the hobo who stole rides on passing trains; he was taken in by a rich and benevolent gentleman and educated in the finest schools—only to return one day and steal the railroad company. Unfortunately, more skills won't solve the self problem. Educated self is still self, and self has to die for marriage to live.

From a biblical perspective, there are three causes of divorce: (1) selfishness, (2) selfishness, and (3) selfishness. And there is only one antidote: covenant's "walk of death." Learning marriage skills is fine; I'm for it. But in order for a marriage to survive and soar over the long term, a proper understanding of covenant and an acceptance of its terms must precede skills-based education.

Learning to Serve

Two questions reveal whether or not you are genuinely taking that "walk of death." The first is, Are you happily serving your mate? It has been said that marriage is like a tennis match; you'll never win consistently until you learn to serve well. For this reason you need to stay on the lookout for big and small ways to practice serving your spouse. And the gauge of your success as a servant will be how you act when you are treated like one! As Jesus said, "The greatest among you will be your servant" (Matthew 23:11). In a successful covenant marriage, both husband and wife serve each other joyfully for life.

The second question is this: Are you graciously submitting to your spouse? Paul tells us in Ephesians 5:21 that we are to "submit to one another out of reverence for Christ." Easy? Not at all! Because we are selfish, it is only by making Jesus the Lord of our lives and relying on the inner power of the Holy Spirit that we are able to mutually submit to and serve one another in marriage. Without Christ, marriage is at best an "iffy" proposition. Self will eventually get out of control and cause chaos. Only Jesus can give us the desire and the determination to be unselfish—not to mention the power to pull it off.

When Jesus went to the cross, he took the ultimate "walk of death." Now, as recipients of his salvation, we are called to imitate his love and display his attitude—in marriage and in all our relationships. We must die to our own fleshly desires daily. In other words, we must continually crucify the urge to selfishly measure every action and decision solely on the basis of what is best for us.

Paul goes on to explain in Ephesians 5:22–33 that a marriage between husband and wife is supposed to mirror Christ's marriage to the church. Christ's commitment to the church is total. He loved us while we were yet sinners. He died in order that we might live. He is faithful to us even when we're unfaithful to him.

As a covenant partner, you must love your spouse as Christ loves you and die to yourself in order for your marriage to live. I guarantee that the following words of Paul, fleshed out in your relationship with your spouse, will revolutionize your marriage:

> If you have any encouragement from being united with Christ, if any comfort from his love, if any fellowship with the Spirit, if any tenderness and compassion, then make my joy complete by being likeminded, having the same love, being one in spirit and purpose. Do nothing out of selfish ambition or vain conceit, but in humility consider others better than yourselves. Each of you should look not only to your own interests, but also to the interests of others. Your attitude should be the same as that of Christ Jesus. (Philippians 2:1–5)

Here's another statement from Paul that should be on the refrigerator of every Christian home:

> Be completely humble and gentle; be patient, bearing with one another in love. Make every effort to keep the unity of the Spirit through the bond of peace.... "In your anger do not sin": Do not let the sun go down while you are still angry, and do not give the devil a foothold.... Be kind and compassionate to one another, forgiving

each other, just as in Christ God forgave you. (Ephesians 4:2–3, 26–27, 32)

In closing this chapter, my mind turns to a beautiful and well-known prayer by St. Francis of Assisi. A selfless servant, Francis was a preacher in Italy during the Middle Ages. As we think about our marriages, why don't we make his prayer our own?

> Lord, make us instruments of peace.
> Where there is hatred, let us so love.
> Where there is injury, pardon.
> Where there is discord, union.
> Where there is doubt, faith.
> Where there is despair, hope.
> Where there is darkness, light.
> Where there is sadness, joy.
> Grant that we may not so much seek
>   to be consoled, as to console.
> To be understood, as to understand.
> To be loved, as to love.
> For it is in giving that we receive.
> It is in pardoning that we are pardoned.
> And it is in dying that we are born to eternal life.

Chapter 8

A COVENANT WEDDING

*Marriage is the greatest institution ever invented! It can be
good, or it can be great, but it should never be ordinary!*

—Neil Clark Warren

Many years ago I performed a wedding ceremony in which the best
man was none other than the famous comedian Bob Hope. At that
time Bob had been married for more than fifty years (it's closer to seventy
as I write this). As you would expect, Bob believes that laughter is an
important ingredient in a lasting marriage. "If you can laugh together, you
can get through anything," he has been known to say.

But Bob also knows that marriage is more than a barrel of laughs.
When asked about the real secret to his long-term marriage, he gives a one-
word answer: "Delores." That is quite a tribute to his lovely wife! But I
have a feeling that both he and Delores have worked hard at their marriage. Here's why I think so: Just before we went out to take our places at
the altar, Bob looked at me and said, "Reverend, don't worry about me. I
won't be telling any jokes tonight. Marriage is a serious and sacred thing."

Way to go, Bob! And congratulations on your long-lasting marriage in
a sector of our culture in which divorce is as common as blue jeans.
Getting married in Hollywood is such a high risk, couples should register
for paper plates!

Unfortunately, an increasing number of Americans do not share Bob's conviction that marriage is a serious and sacred institution. Adopting a more casual attitude, couples now say their wedding vows in strange and unique places. I have heard about weddings in airplanes, helicopters, and boats. Some couples have gotten married while skydiving, parasailing, or even dropping on the end of a bungee cord. Last year I read about a dozen or more couples getting married on a roller coaster!

Granted, marriage, with all its ups and downs, can be a roller coaster ride. But to me, the altar of a church is still the best place for Christians to get married. There, a true covenant wedding can include its three key components: the commitment, the ceremony, and the celebration.

A COVENANT COMMITMENT

Marriage is a huge commitment. Think about it. What could we give anyone that is more significant than giving ourselves? Frankly, I believe it is commitment—even more than love—that is the real "glue" of marriage. Whatever comes, good or bad, we can ride it out if we are forever and unconditionally committed.

The word *commitment* makes many people shiver, but it's actually a softer word than *covenant*. Commitment, in the modern sense, still leaves you in control. You can choose to commit to something and then control the length and depth of that commitment. But covenant, as we discussed in the last chapter, calls for complete surrender. In covenant you give up control; you surrender your personal rights in order to become one with the other person.

In the Old Testament, Ruth said to Naomi: "Where you go I will go, and where you stay I will stay" (Ruth 1:16). That is covenant commitment. In the New Testament, God says, "Never will I leave you; never will I forsake you" (Hebrews 13:5). That is ultimate covenant commitment. And because God will not forsake us, we have the potential to keep our covenant commitment in marriage.

That level of commitment, however, is not automatic. It requires continual work and maintenance. It says: "I have chosen this path with you,

118

and I will give it my absolute best. I am in this for the long haul, and I am determined to make our marriage the best it can be. I will give it one hundred percent. I will do whatever it takes. And I will never, never give up on our relationship." As Scott Stanley explains in his book *The Heart of Commitment,* "Commitment is based on choices on the wedding day and every day thereafter. It involves a continual commitment to the commitment."[1] Ultimately it is the strength of the commitment, not the size of the problems, that determines the success or failure of a marriage.

Stanley uses an old naval expression to convey the essence of commitment. In a battle in which surrender was not an option, the captain would order the "colors to be nailed to the mast." That permanent fixing of the flag meant it was impossible to lower it in the heat of battle in order to raise the white flag of surrender. Says Stanley, "With surrender no longer an option, crew members were motivated to fix their minds on how to best win the battle."[2]

I believe God desires marriage to be based on a covenant commitment in which the "colors are nailed to the mast"—all exits are closed, all doors are shut and locked. We have to be in it "for better, for worse; for richer, for poorer; in sickness and in health; until death do us part." In the face of marital battles, we must refuse to surrender and focus instead on how to win the battle.

A Commitment to Priorities

In a nationwide survey by the FindWhat.com Internet search engine, 46 percent of people surveyed said they would pay a million dollars to discover the secret to taking five strokes off their golf game. On the other hand, only 17 percent said they would pay a million dollars to find out the secret to a happy marriage.[3] I wonder how much happier their marriages would be if those golfers spent as much time, money, and energy on perfecting their marriages as they do on perfecting their golf swings. Just a thought!

Chris Spielman, a veteran football player who made two million dollars a year playing for the Buffalo Bills, loves football. "Nobody in the world loves football as much as I do," he says. But football is not Chris's top priority, and he proved that in a beautiful and touching way that epitomizes covenant commitment. When his beautiful wife, Stephane, was diagnosed with breast cancer, Chris responded by walking away from football and giving up his two-million-dollar salary so he could be with his wife and children. He never missed a doctor's appointment with Stephane, and he held her hand through chemotherapy. When Stephane lost her hair, Chris shaved his head. "When Chris told me that he would be with me through this ordeal," Stephane said, "he meant it. He doesn't go back on any of his commitments."[4]

Chris and Stephane Spielman understand that commitment is a matter of priorities. So does legendary head coach Bobby Bowden of Florida State University. Bowden loves to tell stories about the importance of football in his life—but only as a ploy to get the attention of his audience. During a visit to our church, Bowden said that at one time or another, every coach gets asked this terrible question by his wife: "Do you love me more than football?" When Bowden's wife posed that question to him, his reply was classic: "College or pro?" But as this championship-winning coach is quick to point out, football always takes a back seat to God and family. "Success has followed me, but it's not because I followed football," he told our congregation. "My priorities are God, family, others, and football."

Keeping our priorities straight is not easy, but it's absolutely critical to covenant commitment. Recently our church threw a big party for my fortieth anniversary in ministry. As part of that celebration, my wife and daughters were featured on a surprise video, and each one talked about how family was always the absolute first priority in their husband and father's life. As any busy pastor will tell you, making family a priority doesn't happen accidentally. Because of the myriad demands on my time, I had to work hard at keeping my family number one.

How did I do this? For one thing, I "calendared in" my family. On

Tuesday nights I took one of my girls out on a date, and I reserved Friday nights as date night for Leigh and me. For another thing, I gave my wife and daughters an open-door policy to my office and meetings. I left many a committee meeting to respond to a knock on the door by Leigh or one of the girls. Often the only thing needed was a twenty-dollar bill, but more important than the money was the message that "my dad (or my husband) is available for me." Far too many ministers, with good intentions, have neglected their own families while taking care of the families of others. Some have allowed the ministry to become a mistress. For me, my family is my ministry. The one thing that validates my ministry in the pulpit is my ministry at home with my own family. I'd rather be known as a great husband and father than a great pastor.

Where Parents Fit In

As someone once said, "A marriage kept on the back burner will die from lack of heat." Covenant marriage is a commitment that establishes a primary relationship so important that all other relationships become secondary. It sets the relationship between husband and wife as first priority. Even biological parents must take a back seat. The Bible says clearly that "a man [because of covenant] will leave his father and mother and be united to his wife, and they will become one flesh" (Genesis 2:24). Jesus quoted this verse in the Gospels, confirming that the marriage relationship must supersede all other relationships, past, present, and future (see Matthew 19:5 and Mark 10:7).

Don't misunderstand. Parents are important. Turn a television camera on a three-hundred-pound linebacker, and he will invariably say, "Hi, mom!" The bond between a mother and son ("mama's boy") and a father and daughter ("daddy's girl") is deep and long-lasting. It should be. The Bible calls for a high level of respect for parents and tells us to always honor them. When we read about a grown man acting like a jerk toward his mother and treating her with disrespect or disdain, we're repulsed. But as bad as that is, it is even worse for a man to treat his covenant wife with disrespect, because she is to be more highly honored and respected than his own mother. How many marriages could be radically changed for the better if the husband would simply begin to treat his wife with the same level of respect and honor that he has for his mother? If he were to treat her with an even higher level of respect and honor, I guarantee he'd experience a little bit of heaven in that home.

Of course, a wife is to reverence her husband above her parents as well. For a marriage to not only survive but soar, both husband and wife must continually remind each other of this absolute fact: "You are my number one priority, and you always will be." Then those words must be proved by appropriate actions.

The Preeminence of Christ

I need to add a caveat here. We're talking about priorities among human relationships. Even more important than our relationships with our spouses and families is our relationship with God. Before Leigh and I married, I told her about my conversion experience and my call into the ministry. It was critical for her to know that she was marrying a Christian with an irrevocable call on his life—a fact that would always dictate where we lived and how we lived. At times it could mean great sacrifice.

I expressed to Leigh that my ultimate love and loyalty belonged to my Lord. For Leigh, that was good news. It meant that I would be a better husband and covenant partner that I could ever be without God as the center of my life.

I'm reminded of the overly zealous groom who sang to his bride during the wedding ceremony a song entitled "I'd Rather Have Jesus." I do think he could have chosen a more appropriate song, but at least the place of Christ in his marriage was well established!

Think about your own life and marriage. Is Jesus one priority among many priorities, or is he your absolute Lord? The fact is, Jesus must be more than your priority; he must be preeminent. He is in a class all by himself. As the saying goes, "He is Lord of all or not Lord at all!" In my own marriage I've found that it is only when Jesus is preeminent in my life that I am able to make my wife my first priority and put her needs above my own. Only by yielding our personalities and temperaments to the Holy Spirit's control are we able to unselfishly give ourselves to each other in covenant marriage.

A Commitment to Permanence

Not long ago Leigh asked me, "Will you still love me when I'm old and gray?"

"Sure, why not?" I responded. "I've loved you through three other colors!" Then, sensing an immediate need to say something else, I asked her, "Will you still love me when I'm old, gray, and flabby?"

She smiled and said, "I do!"

Underneath our joking, of course, is a very serious foundation: an absolute commitment to permanence in our relationship. We have made a covenant commitment to *stick it out* and *work it out* "until death do us part." Research shows that couples who enter marriage recognizing that it is a commitment of permanence are much more likely to successfully manage marital conflicts than those who get married without that understanding.

Somewhere I read a cute story about a little boy sitting in the nurse's office at school with his shirt pulled up and his tummy sticking out. He sat like that, rubbing his stomach, for more than an hour. Finding this a bit unusual, the nurse decided to check with his teacher. She went to his classroom, pulled the teacher aside, and described the boy's unusual behavior.

"Oh, my!" the teacher exclaimed. "He said he had a stomachache, and I told him to go to your office and stick it out till noon!" And that's exactly what he did!

Covenant marriage is a commitment to "stick it out." But for how long? I heard of a ninety-year-old husband who filed for divorce. When the judge asked, "Why divorce your wife after all these years?" he answered, "Because I made a commitment to stick it out until all our children died."

That old man had it wrong. Marriage is designed by God to be a permanent relationship "until death do us part"—and that means the death of a spouse. The goal of every married couple should be to finish well. In the 1968 Olympics, Tanzanian marathon runner John Stephen Akhwari limped into an empty stadium more than an hour after all the other runners had crossed the finish line. When asked why he had not just given up, the gutsy competitor replied, "My country did not send me seven thousand miles to start the race. They sent me seven thousand miles to finish it."[5]

Hang in there! Don't let go! A covenant marriage is meant to last. In the appendices at the end of this book, I have included two sample ceremonies that you are free to use or adapt for your own purposes: a covenant wedding ceremony for new brides and grooms, and a covenant recommitment ceremony for couples who are already married but want to renew and "upgrade" their commitment to one another. If you didn't mean these words when you said them to your spouse the first time, why not say them now that you really mean them: "I'm going to give myself to you and you alone—until death do us part."

A COVENANT CEREMONY

The second component of a covenant wedding is the ceremony. Before we look at a modern wedding ceremony, however, let's consider two of its predecessors: the Old Testament ceremony of blood covenant and a typical Jewish wedding ceremony of the first century.

The Covenant of Blood

In ancient times when two Hebrews entered into a blood covenant, they went through a special ceremony. We don't know exactly what such a ceremony was like, since customs varied from time to time and the Bible doesn't spell out the details. However, by putting various Scripture passages together, we can get an idea of what a basic ceremony must have included.

David and Jonathan

The friendship of David and Jonathan presents us with a classic example of a covenant friendship and illustrates one instance of a blood covenant ceremony:

> After David had finished talking with Saul, Jonathan became one in spirit with David, and he loved him as himself. From that day Saul kept David with him and did not let him return to his father's house. And Jonathan made a covenant with David because he loved him as himself. Jonathan took off the robe he was wearing and gave it to David, along with his tunic, and even his sword, his bow and his belt. (1 Samuel 18:1–4)

Here the friends stand opposite one another, remove their robes and tunics, and exchange them. To these two Hebrews, the robe symbolically represents the person who wears it. By taking off his robe and giving it to his covenant partner, each man is saying, "I am giving you my total self, one hundred percent. All that I am, I give to you." Then by putting on each other's robe they are saying, "We are now one. I have put on you, and you have put on me."

Their belts held their weapons, and they had probably been removed first and set aside. Now each picks up his belt and gives it to the other. In the giving of the belt, each is saying, "Here is my strength and ability to fight. When you are weak, I will be there for you." A major purpose of covenant is for two partners to compensate for each other's weaknesses. We all have weaknesses. Covenant says, "I will cover your weaknesses with my strengths, and you will cover my weaknesses with your strengths." When we cover each other's weaknesses, we add incredible strength to the relationship. Together we are strong—much stronger than we ever could have been separately. Whatever we lack as individuals, covenant brings to the relationship.

Next the two friends exchange weapons. In doing so, they are saying to each other, "From this moment on, your enemies are my enemies, and your battles are my battles. Whoever takes you on takes me on. I will fight, defend, and protect you forever."

The description of David and Jonathan's covenant ceremony ends there. But from other parts of Scripture we know that the core element of a blood covenant ceremony is the "walk of death." As we described in chapter 4, the covenant is actually "cut" by sacrificing animals and splitting them down the middle as described in chapter 15 of Genesis:

> But Abram said, "O Sovereign LORD, how can I know that I will gain possession of it?" So the LORD said to him, "Bring me a heifer, a goat and a ram, each three years old, along with a dove and a young pigeon." Abram brought all these to him, cut them in two and arranged the halves opposite each other; the birds, however, he did not cut in half. (Genesis 15:8–10)

The two partners stand between the bloody halves of the dead animals with their backs to each other. They walk through the halves, make a figure eight (which symbolizes eternity), and return to face each other. In taking this "walk of death," they are vowing to each other, "I am dying to myself—giving up my independent living, my rights, and my prior relationships—in order to begin a new walk with you, my covenant partner, until death." And in recognition of the dead animals on either side, they are saying, "God do this to me if I break this covenant. Kill me on the spot. I wouldn't deserve to live."

Pagan Ritual

History records that pagan nations often took the rituals of covenant a step further. At this point in a pagan ceremony, the partners made a cut on their wrists and raised their right arms to meet, mixing their blood. (Blood represents life, and blood intermingled symbolizes two lives becoming one.) Then they rubbed their wounds on the ground or against a stone to make certain a scar formed, thereby providing a constant reminder of their covenant responsibilities. The scar also stood as a signal to any potential attacker that the bearer had a covenant partner, and taking on one meant taking on both.

Please note: This pagan commingling of blood is not a practice that was followed by the Hebrews of the Old Testament, nor should it be practiced by Christians today. The Bible forbids the ceremonial cutting of flesh or drinking of blood (circumcision is the only exception). In the Old Testament, ceremonial blood was shed only by a substitutionary animal and then poured on the ground. In the New Testament, the blood of Jesus Christ was shed as a substitute on our behalf for the forgiveness of sins. My point in including this step is not to promote it, but simply to emphasize the seriousness with which covenants were regarded through the ages.

A New Identity

Next, as another symbol of total bonding, the partners in a covenant ceremony exchange names. Each partner takes the last name of the other as a part of his own name, symbolizing the fact that covenant brings them a new identity. Standing before witnesses, they speak out the terms and conditions of their covenant. They read a list of their assets and liabilities, and each receives the blessings and burdens of the other. From this day on, they share both resources and responsibilities.

The partners sit down to a covenant meal to celebrate the completion of the ceremony. They actually feed each other bread as a symbol of total oneness, saying in effect, "I am coming into you and you into me." Finally, they set up a memorial by piling up stones or planting a tree. This marks the spot and served as a permanent reminder of the covenant they've made. Some of the blood of the dead animals is sprinkled on the memorial.

Keep this blood covenant ceremony in mind as we take a look now at a Jewish wedding in Jesus' time. God used the Jewish wedding ceremony as a prophetic illustration of redemption and Christ's relationship to his bride, the church. The traditions of a modern Christian wedding are rooted in this relationship as well. Both are based on covenant.

A First-Century Jewish Wedding

A young Jewish man tells his father that he is ready to take the hand and heart of a young Jewish girl in covenant marriage. A lengthy father-and-son talk ensues, sometimes lasting hours or even days. Finally the father grants permission, and the details (such as what the payment for the bride will be) are worked out.

Taking the initiative, the prospective bridegroom travels with his father to the home of the prospective bride. Upon arrival the two fathers talk first, and then the son expresses to the father of the potential bride his desire to marry the man's daughter. He then tries to assure the father of his noble intentions to provide for and protect his would-be wife. At this time he presents some sort of payment for the bride. If the father of the future bride accepts the payment, the young man can marry the daughter.

Pastor and educator Ray Vander Laan explains what happens next:

> With negotiations complete, the custom was for the young man's father to pour a cup of wine and hand it to his son. His son would turn to the young woman, lift the cup and hold it out to her, saying, "This cup is a new covenant in my blood, which I offer to you." In other words, "I love you, and I'll give you my life. Will you marry me?" The young woman had a choice. She could take the cup and return it and say no. Or, she could answer without saying a word—by drinking the cup, her way of saying, "I accept your offer, and I give you my life in response."[6]

After the wine is shared, a betrothal benediction is pronounced, symbolizing that a covenant relationship had been established. From that moment it is understood that the bride is set apart exclusively for the bridegroom.

The groom and his father leave the bride's house and return to their own home. The groom remains there for a period of twelve months, separated from his bride. During this time of preparation, he busies himself with the task of building a house for his bride or at least an addition to his parent's home.

Meanwhile the bride is getting together her wardrobe and preparing for married life. She is working to make or find the most beautiful dress available for her wedding day. As the end of the twelve months approaches, she is ready and waiting for her groom. In addition to having her beautiful dress available, she makes sure she is always clean and "well-oiled" with aromatic spices. "Maybe today or tonight my man is coming for me," she tells her friends. She doesn't know the exact day—she only knows that it is coming and that she must be ready at a moment's notice. She awakens each morning with anticipation; throughout the day she looks into the distance, watching and waiting for her groom. In the evening's darkness she leaves her oil lamp burning as a sign that she is ready even if he were to arrive in the middle of the night.

As soon as the groom finishes building the new home or addition for his future family, he returns for his bride. Often the last touches on the house are completed toward the end of the day, so the groom calls together his best man and other male escorts and leads a nighttime procession by torchlight to the house of his bride.

As they approach the bride's home, the groom asks his companions, "Do you see the lamp burning?"

"Yes, we do," his friends answer. "It is burning brightly! She is ready!"

The groom and his friends sneak into the bride's house and announce their presence with a shout. Then he picks up his bride and carries her through the streets, proclaiming his joy.

The bride and her attendants return with the groom to his father's house. Later, the bride and groom enter the room or house he had been building, and in the privacy of that place, they enter into physical union for the first time and consummate the marriage.[7]

Think back over this whole, long, ceremonial process. Do you see how God uses the various aspects of the Jewish wedding ceremony to illustrate redemption and the coming of Christ for his church? Christ left his Father's house and came to earth to gain a bride for himself. The purchase price was his own blood, shed on Calvary's cross. Christ then returned to his Father's house to prepare a place for his bride, the church. Now we are watching and waiting for the day when Jesus will return for his church, and we will be with him forever. You know what I have to say to that? "Amen. Come, Lord Jesus!" (Revelation 22:20).

Ray Vander Laan reminds us that on the night of the Passover meal, Jesus said something that caught his disciples off guard. He ended the normal Passover ritual with these words: "This cup is the new covenant in my blood, which is poured out for you" (Luke 22:20). Says Vander Laan: "There are many meanings to that statement, but one of them, in common, ordinary language, was, 'I love you, and the only picture I can think of that will describe the power of my love for you is the pure love of a husband for his wife.'"

Every time we celebrate the Lord's Supper, we remember in vivid detail that statement of Christ. By grace his offer of love still reaches out to us today. Vander Laan continues: "He still says, 'I love you.' He still says, 'I offer you my life. Will you be my bride?' In a sense our salvation is nuptial. It begins when we say 'I do' to Christ's marriage proposal."[8]

Just like that Jewish bride-to-be, when we take the cup and drink it, we are responding to our heavenly Father's offer. We're saying, "I accept your love, and I give you my life in return." We become engaged to Christ in this present life. "I betrothed you to Christ," Paul writes, "to present you as a pure bride to her one husband" (2 Corinthians 11:2 RSV). When Christ returns for his bride, we will know complete and final union with him and celebrate at the "wedding supper of the Lamb" (Revelation 19:9).

The Modern Christian Ceremony

I have gone into detail about Old Testament covenant rituals and first-century Jewish weddings not to bore you, but hopefully to bless you as you realize that God designed marriage as a beautiful and blessed blood covenant. As we come to understand the history and meaning behind our modern wedding symbols, we can better appreciate the sanctity of marriage and the significance of the vows we speak.

To be painfully honest, I performed several hundred weddings before I had a good understanding of the meaning behind many of the symbols and traditions of today's Christian ceremony. It may well be that in most weddings, neither the preacher nor the bride and groom fully realize why they are doing what they are doing as they embrace the most common wedding traditions. That's a shame. They are cheating themselves out of much of the true beauty and blessing of a covenant wedding. Because one thing is crystal-clear: The principles of covenant profoundly impact the traditional wedding ceremony. And for that, I am grateful.

Let's take a look at the meaning behind some of our most common wedding traditions.

The Seating of Guests

The ushers seat the family and friends of the bride on one side of the sanctuary and the family and friends of the groom on the other side, symbolically recreating the blood covenant "walk of death" between the two halves of the sacrificed animals. As we've said before, this sacrificial "walk of death" is the heart of covenant and the ultimate key to lasting marriage. In covenant marriage, we die to prior relationships with family and friends and create a new relationship that supersedes all others. Death is necessary in order for marriage to live. The seating order also symbolizes the sacrifices made by family and friends to pave the way for the bride and groom to enter into their covenant relationship.

Special Seating of the Parents

The ushers seat the parents of the bride and groom in places of honor at the front of the sanctuary. They are given special seating because the Bible specifically teaches children to honor their parents. In addition, parents play a vital role in the covenant process. They give public support and approval of the marriage and act as witnesses to the covenant ceremony. In so doing they release their authority as primary caregivers and acknowledge the fact that they have given the bride and groom both roots and wings to establish a new primary relationship that transcends all others. From that point on, by covenant, the parents of the bride and groom are not to tamper with, manipulate, or try to control the marriage of their children. They must give the couple space and show sensitivity as they move forever from their position of authority to their new position as counselors (who only give counsel when it's asked for).

The White Runner

A white runner is rolled open down the aisle as a symbol that the wedding participants are walking on holy ground. In the Old Testament, when Moses found himself in the presence of God, he was told, "Take off your sandals, for the place where you are standing is holy ground" (Exodus 3:5). The wedding aisle is holy because God is present and plays an active role in the covenant ceremony. He is the one who joins two people together in covenant marriage. That's why marriage is called "holy matrimony."

The Initiator of Covenant

The groom enters the sanctuary before the bride and waits for her at the altar, because he is the initiator and the facilitator of the covenant. He is the one who popped the question and initiated the agreement. Of course, when a marriage is in trouble, it is not always the man's fault; but it is always his responsibility to do something about it. God holds the man responsible for the spiritual welfare of the home. As the husband, he is accountable for seeing that the marriage covenant is maintained and sustained.

Who Presents This Bride?

The bride's father walks his daughter down the aisle and presents her to the groom as a symbol of his endorsement of the groom and his support for the marriage. The symbolism of this act goes all the way back to the time when the heavenly Father brought the first bride, Eve, to the first man, Adam (see Genesis 2:22).

This giving away of the bride also symbolizes a transfer of authority. Remember, the groom had to initially come to the father and ask for the hand of his daughter in marriage. Now the father is formally bringing her to him.

Something else is significant about this action. According to the Bible, a father is responsible for the purity of his daughter until marriage. By personally bringing his daughter to her chosen groom, he is saying, "I present to you a bride who is pure. By God's grace, and under my supervision, she has saved herself for you and for this covenant relationship." In Bible times, the couple would be given white sheets or cloths for their wedding bed. In the process of consummating the marriage, the bride would bleed on these cloths as proof of her virginity. Then the wedding night sheets would become the possession of the bride's parents in case her virginity was later challenged (see Deuteronomy 22:13–18). Tragically, says pastor and author T. D. Jakes, many couples today cannot wave bloodstained sheets after the wedding night. Instead, he says, "the stains that they wave are battle scars from the past...tear stained pillowcases...unresolved issues."[9]

Lifting the Veil

As I write this chapter, my mind is flooded with memories of the day one week ago when I walked my second daughter down the aisle in our beautiful church and presented her to her groom in covenant marriage. Knowing that Shelby and Jon had saved themselves physically for their wedding night, it was a special blessing to be able to lift Shelby's veil, which represented modesty and purity, and present her to Jon. The veil and the white wedding dress are symbols of the purity and exclusiveness of the marriage covenant. Lifting the veil is a reminder, and in Shelby's case a testimony, that the physical relationship is to be consummated *after* the vows are spoken. Imagine the joy and blessing of a man and woman entering into a covenant relationship and giving themselves sexually to each other on their wedding night with no regrets or painful memories! Doing things God's way always brings us our greatest joy.

After the wedding the husband assumes responsibility for the purity of the heart and life of his bride. He does this by being the spiritual leader of the home and allowing God's Word to be the guide for their lives together. In biblical terminology, he is to "cleanse" her by the Word of God, just as Christ purifies believers by the Word (see Ephesians 5:25– 28). I know of no better exercise for a married couple than to read God's Word and pray together on a daily basis. It is the husband's God-given responsibility to see that this happens. One day every husband and father will answer to God for the spiritual welfare of his family.

Saying the Vows

In recent years more and more couples have wanted to write their own vows, and as a minister I used to go along with them and allow it. No more. I have learned my lesson. Vows should never be cute or crazy; they are supposed to be serious and sacred. (Since you brought it up, I also think the choice of songs should be sacred and not secular. The music in a covenant wedding should enhance the praise and worship of God and point to his miraculous activity in the life of the couple.) For the ceremonies I perform, I have returned to the traditional vows because they originate in God's Word and speak of the very things that represent covenant: "To have and to hold from this day forward; for better, for worse; for richer, for poorer; in sickness and in health; to love and to cherish; until death do us part."

These are all covenant promises, spoken as sacred oaths that characterize permanent bonding. This is blood covenant talk, and it should be. God gives us these vows, and they are non-negotiable.

The joining of right hands before saying the vows is another symbol of covenant, representing the merging of lives that is about to take place. As we've said, the essence of covenant is that two become one, joined at the heart forever. The clasping of hands also symbolizes the merging of resources each one brings to the covenant relationship. Not only are they dependent upon the right hand of God, they are now interdependent—totally dependent upon each other from this day forward.

The groom says the vows first for the same reason he enters the sanctuary first: it symbolizes his position as covenant initiator and facilitator. It also acknowledges the position of the wife as the responder in the relationship. In biblical marriage, there is always a leader and a responder.

For years, the words "and therefore I plight thee my troth" were spoken at the end of the vows. This phrase represented the covenant wrap-up. In today's English we would say, "and you have my absolute word that I am going to keep every promise I have just made to you."

The Unity Candle

Following the saying of vows, many couples move to light the unity candle. Typically there are three candles together, with the two on the outside already lit and the one in the center unlit. The bride and groom each take one of the lighted candles, light the center candle together, then extinguish their individual candles. This is a beautiful picture of two people taking the ceremonial "walk of death" by blowing out the candles of their individual lives and lighting the candle of their new life together as one.

The Exchange of Rings

The wedding ring is probably the most familiar symbol of covenant. It is the outward sign of a commitment made in the heart and should be worn as a continual reminder of that covenant commitment. (In some ancient cultures, the finger would be cut with a knife in such a way as to leave a permanent "ring" scar.) In a covenant relationship, the ring is a sign of identification. It is a bold message to the world that the person wearing the ring is taken; they're off limits. Formed as an unending circle, it symbolizes not only the unending nature of the marriage commitment but also God's love for us that never ends.

The ring is placed on the third finger of the left hand because the heart is on the left side, and it was once believed that a nerve ran from that finger straight to the heart. Covenant marriage is a heart-to-heart connection. Since the heart represents the total being, the covenant partners are saying to each other, "I give you all that I am. I belong to you. I love you with my whole heart."

In a wedding ceremony, I always hold up the bride's ring and say to the groom, "Every time you see this ring on the finger of your bride, let it remind you that on this date you gave this ring as a tangible symbol of a spiritual covenant of commitment. Let it remind you that your love for your bride is endless, and your commitment is forever."

Then I hand the ring to the groom and say, "Please slip this ring on the finger of your bride and say this to her: 'This ring is a symbol of my commitment to you. Wear it for me every day. I believe with all my heart that my love for you is forever. I give this ring to you as my loving wife.'"

Thinking about leaving? Forget it. It's too late. The ring is a constant reminder that a husband and wife have made a forever commitment to always love and never abandon each other.

The Lord's Supper

In the Old Testament, circumcision was the sign of the covenant God made with Abraham and his descendants. In the New Testament the Lord's Supper, with the eating of bread (representing the body of Christ) and the drinking of juice (representing the blood of Christ), serves as the reminder of our covenant of salvation. In many covenant weddings, couples use the partaking of the Lord's Supper as the spiritual climax of the ceremony. I think this is appropriate. It is because of our salvation covenant through the death and resurrection of Christ that we now have the opportunity to achieve a covenant oneness in marriage.

The Public Pronouncement

The powerful words "I now pronounce you husband and wife" are usually prefaced with the phrase "In the presence of God and these witnesses." Contrary to popular opinion, marriage is not a private matter between two individuals. It is a public covenant with an impressive array of witnesses, including God himself. Should we break covenant with a mate, we also break covenant with our family, our friends, and Almighty God. In the Bible, covenant vows between God and his bride, Israel, were spoken publicly. When Moses rehearsed covenant vows with the Israelites, they responded in public, "We will do everything the Lord has said" (Exodus 19:7–8). Covenants, by nature, are public rather than private.

Tying the Knot

It is said that little girls grow up to marry men like their fathers. If that's true, then I understand why so many women cry at weddings! Seriously, I have found that both sets of parents want the minister to "tie the knot" extremely tight for their newly married children. They know that rough times will come for the new couple and only a tight knot will hold them together.

Somewhere I read about two soldiers in World War II who took a rope and literally tied themselves together. They knew that the circumstances around them would get terrible at times, and either one might be tempted to bail out and run. By tying the knot between them, they were making sure they would stay connected when troubles came. They wanted a boundary, a protection—something to help them stay in the battle.

Maybe that's the reason we call marriage "tying the knot." There's great security in knowing that God ties the strongest knot possible in covenant marriage. In an old movie I saw a marriage ceremony in which the minister tied a cloth or sash around the wrists of the bride and groom, symbolically tying them together forever. I think that's a perfect illustration of what the Bible means when it says, "What God has tied together, let not man untie" (Matthew 19:6, my paraphrase).

Ultimately, what makes a marriage succeed is not just that the husband and wife are tied to each other but that both individually are tied to the Lord. As individuals, they must be tied to God in relationship before they can be tied to one another with any guarantee of permanence.

A COVENANT CELEBRATION

After most modern weddings comes the reception. This event is much more than an after-the-fact add-on. It is the important third component of a covenant wedding: the celebration. And like the ceremony, it is filled with covenant symbolism.

On a recent trip to Israel, I observed several Jewish weddings. One thing was evident in each of them: After the ceremony came the celebration! Happy music played, and all the participants and guests laughed, sang, danced, kissed, ate, and drank. I didn't even know the people, but I felt happier just watching them celebrate!

During a typical Jewish wedding celebration, the groom takes a glass, places it under his foot, and smashes it into a thousand tiny pieces. In ancient times this "breaking of glass" symbolized the destruction of the temple in Jerusalem. In modern times, however, it has come to denote the desire of the couple to remain married until the glass is repaired (meaning forever). It also represents a clean break with the past and the beginning of something new. Some grooms break a light bulb, making a loud noise. The point is that marriage demands attention. Listen up!

Martha Williamson tells a story about an acquaintance who got married to a Lithuanian woman in his fiancée's hometown in Europe. At the reception, though he did not speak the language, the groom somehow understood that he was supposed to hold his new bride in his arms as he stepped on a china plate. Remembering the Jewish tradition of the broken glass, he stomped repeatedly and enthusiastically on the plate in an effort to break it into as many pieces as possible. Williamson recalls, "The horrified matrons of the town rushed to stop him, for the number of breaks in the plate represented to the Lithuanians something very different: the number of children you will have!"[10]

Traditions are great. We just need to make sure we know exactly what they mean! Let's look at a few of the traditions of a typical wedding celebration to discover the special meaning behind them.

The Wedding Feast

I am told that one of the root meanings of the word *covenant* is "to feed." In Bible times a covenant meal followed the wedding ceremony. This feast illustrated the joy and unity of the newly married couple. Often it lasted for a full week!

I think it's significant that Jesus chose the setting of a wedding feast in Cana of Galilee to perform his first miracle (see John 2:1–11). When the wine ran out, he turned water into wine and prevented the celebration from being cut short. In this way he not only honored his mother, who had asked him to do something about the problem; he also honored the covenant wedding traditions of the day.

The truth is, every marriage needs Jesus, and most need a good miracle or two to make it! Fortunately, when we invite Jesus to the wedding, we can expect him to stay for the marriage.

Feeding Each Other Cake

Have you ever wondered why newlyweds feed a bite of cake to each other at their reception? I have. The cake feeding was my least favorite part of my own wedding. I thought it was silly—a photographers' conspiracy. Of course, I didn't have a clue what it meant. I missed the whole point.

Now I know that this tradition symbolizes a husband and wife becoming one. By feeding cake to each other, the couple is saying, "This cake represents my body. As you eat it, I am coming into you; and as I eat the cake that you give me, you are coming into me. We have become one flesh." The Lord's Supper in the New Testament provides this same type of symbolism (see 1 Corinthians 11:23–26).

Throwing Rice

At the conclusion of the festivities, the wedding guests typically stand outside the church or hall and throw rice at the couple as they exit. This gesture symbolizes their hope for the couple's fruitfulness in childbearing.

In ancient times, the parties to a blood covenant often ended the ceremony by planting a tree or garden. In a marriage covenant, the garden represents the children who will be born to the couple and grow up as "olive shoots" around the family table (Psalm 128:3). I like the way the Psalmist puts it: "Sons are a heritage from the LORD, children a reward from him. Like arrows in the hands of a warrior are sons born in one's youth. Blessed is the man whose quiver is full of them" (Psalm 127:3–5).

The Honeymoon

Sexual intercourse seals the marriage covenant. Two become one by actual physical union, thereby consummating the marriage. A sexual relationship is meant to exist only in marriage; it is the privilege of complete intimacy that is earned by a commitment to marriage as a permanent covenant. In sexual intercourse, you not only give your body, you give your whole self. Such absolute intimacy requires absolute covenant.

In the marriage conferences Leigh and I conduct, Leigh uses a powerful illustration to show the significance of sexual intimacy. In front of the audience, she takes two pieces of construction paper—one blue and one pink—and glues them together. The blue sheet represents the man in an intimate sexual relationship, and the pink sheet represents the woman. Then, as the audience watches, she tries to pull the sheets apart. But they don't separate cleanly. The blue sheet takes little, torn pieces of the pink sheet with it, and the pink sheet takes little, torn pieces of the blue. It's a mess! The same thing happens when you try to get out of an intimate sexual relationship: You take little, torn pieces of the other person with you, and vice versa. It's always a mess. No wonder God is opposed to premarital sex and hates divorce!

MAKING IT WORK

With this conclusion of this chapter, we move from our discussion of the foundational concepts of the marriage covenant to a consideration of some of the practical ways in which we can live, love, and grow as covenant marriage partners. How can we make covenant marriage work day in and day out, month after month, year after year? Before we turn the page and begin answering that question, I want to quote a statement from David Atkinson's excellent book *To Have and to Hold,* which I think summarizes everything we've said about covenant marriage to this point. Come back to it whenever you need to be reminded of exactly what it means to have a covenant marriage:

> The marriage covenant, as we have sought to understand it from the biblical perspective, includes the following features: Its central theme is the commitment of a man and a woman to each other in an exclusive relationship of moral "troth" which is intended to be permanent, and to be patterned on and in its turn display the meaning and character of God's relationship with his people, Christ's with his church. The marriage relationship is intended to be—and increasingly to become—the "one flesh" union of total love commitment, person to person, at all levels of life and experience, symbolized by, expressed in, and deepened through sexual union. This permanent personal and sexual partnership is publicly known, witnessed and accepted as such by society, and becomes within society the basis of a new family unit within which (normally and normatively) children are to be born and reared.[11]

Long live covenant marriage!

Chapter 9

THE POWER OF COVENANT LOVE

It is not love that sustains your marriage,
but marriage that sustains your love.

—*Dietrich Bonhoeffer*

Some time ago a news organization prepared a special presentation on love and marriage. The reporters talked to more than one hundred people from various cultures that practice arranged marriage—Indians, Koreans, Pakistanis, Iraqis, Orthodox Greeks, and Orthodox Jews. Over and over again they heard the same thing: "You Americans fall in love and then marry. We marry and then fall in love."

Which way is best? Let's just say I don't know many people in America who would want their parents to pick a spouse for them. But whether you fall in love before the wedding ceremony or after, the fact remains that love is a crucial ingredient of any marriage. Love alone, however, will not make a marriage last. It is the *marriage covenant* that sustains a marriage over the long run.

Love is something that, because of covenant, you keep choosing to do, both when you feel like it and when you don't. According to Douglas Minson, covenant love "is a view of love or a settled disposition on the part of the lover to seek the good of the loved—and that for the sake of the loved one, not as a byproduct of self-fulfillment."[1] Gary Smalley puts it another way: Genuine love is "honor put into action regardless of the cost."[2]

WHAT IS LOVE?

The word *love* is used casually and flippantly in our modern culture. Limited by our language, we use the same word to describe our love for God as we do our love for a spouse, a dog, or a bowl full of Blue Bell ice cream. When we say, "You gotta love it," we could just as easily be referring to circumstances or things as to people.

The Greek language is much more descriptive than English and uses four words to describe different kinds of love. Let's look briefly at each of these.

Storge: *"I Like You"*

One of the major reasons for the skyrocketing failure of marriage today is a flawed selection process. Simply put, people are making poor choices, and those choices are producing terrible consequences. May I be crude with you for a minute? Ladies, don't marry a jerk! Guys, don't marry a jerkette! A handsome jerk is still a jerk. A rich jerk is still a jerk. A beautiful jerkette is still a jerkette. A sexy jerkette that sends your hormones through the ceiling is still a jerkette. Got it? Good!

One of the Greek words for "love" is *storge,* and it means "I like you." Liking the person you marry is very important if you want your marriage to last. A husband and wife should share similar interests and values. They should enjoy being around one another in good times and in bad times, in pressure times and in play times. Not long ago a woman said to me, "My husband is a great guy until he gets upset, and then he turns into a monster." What she was really telling me was that her husband is sick. He has emotional issues and baggage that will ultimately poison their relationship. If he doesn't get help, the marriage will be miserable. How can she enjoy a long-term relationship with a spoiled child in an adult body or an insecure egomaniac who is a control freak? Where is the companionship in that? A marriage will never be any healthier (or happier) than the least healthy partner.

In the great old Jimmy Stewart movie *Shenandoah,* young Sam asked

Mr. Anderson (played by Jimmy Stewart) for his daughter's hand in marriage. When Mr. Anderson questioned Sam about why he wanted to marry his daughter, Sam stammered, "Well, I love her, Mr. Anderson."

"Well, that's not good enough," Mr. Anderson replied. Then, in that wonderful Jimmy Stewart drawl, he went on to explain: "When I married Jenny's mother, I didn't love her; I liked her. I liked her a whole lot. I liked Martha for at least three years after we were married, and then it dawned on me I loved her. I still do. You see, Sam, when you love a woman without liking her, the nights can be long and cold, and contempt comes up with the sun."

Sam assured Mr. Anderson that he liked Jenny as well as loved her, and the marriage was approved. As Jimmy Stewart's character knew, it is much easier to grow to love someone you like than to keep loving someone you don't like.

Eros: *"I Want You"*

I often hear people say they want to get married because they are in love. The truth is, many of these folks are not so much "in love" as "in lust." No wonder so many marriages fail! Marriage is not the cure for lust; self-control is.

In our modern, sex-crazed culture, we tend to have a "Love Boat" mentality that worships fun and fantasy in the pursuit of a love that feels good. In the words of the old 1970s mantra, "If it feels good, do it." The Greek word for this kind of love is *eros,* and it represents a selfish, sensual, and sexual love. Driven by raging hormones, *eros* produces chills and thrills. It takes you to the edge. The problem is, the hormones that produce these ecstatic highs cannot be sustained. They eventually tone down. Level off. Wear out.

It takes a lot more than body chemistry to keep a couple together for life. As Gary Thomas says, romantic, *eros* love has "no elasticity in it. It can never be stretched; it simply shatters."[3] Passion and romance come (and go) quickly and easily; real covenant love, on the other hand, is hard work.

According to Bob Moeller, "Love is not the rush you feel when you see the other person. That rush eventually gives out. That is where real love just begins."[4] Thomas Jones explains the difference between romance and love this way: "Romance is based on sexual attraction, the enjoyment of affection and imagination. Love is based on decisions, promises, and commitments. It is not romantic—not up and down. It is unflappable and unchangeable—solid as a rock."[5]

Marjorie Holmes, in *Turning Sweet Nothings into Sweet Somethings*, offers this beautiful contrast between the romance of *eros* and true love:

Romance is fleeting. Love is long.
Romance is seeking perfection. Love is forgiving faults.
Romance is flattering attentions. Love is genuine thoughtfulness.
Romance is delicious. Love nourishes.
Romance can't last. Love can.[6]

Eros is not a New Testament word, and it's definitely no basis on which to build a lasting marriage. Dr. Owen Morgan, director of the Center for Family Life Studies at Arizona State University, makes the point that "less than one-tenth of one percent of the average couple's time is spent in any kind of direct sex play."[7] Yes, we want passion and romance in marriage, but these must not be the defining qualities of the relationship. To base love on physical attraction and sex appeal is to guarantee that a marriage will not go the distance. Any time another attractive person comes along and hormones begin to race, the relationship is threatened. You do not marry a cute face or an attractive body; you marry a complete and complex person, inside and out. Beauty fades and bodies sag. People who marry based solely on *eros* love are bound to be disappointed sooner or later.

Phileo: *"You Are My Friend"*

Another Greek word for love is *phileo*, which denotes friendship. Defined by H. Norman Wright, friendship is "an unselfish dedication to your partner's happiness. Friendship means you do some things together, but you are also comfortable with having your own individual interests and you encourage each other in these. There is a balance between togetherness and separateness."[8]

In the Bible, friendship is a covenant term. Jesus used this term when he said to his disciples, "I no longer call you servants, because a servant does not know his master's business. Instead, I have called you friends, for everything that I learned from my Father I have made known to you" (John 15:15). Jesus calls us friends today because he is in covenant with us. He shares his heart and his life with us because of covenant.

In the covenant of marriage, *phileo* plays a significant role as spouses share their hearts and lives with one another as friends and partners. Interestingly, a national survey confirmed the bonding power of friendship between mates. Hundreds of couples who claimed to have successful and fulfilling marriages were asked to identify the factors that best explained their marriage success. Amazingly, the top seven answers were the same for both husbands and wives; and of those, the top two answers were "My spouse is my best friend" and "I like my spouse as a person."[9]

Agape: *"I Love You Unconditionally"*

Agape is a word coined in the New Testament to describe God's love for us. It also describes the way God wants us to love one another. It is unselfish and unconditional in nature—love with no strings attached. It loves regardless of the other person's behavior and without the expectation of something in return. However, you and I can't be a vessel or conduit of God's *agape* love toward someone else until we first belong to God. *Agape* is only available through God (see 1 John 4:7); it is a God-given capacity. Without the power of the Holy Spirit, we are incapable of making such an unconditional commitment to another imperfect person!

Agape love requires honesty, openness, and intimacy, and it operates on the basis of covenant. It is the kind of love that makes a lasting covenant relationship possible. It *is* covenant love. Without a doubt, companionship (*storge*), romance (*eros*), and friendship (*phileo*) play important roles in a marriage relationship, but it is *agape* that provides a lasting foundation. To build a marriage on anything else is to build a castle of sand.

God's Tenacious Love

The Old Testament is filled with references to another word for love: *hesed*, which is translated "loving kindness" or "steadfast love." For example the Psalmist says, "But the loving kindness (*hesed*) of the Lord is from everlasting to everlasting to those who reverence him; his salvation is to the children's children of those who are faithful to his covenant and remember to obey him" (Psalm 103:17–18 TLB). *Hesed* is the Old Testament Hebrew word for the deepest form of committed love that can be expressed in human language. It is a covenant term for the kind of divine love that led God to initiate and guarantee an irrevocable covenant with his people— despite their sin and rebellion.

Hesed is a tenacious love that refuses to leave or let go. It keeps covenant regardless of what the other party does or fails to do. That's why the Bible uses adjectives such as *everlasting* and *irrevocable* to describe God's *hesed* love. There is nothing you or I could ever do to cause God to stop loving us or stop being faithful to us. His covenant is based on his unchanging character of love and grace. We have absolutely nothing to offer God that would merit his covenant with us—but that's okay. He doesn't love us because of who we are, but because of who he is. And, as the Scriptures state emphatically, "God is love" (1 John 4:8).

A covenant marriage is bound by this same kind of unconditional *hesed* love, along with the *agape* love we discussed earlier. A spouse who loves with *hesed* and *agape* love doesn't say, "If you measure up as a partner and perform as I think a spouse ought to perform, then I will love you." The love of covenant marriage is love that is freely given; it is totally selfless and seeks what is best for the other person. Whether or not it is earned or deserved has no bearing on the commitment.

Who wouldn't want to be loved so unconditionally? When participants in a national survey by Gary and Barbara Rosberg were asked to name their number one need in marriage, the top answer among men was not "sex," and the top answer among women was not "communication," as some might expect. Rather, a majority of both men and women identified "unconditional love" as the one thing they needed the most from a mate.[10]

THE WORLD OR THE WORD?

The secular world would have us believe that love is a feeling. As I've heard it described, love is "that feeling you feel when you feel like you have a feeling you never felt before." According to the media spin, love is emotional and uncontrollable—something that happens to you. The term "falling in love" is used as if love is an accident, like tripping over a suitcase in the hallway. The problem with this definition is that if you can accidentally fall in love, you can accidentally fall out of love too. You simply follow your feelings, and when the feelings are gone, love is gone.

But covenant love is not a feeling. It is not defined by the presence of "warm fuzzies." As a minister I do not ask a bride or groom during a wedding ceremony, "How do you feel about taking this person to be your wedded husband or wife?" It's not that feelings don't matter. They just can't be the basis for a lasting marriage. If you marry on the basis of feelings and those feelings change, then the relationship changes. You're tempted to say, "I don't feel the way I used to. I must not love you anymore. I want out." Unconditional covenant love overrides such feelings and fickleness.

According to the Bible, love is not something that happens to you; it's something that you can make happen. We have a choice. When it comes to love, we can follow the world or we can follow the Word. We can accept and apply the culture's definition of love, or we can accept and apply Christ's.

Love According to God

The Bible tells us four important things about love as defined by God: First, love is a matter of *choice*. Falling in love is not an accident but a

149

choice. The Bible says we "put on" love in the same way we put on our clothes. We suit up. We don't just fall into the closet and come out dressed. Colossians 3:14 says, "And over all these virtues put on love, which binds them all together in perfect unity."

Second, love is a matter of *conduct*. It's "show and tell." Just do it! Love is a verb; it requires action and hard work. First John 3:18 tells us, "Dear children, let us not love with words or tongue but with actions and in truth."

While channel surfing one day, I discovered Steve Irwin, best known as television's "Crocodile Hunter." He wrestles crocodiles, chases wild animals, and sticks his hands in dark holes to pull out poisonous snakes— just to mention a few of the dangers he submits himself to on a routine basis. Steve appears to be the most courageous (some would say stupid) man in the world. With nerves of steel, he is afraid of nothing. Well, almost nothing. Steve finally came across one thing that made him shake in his steel-toed boots: marriage. On a talk show I heard Steve describe the feelings and fears he experienced as he approached marriage to his beautiful wife, Terri, the woman who partners with him on his dangerous adventures. In his thick Australian accent, he said something like this: "Thinking about the responsibilities of marriage made me dead sick. I was sweating bullets. Shaking! Man! Never has anything scared me as much as getting married. I had rather have a sixteen-foot crocodile striking at me."

As the fearless Crocodile Hunter understood, married love demands bold action and hard work unparalleled by anything else in life. You don't just love and sit back. You love and jump headlong into the adventure.

Third, love is a matter of *commitment*. It sticks. It stays. It predetermines to act in loving ways and to be there for the loved one through thick and thin. Author Mike Mason nails it when he talks about a commitment of love that is strong enough to hold a relationship together in good times as well as in bad times:

It is not that the vows hold any guarantee that a couple shall always be "in love," but rather that through God's grace and strength they may continue in faith "to love." For that, once again, is the peculiar meaning of Christian love: not a feeling, but an action, and not a human and limited action, but a supernatural and eternal one. Love is a deep, continuous, growing, and ever-renewing activity of the will, superintended by the Holy Spirit. A wedding, therefore, declares openly and robustly that there is nothing romantic about love, nothing the least bit chancy or changeable. It is a gift from the Lord, whole and intact forever, a sure rock.[11]

Our commitment to love is a mirror of God's commitment to love and care for us. The apostle Paul says it best: "For I am convinced that neither death nor life, neither angels nor demons, neither the present nor the future, nor any powers, neither height nor depth, nor anything else in all creation, will be able to separate us from the love of God that is in Christ Jesus our Lord" (Romans 8:38–39).

Finally, love is a matter of *covenant.* It says, "I will give you my love, my loyalty, and my life until death." When we make this kind of covenant, we are mirroring our covenant God who promises, "Never will I leave you; never will I forsake you" (Hebrews 13:5). Jesus was forsaken on a cruel Roman cross so that you and I would never be forsaken—and so that we, through his power, could have the ability to not forsake those we love.

Elizabeth Achtemeier has written a beautiful description of covenant love:

I will be with you, no matter what happens to us and between us. If you should become blind tomorrow, I will be there. If you achieve no success or status in our society, I will be there. When we argue and are angry, as we inevitably will, I will work to bring us together. When we seem totally at odds and neither of us is having needs fulfilled, I will persist in trying to understand and in trying to restore our relationship. When our marriage seems utterly sterile and going nowhere at all, I will believe that it can work and I will do my part to make it work. And when all is wonderful and we are happy, I will rejoice over our life together, and continue to strive to keep our relationship growing and strong.[12]

151

Life-and-Death Loyalty

One of the key elements of any covenant is loyalty. In Bible times, armies of cooperating allies would make blood covenants, pledging allegiance to each other and vowing to fight together on the battlefield against a common enemy. King Ahab of Israel and King Jehoshaphat of Judah made such a covenant in 2 Chronicles 18:3. Jehoshaphat said to Ahab, "I am as you are, and my people as your people; we will join you in the war." Theirs was a pledge of life-and-death loyalty.

In 2 Samuel 23, King David and his men found themselves near Bethlehem, which was a Philistine garrison at the time. Probably standing around and chatting casually with the group, David said out loud, "Oh, that someone would get me a drink of water from the well near the gate of Bethlehem!" (v. 15). He was expressing a *want*, not a *need*, and probably didn't expect to be taken seriously. Nevertheless, three of David's men immediately went out and risked their lives to break through the Philistine lines and draw water from the enemy well for their king. Wow! Their covenant loyalty to David was so strong that they were willing to die if necessary to make sure David got what he wanted. That's life-and-death loyalty.

The last book in the New Testament records a vision of people who gave their lives for the sake of God's kingdom: "They overcame him by the blood of the Lamb and by the word of their testimony; they did not love their lives so much as to shrink from death" (Revelation 12:11). The word *testimony* refers to their covenant oath with Jesus. These people were loyal to the point of giving their own lives for the sake of their covenant with Christ. That's life-and-death loyalty.

Marriage is a blood covenant that requires this same kind of loyalty toward a spouse. "But my wife lied to me!" I've heard husbands object. "But my husband had an affair!" more than one wife has complained. Do you really have to be loyal to a spouse who hasn't been loyal to you? Yes, if your marriage is based on covenant's *hesed* and *agape* love.

In the Old Testament story of Joshua and the Gibeonites, God honored his covenant with Israel even though Joshua and the Israelites did not honor their covenant with him. As the Israelites entered the Promised Land under the leadership of Joshua, God told them unequivocally to destroy all its current inhabitants: "And when the LORD your God shall deliver them before you, and you shall defeat them, then you shall utterly destroy them. You shall make no covenant with them and show no favor to them" (Deuteronomy. 7:2 NASB). There was to be no friendship. No covenant. No sleeping with the enemy. God had two reasons for this command. First, he wanted his chosen people to be instruments of his judgment on pagan idolatry; and second, he wanted to eliminate any temptation for Israel to be led away from the one true God.

God gave Joshua and the Israelites many victories in battle, including a great military success at Jericho. Afterward, Joshua and the Israelites approached the land of Gibeon. Not wanting to be next in Israel's line of conquests, the Gibeonites disguised themselves, approached Joshua, and tricked him into making a treaty (or covenant) with them. True to that covenant, when Israel went out to battle, Joshua did not attack the Gibeonites because they had sworn an oath before God. And later, when Gibeon came under attack by the Amorites, Joshua marched in his entire army to fight beside the Gibeonites because of the covenant he'd made.

What about God's command that Israel not make any covenants with the inhabitants of the Promised Land? Not only did Joshua disobey that command, he failed to seek God's direction when the Gibeonites came to him and tricked him into the agreement. But even though Joshua was not loyal to God, God remained loyal to him. God honored Joshua's treaty with the Gibeonites and helped Israel defeat the Amorites. At Joshua's request, he even performed the greatest miracle in the Old Testament—he caused the sun to stand still for nearly a full day so Israel could finish the battle. The Bible says, "There has never been a day like it before or since, a day when the LORD listened to a man. Surely the LORD was fighting for Israel!" (Joshua 10:14).

Absolute, life-and-death loyalty is never dependent on a positive response from the other party. It stands alone. God's covenant love means that he is loyal to those who are disloyal to him and faithful to those who are unfaithful to him. Yes, that kind of love and loyalty is hard to come by in marriage. Keeping covenant with someone who is faithful and true is one thing; keeping covenant with someone who has deceived you, lied to you, and hurt you is a far different thing.

Loving like Jesus

Is it possible to love your spouse no matter what he or she does? No, if your love is based on feelings. Yes, if your love is based on covenant. Once a covenant is made, it no longer matters how you feel. You keep covenant when you feel like it, and you keep covenant when you don't. The greatest example of covenant love was Jesus' death on the cross. Did he feel like being crucified? Of course not! In fact, he acknowledged his feelings in the Garden of Gethsemane when he prayed, "My Father, if it be possible, may this cup be taken from me. Yet not as I will, but as you will" (Matthew 26:39). He chose to act not on the basis of feelings but on the basis of covenant.

To hang in there with a spouse who has been disloyal or unfaithful requires nothing less than the power of the Holy Spirit and the grace of God in your life. But just as he did for Joshua, God will fight for you. He will fight for your marriage. He will perform whatever miracles are necessary to make it possible for you to keep the covenant you have made.

REBUILDING A MARRIAGE

Trouble, tragedy, or even an adulterous affair does not have to mean the end of a marriage. Adultery is the ultimate betrayal; it's a breach of trust and a terrible sin. It shakes a marriage covenant to the core. It is difficult for any relationship to handle—but it is not impossible to overcome. I've talked with many couples who survived an affair and now have a stronger and more intimate marriage than before. In such cases, the guilty party has had to admit his or her guilt, ask for forgiveness, repent, stop the affair, and patiently seek to rebuild shattered trust.

Rebuilding a spouse's trust takes patience, determination, humility, and a lot of time. It's not easy. A couple needs God, good counseling, the support of family and friends, and a determined willingness on the part of both spouses to get to the root of their problems and seek well-defined solutions. Moving beyond the anger, rejection, and hurt of adultery requires a lot of hard work, but it can be done. And the end result is worth it. A marriage saved is a marriage that has the potential to finally become what God designed it to be.

Unfortunately, "most people wait for love to return before they'll recommit to their marriage," says Janis Abrahms Spring, author of *After the Affair.* "I say just the opposite—the couple has to recommit to the marriage before love will return."[13] Most experts agree that even the most troubled marriages can be salvaged if both spouses are willing to work at it.

Covenant Forgiveness

Anytime covenant is threatened or broken, forgiveness must be initiated. Covenant and forgiveness are inseparable twins. You cannot have one without the other.

Forgiveness isn't easy, however. A couple I knew, Tom and Ann, had a good marriage. In fact their marriage was so good that they had begun to take it (and each other) for granted. Another man picked up on some of Ann's unmet needs and talked her into spending the afternoon with him. Before Ann left home, she took off her wedding ring and laid it on the kitchen sink. She had never been unfaithful before.

Her brief tryst ended that evening in a motel room where Ann died suddenly from a heart attack. Imagine Tom's pain and agony as he went to that motel to identify the body of his unfaithful wife! The grief, rejection, anger, and disappointment was almost too much for him to handle; but with God's help, Tom worked through his emotions. At the funeral he walked up to the casket for a last goodbye. With tears flowing, he bent down, kissed his wife, and said, "My darling, I love you with all my heart. I forgive you." Then he reached in his pocket, pulled out her wedding ring, and slipped it on her finger. "I love you. I forgive you. You are my wife," he said. Wow! What an example of the power of covenant love!

I remember one night years ago when, as a student pilot, I was flying high above the Six Flags Over Texas amusement park. Suddenly my airplane went into a spin. Only two things could keep me from spiraling right into the ground at that point: (1) being high enough to have time to break the spin; and (2) knowing what to do to pull the plane out the deadly spiral. Fortunately I was flying high, and my instructor had prepared me well. He had alerted me to this worst-case scenario and drilled into my head the appropriate response, even though we both hoped it would never happen. In this way he had built my confidence and sense of security as a pilot. And that evening over Six Flags, when every pilot's worst nightmare came true, I was able to respond automatically, right the plane, and get back to smooth flying.

What happens in a marriage when your worst nightmare occurs? You need to know in advance that it is possible to get through such a worst-case scenario. You don't have to crash and burn. It is not the end of the world. In fact, it is possible to survive and soar again—you just need to know how to pull out of the spiral and set things back on course. As Mike Mason states:

> One thing that is very important to know in marriage is that there is always a way out. And the way out is not divorce! No, the way out in marriage (no matter how bad things may get) is simply to put everything we have back on the line, our whole hearts and lives, just as we did the moment we took our vows. We must return to an attitude of total abandonment, of throwing all our natural caution and defensiveness to the winds, and putting ourselves entirely in the hands of love by an act of the will. Instead of falling in love, we may now have to march into it.[14]

A friend and his wife have made a commitment to allow each other "one free spin." If one of them ever makes a terrible or stupid choice at some point, the other spouse will not assume that the marriage is over. People in good marriages can and do make mistakes. The fact that a spouse strays does not necessarily mean that he or she wants the marriage to end or that it has to end. In my experience as a pastor and counselor, I've observed that most people who have affairs do not intend to get caught, and they have no desire to end their marriages. Unfortunately, selfishness gains control, and they choose to get their needs met outside the marriage rather than facing and dealing with the issues that exist within the marriage. The good news is, a return to covenant love and commitment, coupled with covenant forgiveness, can pull any marriage out of its tailspin—and even cause it to fly higher than ever before.

A Flash of Hope

When marriage is a covenant commitment between a husband, a wife, and God, there is always hope. Madeline L'Engle, in her book *The Irrational Season,* reflects on her own marriage in a beautiful chapter titled "To a Long-Loved Love." The word *covenant* is missing, but there is no doubt that what L'Engle so eloquently describes is the invisible foundation that the Bible refers to as covenant:

> My love for my husband and his for me is in that unknown, underwater area of ourselves where our separations become something new and strange, merge and penetrate like the drops of water in the sea. But we do not lose our solitudes, or our particularity, and we become more than we could alone.
>
> This is mystery. I cannot explain it. But I have learned that it makes up for our clashes, our differences in temperament, our angers, our withdrawals, our failures to understand.
>
> No long-term marriage is made easily, and there have been times when I've been so angry or so hurt that I thought my love would never recover. And then, in the midst of near despair, something has happened beneath the surface. A bright little flashing fish of hope has flicked silver fins and the water is bright and suddenly I am returned to a state of love again—till next time.

I've learned that there will always be a next time, and that I will submerge in darkness, but that I won't stay submerged. And each time something has been learned under the waters; something has been gained; and a new kind of love has grown. The best I can ask for is that this love, which has been built on countless failures, will continue to grow. I can say no more than that this is mystery, and gift, and that somehow or other, through grace, our failures can be redeemed and blessed.[15]

That's the power of covenant love.

Chapter 10

DO YOU HAVE A PURPOSE-DRIVEN MARRIAGE?

If you don't know where you are going,
you will wind up somewhere else.

—Yogi Berra

Here's an important principle every married person—and every person thinking about marriage—should know: A good marriage doesn't happen by accident. In fact, to survive amidst all the pressures, pains, and pitfalls of life in the twenty-first century, a marriage today must be more proactive and more intentional than ever before. It must be *purpose-driven.* Living and loving purposefully, as relationship coach Ed Shea says, is the "way to take your relationship from functional to exceptional; from the ordinary to the extraordinary."[1]

What does it mean to have a purpose-driven marriage? It means that you and your spouse have a basic understanding of the kind of marriage you are trying to build and what it will take to make it happen. It means that you are willing to work together—hard—toward that common goal. But most couples I talk to in premarital counseling haven't got a clue what the purpose of their marriage is. "I do" what? For how long? In what way? *Who knows?*

When I say to the typical prospective groom, "What is the purpose and goal of your marriage?" he shifts his feet around, makes strange, guttural noises, and finally blurts, "I dunno. I just love her" (which is a

159

hormonally driven expression for, "I want sex without guilt"). When I ask the typical bride-to-be the same question, she rolls her eyes, giggles, and utters a few words in fairy-tale language about finally finding her "knight in shining armor." (That's female-speak for, "I am being rescued from my home by one who will wow me and worship me for the rest of my life.")

In a magazine article titled "Marriage: What's the Point?" author Susan Dixon admits that she stood at an altar in a beautiful white gown and said "I do" without having the slightest idea of what she was getting herself into. "It took nearly twenty-five years and a divorce before I began to understand something I should have known before that ceremony ever took place," she writes. "In the quarter century that has passed since I naively repeated my wedding vows, I have become more and more aware that relationships die from lack of purpose.... If there is no valid, defined, and acknowledged purpose for our relationship—chances are we'll have trouble keeping it alive."[2]

Do You Know?

What is the purpose of marriage? Of *your* marriage? Do you have a well-defined purpose? Do you and your mate agree on goals? Do you know where your relationship is headed? Do you know where you want your marriage to be five years from now? Ten? Thirty?

Hopes and Dreams

Do you have common hopes and dreams for the future? This is an important question because, as Neil Clark Warren writes in *The Triumphant Marriage*, without a shared dream a marriage relationship "will eventually die." According to Warren, dreams inspire hope and thereby "stimulate the brain and mobilize the action centers.... [Hope] stimulates planning. Planning produces behavior designed to move you forward." The end result is positive progress in a marriage relationship.

If you can answer "yes" to these three essential questions, Warren asserts, you have a healthy dream that will serve your marriage well:

- Is the dream equally inclusive of both you and your spouse and your life together?

- Is the dream broad enough?

- Are both of you strongly committed to the dream you have for your life together?[3]

Values and Beliefs

What about values and beliefs? Do you and your spouse share the same values? Do you have similar religious beliefs? What is really important to each of you? These are critical questions. Even secular counselors acknowledge the importance of shared beliefs and values in building a successful marriage. If you're not sure what you value, ask yourself:

- What do I really want to *be?*

- What do I really want to *do?*

- What do I really want to *have?*

Get your spouse to answer the same questions, then discuss your responses together. What values and beliefs do your answers reflect?

Expectations

What are you expecting out of marriage? What are the expectations of your mate? Ecstatic bliss? A romantic paradise? Do you both want children, and if so, how many? Do you expect to make enough money to buy a Suburban? To build your dream house?

How realistic are your expectations, and what happens when they're not met? What happens when your relationship gets *blah* or boring? When it gets bumpy or bitter? What price are you willing to pay in order to have a great marriage that goes the distance? Are you both willing to make the relationship an absolute priority? Are you willing to hang in there, even through the bad times?

Approach to Marriage

Is your marriage self-centered or God-centered? Is your first thought, "What will make me happy?" Or is it, "What will make my Lord happy—and ultimately strengthen my relationship with my spouse?"

Author Gary Thomas says that marriage is designed to reflect or model Christ's love for his church. He writes:

> If I believe the primary purpose of marriage is to model God's love for the church, I will enter this relationship and maintain it from an entirely new motivation.... If my "driving force" is as Paul said it should be (to please Christ—see 2 Corinthians 5:9), I will work to construct a marriage that...incarnates this truth by putting flesh on it, building a relationship that models forgiveness, selfless love, and sacrifice. The last picture I want to give the world is that I have decided to stop loving someone and that I refuse to serve this person anymore, or that I have failed to fulfill a promise I made many years before.[4]

This leads me to a question I asked back in chapter 6. It bears repeating here: Do you approach your marriage as a contract or a covenant? The Bible clearly reveals that covenant oneness with your mate—a oneness that is spiritual, emotional, and physical—is God's ultimate goal and purpose for marriage. Two become one. If you approach marriage as a covenant, you already have this built-in purpose. Your relationship with your spouse (next to your relationship with God) is the most important thing in your life.

If you approach marriage as a contract, however, you're likely to emphasize rules and regulations over relationship. Many self-help books on the market offer practical rules for living with a spouse and promise that if you'll just follow those rules, you'll have a happy marriage. The problem is, when you emphasize following rules over building relationship, you only breed resentment and rebellion in your mate. Rules without relationship equal disaster in a marriage.

In the Bible the old covenant (Old Testament) put rules and regulations as the top priority of God's people, while the new covenant (New Testament) set forth "a better covenant" that elevated relationship to top priority. Jesus cut covenant with God for us on the Cross—something that all the rules and regulations in the world could never do. Ultimately it is our relationship with Christ that makes possible our reconciliation with our heavenly Father. The greatest blessings of our lives always flow out of relationship!

MAKING A PLAN

Do you have a plan for your marriage relationship? You need one! Marriage is a journey into previously undiscovered territory. Other people may give you some helpful travel tips; they may even point you in the right direction. But once you agree with your spouse on purpose, values, expectations, and approach, the two of you need to plan your route. Gary Smalley can't plan it for you. Neither can Kevin Lehman. John Gottman can't, and John Gray can't (he'll end up sending one of you to Mars and one of you to Venus). Even Fred Lowery can't. You are the only ones who can do it.

We've already said that a wonderful, lasting marriage doesn't happen by accident. It doesn't happen by chance or luck either. Rather, it is the result of wise decisions, hard work, and careful planning. The old axiom is as true for marriage as it is for other areas in life: If you fail to plan, you plan to fail.

A good plan includes short-term and long-term goals. It enumerates specific actions necessary to achieve those goals. It takes into consideration obstacles that are likely to rise up and determines how to deal with them in advance. And it builds in opportunities to stop and celebrate when certain milestones of success are reached.

A good plan is also smart. I remember a time early in my marriage when a relatively small problem escalated to gargantuan proportions. In frustration I said to my wife, "Well, I'm working as hard as I can at this marriage. This is the best I can do. It is all I can do—and it will have to do!" Looking back, I think, *How insensitive! How stupid!* Leigh was working as hard or harder than I was. Unfortunately, neither of us realized at the time that simply working harder would never get us where we wanted to go in our relationship. We had a shared vision of what we wanted our marriage to be, but we didn't have a clue about how to get there. We needed to work smarter, not necessarily harder.

Try this project: Ask your spouse to list ten things you could do, or both of you could do, to make the quickest and greatest improvement in your marriage. You make a similar list. Then sit down together and carefully go over each item. Be realistic. Determine the top two or three things that will make the greatest difference in the quality of your relationship over the long term.

Our natural temptation is to compile such a list and then try to work on all the items on the list—all at the same time. When I was growing up in Alabama and somebody asked, "What are you doing?" the down-home response was, "A little bit of everything, not much of anything." That is often our approach to marriage. We work a little bit on all of our problems, but never enough on one problem to get it solved.

Another thing we do: We get overwhelmed by the sheer number of things on the list. Then, feeling alternately paralyzed and guilty, we tackle none of it. Or we succumb to the tyranny of the urgent and do the loud things first, only to leave the important things unfinished. Or we wimp out and do the easy things first, never getting around to the hard but crucial things. Or we take a stab at something on the list, and when the result falls short of our expectations, we tear up the list. No wonder our marriages have a 75 percent failure rate!

But, there's a better approach. A few years ago my friend John Maxwell, an expert in leadership training, introduced me to a concept known in the business world as the "Pareto Principle." Vilfredo Pareto, twentieth-century economist and sociologist, observed that in any group of objects, a small number tend to contribute most of the value. If, for instance, a company sells five products, one product will account for most of the sales. If the company has a hundred customers, twenty will make most of the purchases.

Since Pareto's time, other researchers have made similar observations in various fields. Some people call it the 80-20 rule: Eighty percent of the total value or impact of any group of people or things will come from 20 percent of those people or things. Twenty percent of a book will contain 80 percent of the critical content (except this one, of course, which is *all* critical!). Twenty percent of a congregation will do 80 percent of the volunteer work. Twenty percent of our time produces 80 percent of the desired results. In terms of relationships, if you have ten friends, you will do 80 percent of your socializing with two of them. It's true, isn't it?

The Pareto Principle leads to success in many arenas because it provides focus. It helps set priorities. Sometimes deciding what not to do is as important as deciding what to do! As Secretary of Defense Donald Rumsfeld says, "Success tends to go not to the person who is error-free, because he also tends to be risk-averse. Rather it goes to the person who recognizes that life is pretty much a percentage business."[5]

The Pareto Principle can be applied to marriage as well. A marriage doesn't have to be better at everything to be great. It only needs to be better at the vital few things that make the critical difference. Isn't that good news? By focusing on doing just a few things well, your marriage can be a wonderful success!

What are those few things you can do that will give you the greatest return in your marriage? In *The Triumphant Marriage,* Neil Clark Warren identifies five basic skills he thinks are critical:

- Learning to dream together

- Learning how to communicate at a deep level together

- Learning how to resolve conflict when it first occurs

- Negotiating a mutually satisfying sexual relationship

- Pursuing spirituality together[6]

I think Warren is pretty much on target. A few months ago I wrote to four of the best professional marriage counselors I know and asked them to give me their lists of those vital few things they think improve a marriage the most. Like Warren's list, the bulk of what they shared with me was directly or indirectly related to better communication and conflict management, which lines up with conventional wisdom. Without a doubt, one of the quickest ways to change any marriage for the good is to improve in these two areas. That's why I've devoted the last two chapters of this book to those subjects.

Combining the response of the professionals with my own experience of working with couples for the past forty years, I've come up with four essentials that I believe, if worked on purposefully, will give a couple 80 percent of the satisfaction and fulfillment they want in their marriage. They are: (1) covenant, (2) companionship, (3) communication, and (4) conflict management.

The first two, covenant and companionship, are foundational; they give marriage its *security*. The last two are practical; they give marriage its *sizzle*. Of course, we've already talked a great deal about covenant. You know by now that covenant is the core element of marriage done God's way. Building your marriage on the rock-solid foundation of covenant is what will allow you to survive the inevitable storms of life. It's the closest thing you can get to a guarantee of a long-lasting, fulfilling, and happy marriage.

So let's turn our attention now to the final three essentials: companionship, communication, and conflict management. I'm convinced that if you focus your efforts in covenant marriage on success in these three areas, your relationship with your spouse will become everything you always hoped and dreamed it would be.

Chapter 11

COVENANT COMPANIONSHIP

Marry someone whose soul you love.
Passion fades, but friendship remains forever.

—*Lynne Ames*

Do you have a best friend? Is it your spouse? Friendship, one of the most beautiful words in the lexicon of language, is marriage's great enhancer. The happiest couples are those who have developed lifestyles that allow them time and opportunity to become best friends and true covenant companions.

In chapter 9 we talked about the different Greek terms that translate into the single English word *love.* One was *storge,* the kind of love that says, "I like you." Another was *phileo,* the kind of love that says, "You are my friend." Both of these types of love are involved in companionship—one of those essential elements that deserves special, purposeful focus in a marriage because it has the potential to make or break the relationship.

In the Bible, marriage is specifically called a "covenant" twice, and both times the marriage relationship is depicted as a covenant of companionship. The prophet Malachi, reproving God's people for their harshness in dealing with their wives, said, "The LORD has been witness between you and the wife of your youth, with whom you have dealt treacherously; yet she is your *companion* and your wife by *covenant*" (Malachi 2:14 NKJV, emphasis added). Solomon, the wisest man to ever live, used the same two words together in warning his son to avoid women who might tempt him: "...to deliver you from the immoral woman, from the seductress who flatters with her words, who forsakes the *companion* of her youth, and forgets the *covenant* of her God" (Proverbs 2:16–17 NKJV, emphasis added).

As these scriptures attest, companionship is at the very heart of covenant. It's a critical element in any marriage relationship. And while many marriage experts say that good communication and conflict management skills are the most important keys for a lasting marriage, I beg to differ. So does John Gottman, a University of Washington psychology professor who studied married couples during a period of twenty-five years. Based on his research, Gottman says he can predict with 91 percent accuracy which married couples will stay together and which will not. "Even happy couples can't 'validate' each other in the middle of an argument or use the rules for fighting fair," Gottman says. "The key to staying married is a beautifully simple concept with a profound impact: friendship. Happy and successful couples have 'a mutual respect for and enjoyment of each other's company.'"[1]

In other words, couples that stay married *like* each other. They have similar interests. They enjoy a deep, sweet companionship. Sure, they can master each other's love languages and practice the ten steps for better communication; they can memorize the twelve rules for fighting fair and learn the eight keys for resolving conflicts. But unless they like each other, unless they have common interests and other similarities, the relationship is toast!

WHICH PLANET ARE YOU FROM?

A hugely popular marriage book sets forth the idea that men and women are so different, they must be from different planets. And it's true: We are different in significant ways.

Different by Creation

In the beginning God created man, and from man he created woman. "Male and female he created them," the Bible says (Genesis

1:27). The man and woman were designed to be different in significant ways. From science we know that in every cell of every organ in a man's body, there is an x chromosome and a y chromosome; while in every cell of every organ in a female's body, there is an x chromosome and an x chromosome—no y. This difference at the most basic cellular level is why the first two human beings were named Adam and Eve, not Adam and Steve.

Even the most casual observer knows that men and women are radically different, both physically and emotionally. But contrary to popular opinion, men are not from Mars and women are not from Venus. Men are from God and women are from God. Unfortunately too many of us know more about Mars and Venus than about Eden and Calvary.

Different by Chemical Bath

Medical science tells us that between the eighteenth and twenty-sixth week of gestation, something significant happens to a male baby in the womb. A chemical bath of hormones washes his brain, possibly destroying certain connectors and causing other important changes. The result: male brain damage—at least that's what some women say!

What we know is that men favor the left side of the brain and are lateral in the way they think, while women favor the right side and are bilateral in their thinking. In other words, men think, talk, and listen using only one side of their brain, while women use both sides to communicate. Perhaps that's why women tend to talk twice as much as men (just a thought!). It may also be why women are naturally better listeners.

This difference in brain function has led some women to conclude that when it comes to domestic details, men suffer selective memory syndrome. One woman I know is convinced that men deliberately train their minds not to retain the one thousand details of family life that float around in every woman's brain. Many men, meanwhile, can't understand why women obsess over details and minutiae. They tend to focus more on the big picture. It's a matter of brain chemistry.

Different by Caricature

In America, men are supposed to be "macho." They must be strong rather than sensitive, tough rather than tender, and rude rather than relational. Real men don't cuddle, cry, or crack. Instead, they leap tall buildings in a single bound and catch bullets in their teeth.

Balderdash! Jesus, the strongest man to ever live, freely displayed his emotions during his life on earth. He was the ultimate man's man—and he cried. He cared deeply about people and reached out to them with sensitivity. Many men are simply hiding behind the "macho" mask. In reality they are needy and afraid. They have fragile egos and only put up the "tough guy" wall in order to protect themselves.

Women also have a mask they sometimes hide behind. They must be soft and sweet, sexy and silent. They must not have strong opinions or express personal needs. That's balderdash too. But sometimes cultural images are hard to overcome.

Validating the Differences

Often we think of the differences between men and women as faults or problems. A husband will look at his wife and think, *How can I fix my woman?* So he jumps in, offers simplistic solutions, and makes any situation ten times worse. She is not broken—just different! A wife will look at her husband and think, *How can I change my man?* She jumps in to improve him by offering advice and criticism. He is not crazy—just different!

We must learn to validate the differences between men and women and value each other. Differences can be a blessing or a burden, destructive or dynamic. It's all in how we choose to look at them. You can see your mate as defective and complain or as different and celebrate. It's your choice. I tend to agree with Groucho Marx's assessment: "I am a man, and you are a woman. I can't think of a better arrangement."

The Bible says, "As iron sharpens iron, so one man [or woman] sharpens another" (Proverbs 27:17). God wants to use marriage as a refining tool to bring out the best in both you and your spouse. Your differences can work for you instead of against you if you will:

- Acknowledge the differences.
- Accept the differences.
- Analyze the differences.
- Appreciate the differences.
- Adjust to the differences.

These days we hear of many people getting divorced because of "irreconcilable differences." That's a cop-out. The truth is, these folks are unwilling to change. They are unwilling to put someone else's interests before their own. Their selfishness is on parade.

Of course we have differences! The fact that we are different means that we have opposing strengths and weaknesses. One of the great things about covenant is that major weaknesses can often be eliminated as partners cover for one another. Leigh is strong in some areas where I am weak, and I am strong in some areas where she is weak. Together we are much stronger than we could ever be alone. For instance, Leigh has a personality that is bubbly and exciting, while mine is cautious and cool. Put us together and we are a dynamite team. We fill each other's personality gaps. Together we reflect the character of God more fully and accurately than either one of us could alone.

More Alike than Different

Despite our differences, however, there are still many areas in which men and women can be very much alike. In the last chapter we talked about the importance of a husband and wife having similar goals, dreams, values, and beliefs. Companionship in marriage thrives on these and other similarities. Men and women are not so different that we can't understand and relate to one another as companions and friends.

The truth is, men and women both want one thing more than anything else: to be known and accepted, understood and loved. Something deep inside each of us cries out for a best friend, a soul mate, a close companion. That was Creation's cry when God acknowledged that it was not good for man to be alone.

In the covenant relationship of marriage, that cry is answered. Body answers body, spirit answers spirit, and soul answers soul. Two persons unite and become one, forming earth's closest and dearest relationship— friends bonded in companionship and blessed for life.

ONE ESSENTIAL FRIEND

Apart from salvation, no gift is more precious or lasting than the gift of an intimate friendship. As Dr. William Glasner writes in his book *Reality Therapy,* "Every person needs one essential friend."[2] Except for your relationship with Christ, nothing can meet your deepest emotional needs the way a close friendship can—and if that friend is your spouse, all the better. An old Celtic saying puts it this way: "Anyone without a soul friend is like a body without a head."

What is a friend? A friend is someone who knows what you are really like, loves and accepts you just the way you are, and patiently gives you time and space to grow. A friend loves you unconditionally—and that's a good thing, because all of us can be unlovable at times. A friend is not sporadic or impulsive in loving, but continual and tenacious. He or she can know the worst about you and still believe and love the best about you. A true friend is someone who walks in when others walk out—someone who believes in you even when you have ceased to believe in yourself.

A friend is someone who understands your silence. Someone who hears your stories and values them. Someone who "doubles your joy and halves your grief," as the saying goes. I think it was humorist Erma Bombeck who said, "A friend is somebody who doesn't go on a diet when you are fat."

A true friend is someone you invite into your heart. Someone with whom your soul can be naked. Someone with whom you have a mutual commitment to the four basic tenets of close friendship: openness, intimacy, loyalty, and confidentiality. The wise philosopher Aristotle said, "Friendship is a single soul dwelling in two bodies." But it is the Bible that gives us the best summary statement: "A friend loves at all times" (Proverbs 17:17).

Abraham was called a "friend of God." Moses was referred to as a friend with whom God spoke face to face. Jesus placed great value on friendship and became transparent with trusted companions. He knew that transparency results in authenticity. In reality, you can never really know yourself without disclosing yourself to others. Jesus called believers his "friends." And he defined the essence of friendship when he said, "Greater love has no one than this, that he lay down his life for his friends" (John 15:13).

The greatest example of covenant friendship in the Old Testament has to be the relationship between David and Jonathan. The Bible says that "the soul of Jonathan was knit with the soul of David, and Jonathan loved him as his own soul" (1 Samuel 18:1 KJV). Jonathan made a covenant of friendship with David. So strong was this friendship that Jonathan gave up his father's kingdom for his friend. David's protection meant more to him than his own safety or position. You see, true covenant friendship knows no bounds of sacrifice. In this case, the bond of friendship was stronger even than blood. Jonathan risked his life again and again on David's behalf.

In life there is no adequate substitute for this kind of friendship. Abraham Lincoln said, "If we have one true friend, we should consider ourselves wealthy." As the old saying goes,

Happy is the man who has a friend.
Happier is the man who is a friend.
Happiest is the man who has a friend and is a friend.

The Joy of Being Best Friends

Over lunch this week, Leigh and I talked about our relationship. Why is it a good one? What gives it its strength and longevity? Is it that we love each other? Certainly love plays a definitive role, but love is a continuous choice that we make. Perhaps a better explanation is that we really like each other. We must keep choosing to love because we have made a covenant with each other. But liking each other makes it so much easier!

The truth is, Leigh and I are best friends. We talk and pray together every day. We share our feelings, our fears, and our fantasies. We are travel mates, play mates, shopping mates, sex mates, and soul mates. The covenant companionship we enjoy is the golden key that has unlocked the doors of blessing in our marriage.

Having a spouse who is your best friend can get you through even the toughest times in life. When author Gary Rosberg was grieving over the death of his father, his wife, Barbara, told him, "I am sticking to you like glue, and nothing can separate me from you. We are one. Those wedding vows are the real thing. That covenant is true. 'For better or worse' means that even at the worst of times, we are a team."

With Barbara at his side, Gary was able to survive his time of crisis. He writes:

> As a result, the intimacy forged in our marriage is so deep and impenetrable that only God will be able to peel one of us from the other when he is ready to call one of us home.... That is ultimate friendship. That is marital oneness. That is what Barb and I have, and that is what we want for you. Why? Because this is God's plan...a marriage friendship of three: the Lord, your husband (wife), and you.[3]

It is often in the darkest moments of life that we discover the value and strength of true friendship. Indeed, if your spouse is your best friend, those dark times only serve to deepen your covenant companionship.

Knit Together in Love

So let me ask you again: Is your spouse your best friend? Are you true companions? Pastor Steve Carr identifies six practical areas of companionship in marriage. Think about how your own marriage measures up as you consider each one:

- Spiritual companionship (praying together)
- Verbal companionship (talking together)
- Emotional companionship (expressing feelings together)
- Recreational companionship (playing together)
- Parental companionship (parenting together)
- Sexual companionship (loving together)[4]

Once you understand and accept that marriage is a sacred and permanent covenant, nothing is more important than becoming best friends with your spouse. In the New Testament, Paul's prayer for the Colossian church was "that their hearts may be encouraged, being knit together in love" (Colossians 2:2 NKJV). If that was God's desire for believers in the church, certainly it is his desire for two believers in marriage. Companionship fortifies marriage. It knits spouses together in love. It is essential for a long and fulfilling life together.

After all, every heart longs for a true friend. And covenant companionship between a husband and wife is the greatest friendship on earth.

Chapter 12

.

THE CRITICAL ROLE OF COMMUNICATION

One always loves the one who understands you.

—*Anais Nin*

A woman noticed that the husband next-door always came home from work with flowers, candy, and a big kiss for his wife. Feeling a little jealous, the lady wondered if a hint might motivate her own husband to do the same. So one day when her husband came home after a long day at the office, she said, "Honey, have you noticed that the husband next-door is always kissing his wife and bringing her flowers and candy? Why don't you do that?"

"Because I hardly know the woman," he responded.

Have you ever been misunderstood when you've tried to communicate something to your spouse? Have you ever told your mate something as clearly as you could, and he or she still got it all wrong?

Welcome to marriage, where there is nothing more important than the ability to communicate—and nothing more difficult.

The word *communicate* means "to impart, to make known." *Communication* is the process of revealing yourself or making yourself known to another person in verbal and nonverbal ways so that the person understands and accepts what you are communicating. It doesn't mean that the other person necessarily agrees with you, just that he or she understands and accepts how you think or feel. "It is impossible to overemphasize the immense need we have to be really listened to, to be taken seriously, to be understood," writes renowned Swiss counselor Paul Tournier. "No one can develop freely in this world and find a full life without feeling understood by at least one person."[1]

Communication is the lifeblood of a marriage relationship. In fact, a marriage will never rise above the level of communication that transpires within it. Before you can really love another person, you must get to know that person; there can be no unity or oneness otherwise. And marriage is intended to be a safe place for communication to happen. Husbands and wives should be able to share their deepest hurts, fears, and failures as well as their greatest hopes, dreams, and successes—all without the threat of resentment, rejection, or retaliation. One of the greatest gifts love can offer is genuine communication within the safety and protection of the marriage covenant.

As we learned in the previous chapter, however, men and women are very different, and those differences become natural barriers to communication. Some differences were designed by God at creation. Other differences are less gender-related and more the result of differing backgrounds, needs, personalities, and temperaments. But because husbands and wives are so different, the possibility of *misunderstanding* is always greater than the possibility of *understanding*.

According to family counselor Norman H. Wright, everything you say to your spouse has more than one message—and that's where the problem begins. Each communication includes:

- What you mean
- What you are actually saying
- What the spouse actually hears
- What your spouse thinks he or she hears

- What your spouse says about what you said

- What you think your spouse said about what you said[2]

As one husband said to his wife, "I know you believe you understand what you think I said, but I'm not sure you realize that what you heard is not what I meant." No wonder we have to work at communication in marriage. We are too different—and too complicated—for it to be easy! And modern cultural trends only make it harder. "With the appearance of the two-bathroom home," Dr. John Bachcom notes, "Americans forgot how to cooperate. With the appearance of the two-car family, we forgot how to associate. And with the coming of the two-television home, we forgot how to communicate."[3]

This "forgetfulness" when it comes to communicating honestly and effectively is at the root of nearly all marriage problems and broken relationships. It is the core issue in virtually every separation and divorce. The fact is, communication is critically important for building a marriage that goes the distance. In a poll done by the Roper organization, both men and women rated "the ability to talk to each other about feelings" as one of the three most important elements in a good marriage.[4]

Without communication, a marriage will surely die. On the flip side, improving communication is the easiest and quickest way to make any marriage better.

In preparation for this book, I surveyed a cross-section of married couples in our church. My first question was, "What do you think is the biggest problem in most marriages?" Both men and women overwhelmingly answered, "Communication." My results mirrored those of Dr. Gary Smalley, who for more than twenty years has asked couples attending his marriage seminars to name one thing they believe could improve their marriage above anything else. "Without exception," he says, "...and from more than three hundred thousand people, the answer has come through loud and clear: 'We need better communication.'"[5]

WORDS THAT TOUCH THE HEART

It is often said, "One picture is worth a thousand words." Because that is true, great communicators often use powerful word pictures to drive home their messages. Word pictures touch the heart, making them a dynamic tool for facilitating understanding. I know I try to use word pictures in my preaching and teaching ministry. A good story or analogy always seems to be the thing that drives home a point best and locks a concept into my listeners' memories. They quickly forget my sermons, but they remember my illustrations!

More than a decade ago, Smalley and John Trent wrote a powerful and practical book, *The Language of Love*, in which they promoted emotional word pictures as a form of love language that any person can speak. "An emotional word picture is a communication tool that uses a story or object to activate simultaneously the *emotions* and *intellect* of a person," they wrote. "In so doing, it causes the person to *experience* our words, not just hear them."

According to Smalley and Trent, word pictures grab our attention and bring communication to life, locking important thoughts into our memory banks. Furthermore, the authors assert, "word pictures open the door to very meaningful and intimate relationships."[6] They believe that learning what to say and how to say it can revolutionize a marriage relationship.

Ronald Reagan, our nation's fortieth president, was often called "the Great Communicator." He punctuated his speeches and public conversations with stories, analogies, and great phrases such as, "Let's win one for the Gipper!" Privately he was a master of communication with those he loved. I discovered this when I picked up his wife Nancy's book *I Love You, Ronnie*, which contained many of the beautiful letters he wrote to her. To be honest, I couldn't put the book down. The letters paint beautiful word pictures of a man deeply in love with his wife. Here are some examples:

> I suppose some people would find it unusual that you and I can so easily span three thousand miles, but in truth it comes very naturally. Man can't live without a heart and you are my heart, by far the nicest

thing about me and so very necessary. There would be no life without you nor would I want any.

> I love you,
> The Eastern Half of Us

Probably this letter will reach you only a few hours before I arrive myself, but not really because right now as I try to say what is in my heart I think my thoughts must be reaching you without waiting for paper and ink and stamps and such. If I ache, it's because we are apart and yet that can't be, because you are inside me and a part of me, so we aren't really apart at all. Yet I ache but wouldn't be without the ache, because that would mean being without you, and that I can't be because I love you.

> Your Husband

Oh, what warm and powerful words of covenant love—beautiful, blessed, and binding! Here's one more Reagan word picture that was a message on a Thanksgiving card on Nancy's breakfast tray at the White House:

You are the real whipped cream on the pumpkin pie of life! And boy am I a dessert man?!

> Prexy[7]

The biggest problem is many marriages today is a language barrier. Of course, all of us aren't going to be able to express ourselves like Ronald Reagan. But each of us needs to learn how to communicate love—the language of the heart. To maximize your relationship with your spouse, you need to learn how to speak the love language of your mate. As with any new language, it takes time and practice.

Not long ago I happened to be on a plane with Gary Chapman, author of *The Five Love Languages.* I took advantage of that opportunity to tell him how much I appreciated his wonderful book. (Read it with your spouse and take the love language quiz. You'll be glad you did.) After twenty-five years of counseling, Chapman is convinced there are five basic languages of love that you can use in communicating love to your spouse:

- Words of affirmation—verbally affirming your spouse for the good things he or she does.

- Quality time—giving your spouse your undivided attention. This may involve going out to eat, taking a walk together, or planning an extended weekend for just the two of you.

- Gifts—giving gifts that say, "I am thinking about you."

- Acts of service—doing things for your spouse; serving in a way that you know is meaningful to your mate.

- Physical touch—kissing, embracing, a pat on the back, holding hands, sexual intercourse.[8]

According to Chapman, one of the five is your *primary* love language. This means that when love is expressed to you in that form, you receive it with the full understanding that you are loved. In most cases, however, a husband and wife do not speak the same love language. In other words, if you are trying to love your spouse the way you want to be loved, you're probably not getting your message across.

Do you know your spouse's primary love language? Do you know your own? If not, find out! Make it a goal of your marriage to identify your mate's primary love language, and learn to speak it fluently and regularly. Love your mate the way he or she wants to be loved. Make a conscious effort to help your spouse learn *your* love language as well.

For Men Only

Let me speak directly to men for a few moments. I do not claim to understand women. Any man who claims to understand women will also lie about other things. However, after years of living in a girls' dorm with a wife and two daughters, I have come to realize one important thing: women love to talk.

In fact, experts agree that women talk more than men. The statistic I've heard is that men use about twelve thousand words a day compared to twenty-four thousand for women. Granted, it can be a challenge when a husband uses his twelve thousand words during the day and comes home to a wife who has twelve thousand words left to use. Would anyone like to testify? But women talk naturally and easily. They talk to feel better, to sort things out, to open up for intimacy, and sometimes to make a point or solve a problem. They not only love to talk; they *need* to talk. They are relational and auditory in the way they process information.

One of the major reasons women like to talk is that it helps them process stress. Often men try to interrupt the process by jumping in and offering quick, cut-and-dry solutions. But that effort at "helping" only creates more stress in a woman's mind. She needs to talk things out. She wants and needs to be heard. The last thing she wants is advice!

Let me stop right here and tell you something that is worth the price of this book. Get this down, and it will revolutionize your marriage. Here it is: When a woman is stressed out and talking ninety miles an hour, there are only two things you need to say. First, when she finally pauses and looks up at you for a response, say, "Tell me more!" And then when she has talked it all out and collapses, exhausted, in your arms, say, "Poor baby. My, how you have suffered!" I guarantee that you both will feel better. Try it!

With women, you cannot overdo kind and loving words. They need to hear the words "I love you" several times a day. Unfortunately, men can talk all day and never share feelings. If a wife wants to put fear and terror in her husband's soul, all she needs to do is say, "Honey, we need to talk." Men would rather eat dirt than talk about problems or issues in marriage.

Someone has said, "Listening to a woman tell about her day is like ordering pizza one pepperoni at a time." Men plead, "Spare me the details. Get to the point." But women love details. Men want the bottom line; women want all the lines. Unfortunately, most men know how to "court and conquer" but not how to "marry and maintain." We're more into *facts* than *feelings;* into *rules* more than *relationships;* more into *courting* than *cherishing;* more into *looks* than *listening;* more into *sex* than *sensitivity;* and more into *tasks* than *touch.* Houston, we have a problem!

Let's face it. When it comes to communication, we men tend to hover at the grunt level or the facts-and-information level, as if we are put on earth to make noises and dispense information. Yet it is at the next level, the feeling level, where women hang out. Have you ever been to a ball game and spotted an ugly man with a beautiful woman on his arm? You think, *How can this be? Does she owe him money and can't pay?* Not at all! This man just knows how to talk. He uses beautiful word pictures, and his words penetrate the surface level and touch her emotions. Any redneck can grunt and spit facts. This dude communicates. He goes auditory, and she goes limp. Get the picture?

Women accuse men of being emotionally absent. One woman said, "My husband has taken a vow of silence. The only time he opens his mouth is to eat and yawn." The truth is, while most men need work in this area, we have not all had emotional bypasses. We are emotional beings. We have feelings. We can talk. We are just different.

Psychologist David Clarke explains the difference between male and female communication this way: "Men are clams and women are crowbars." A wife will pry, prod, and probe information from her husband because she wants *closeness*. Without closeness, she feels that she has nothing. On the other hand, her husband will shut up, shut down, and deny her closeness because he wants *control*. If the man has no control, he thinks he has nothing. (By the way, that's why a husband will stall before doing a chore or coming to dinner when his wife calls—he wants to feel in control.)[9]

As men we can learn a lot about communication from women. They are good at it. We are not. So let's allow them to teach us how to communicate our feelings, fears, and fantasies, and not just the facts. My wife is my mentor in this area. She has taught me so much, but I still have a long way to go.

For Women Only

Let me address my women readers now. Please recognize that your ease with talking and your desire to improve the world around you sets you up for something men hate: nagging. Being nagged, as someone once said, is like being "nibbled to death by a duck." The Bible compares a nagging wife to a dripping faucet (see Proverbs 19:13 TLB). The bottom line is that nagging not only doesn't work, it actually works against you. It is demotivating. Give it up. Stop it! If you want to motivate your spouse, thank him and praise him for the things he does—even the little things—instead of nagging him about the things he doesn't do.

Nagging is one of the most common enemies of good communication. But there are others, and both men and women fall into them:

- Criticism

- Blame

- Condemnation

- Sarcasm

- Interrogation

- Argument

- Correction

- Threats

- Intimidation

Avoid these like the plague! Instead, put into practice the keys to better communication shared by Josh McDowell in his book *The Secret of Loving.* His list includes eleven items; but to round it out to a dozen, I've added one final key that I think is important:

- Work at it.

- Learn to compromise.

- Seek to understand.

- Affirm your spouse's worth, dignity, and value.

- Be positive and encouraging.

- Practice confidentiality.

- Wait for the right time.

- Share your feelings.

- Avoid mind reading.

- Give a response.

- Be honest.[10]

- Become a great listener.

HIS NEEDS, HER NEEDS

For more than twenty years I have told the story of a man and woman who had fussed and fought for fifty years of their married life. Finally, on the occasion of their fiftieth wedding anniversary, their grown kids got together and presented them with a lovely gift: a trip to the psychiatrist. The couple argued about whether or not to accept the gift and then about who would drive them to the appointment. When they arrived at the psychiatrist's office, they argued about which one would tell the doctor the "real" story. After listening to the couple for about fifteen minutes, the doctor got up, walked over to the old lady, and planted a long Hollywood kiss on her. Then he turned to the husband and said, "Now this is what she needs three times a week."

"Good," the old man replied. "I'll bring her by Monday, Wednesday, and Friday."

What is the biggest little word in marriage? *Needs.* Husbands and wives have basic needs that must be met by their mates. As clinical psychologist Willard Harley writes in his classic book *His Needs, Her Needs,* at least five of these needs are dominant according to gender:

Her Needs Tend to Be:
1. Affection
2. Conversation
3. Honesty and openness
4. Financial support
5. Family commitment

His Needs Tend to Be:
1. Sexual fulfillment
2. Recreational companionship
3. Attractive spouse
4. Domestic support
5. Admiration

According to Harley, "If any of the spouse's basic needs go unmet over a long period of time, that spouse becomes vulnerable to an affair."[11] Wherever there is separation and divorce, you can bet there is somebody whose needs haven't been met.

God designed covenant marriage as the perfect environment for husbands and wives to meet one another's needs. But we're not mind readers. Knowing what those needs are is not always easy. That's where communication comes in. We need to go to school on the opposite sex in general and on our spouses in particular. Then we must learn to talk about our needs with each other.

Husbands and wives often fail to meet one another's needs for two reasons: (1) They don't know what those needs are; and (2) Because of gender differences, they don't share the same interest in a particular need. "Men want marriage to meet the needs they have, such as sex," Harley says, "and women want marriage to meet the needs that mean most to them, such as affection and conversation."[12] As the saying goes, "Different strokes for different folks."

Light Bulbs and Crockpots

It's important to understand that women crave affection and conversation the way men crave sex and recreational companionship. Eighty percent of a woman's needs are nonsexual. She wants to be hugged, held, and heard. He wants sex. She wants flowers, notes, dates, and long walks in order to feel special. He wants sex, sex, sex, and sex in order to feel satisfied. In fact, I have it on good authority that men want sex on all days that start with a T: Tuesday and Thursday, Today and Tomorrow, and Taturday and Tunday. As one (frustrated) husband once said, "Maybe women are called the opposite sex because men want sex, and women want the opposite."

When it comes to sex, it seems, men turn on like light bulbs, while women are more like Crockpots. No wonder sex is often the source of conflict in marriage! As someone has wisely said, "If sex is going well, it is 10 percent of the marriage; if sex is not going well, it's 90 percent of the marriage."

I like the instructions Barbara and Allen Pease have come up with for keeping a man and a woman satisfied:

> To satisfy a woman: Caress; praise; pamper; relish; savor; massage; fix things; empathize; serenade; compliment; support; feed; soothe; tantalize; humor; placate; stimulate; stroke; console; hug; ignore fat bits; cuddle; excite; pacify; protect; phone; anticipate; smooch; nuzzle; forgive; accessorize; entertain; charm; carry for; oblige; fascinate; attend to; trust; defend; clothe; brag about; sanctify; acknowledge; spoil; embrace; die for; dream of; tease; gratify; squeeze; indulge; idolize and worship.
>
> To satisfy a man: Arrive naked.[13]

It's not that men are right in their approach to sex while women are wrong. Nor is it the opposite. Men and women are just different. Men tend to be driven sexually while women tend to be driven relationally. As a result, they view sex differently, as the following chart shows:

Men view sex as:	Women view sex as:
1. Performance and release	1. Play and romance
2. An event	2. An encounter
3. The act	3. The atmosphere
4. A single item	4. A package deal
5. Tied to masculinity	5. Trade for attention and affection
6. Stress relief	6. Comfort and closeness
7. Pleasure	7. Potential pleasure

For women, I've been told, sex begins in the kitchen. How good the sex act is at night depends on the atmosphere at breakfast and the affection expressed during the day. So let me ask you, men: How are you in the kitchen? How do you express love to your wife throughout the day? Experts say it takes men an average of 2.8 minutes to reach climax/orgasm. It takes women 12.8 minutes. Men, what are you doing to make that ten-minute difference exciting and fulfilling? With that question not far from your mind, let me give you seven essentials (from a woman's perspective) that precede great sex. Think of this as your wife speaking:

- *Time*—I spell love T-I-M-E. Spend time with me, and I'll believe that I am your number one priority.

- *Talk*—Listen to me and try to understand me. Listen non-defensively and without an agenda. This tells me that I am important to you. Talk to me and tell me you love me. Look me in the eyes and tell me I'm wonderful. And then tell me more!

- *Tenderness*—Treat me tenderly. When I feel comfortable sharing with you because I know you accept me and understand me, I want to be close to you. I need hugs, and lots of them.

- *Transparency*—When I know I can talk about anything and share my secrets with you, I develop intimacy with you and an openness that brings release, comfort, and joy.

- *Trust*—When you listen to me without judging me, I trust you and feel secure in giving myself to you.

- *Touch*—When I know I have found someone who listens to me, understands me, and does not judge me—someone who accepts me as I am—that turns me on. I want to touch you and be touched by you.

- *Ten minutes*—If you will fill in the ten-minute gap with exciting foreplay, forgetting about yourself, pleasuring me in the way I want, and focusing entirely on my need to feel loved, I promise the result will be great sex!

You Can Do It!

Let me encourage you to read Willard Harley's book *His Needs, Her Needs*. You'll learn a lot about your spouse's needs as well as your own. For now I'll just give you the good news that's found at the bottom line: Although you are different, you and your spouse can successfully meet each other's needs. As Harley asserts, "Marriage can meet a man's need for sex and a woman's need for affection and conversation, even when the wife has little interest in sex and the husband has little interest in affection and conversation." In other words, "You don't have to share the need to meet that need in someone else. A man who has no need for affection can learn to be an affectionate husband, and a woman with no need for sex can learn to be a great sex partner."[14]

How can you possibly meet your spouse's needs when they are so different from your own? Here's how: On the basis of covenant, allow God's Holy Spirit to work in you, enabling you to become unselfish enough to truly give yourself to meeting your mate's needs. You take that "walk of death." You put your spouse's needs first.

The story is told of a man who was having some major health problems. His wife accompanied him to the doctor's office. After putting the man through a battery of tests, the doctor went to the waiting room and summoned the wife into his private office. Speaking in hushed tones, he said, "Your husband is a very sick man. In fact, there are some things you have to do for him or he will die."

"Oh," said the startled wife, "and what are those things, doctor?"

"Well, you need to fix him three home-cooked meals every day, give him a full body massage twice a week, and have sex with him every other day," the doctor said.

Shocked and confused, the lady mumbled, "Thanks," and quietly returned to the waiting room. Immediately her curious husband asked, "Well, what did the doctor say?"

The wife replied, "He said you are going to die!"

I don't know if that man died, but I can guarantee that unless a husband and wife give themselves to meeting each other's needs, their marriage will die. Covenant marriage calls for practicing the Golden Rule: Meet your spouse's needs as you would want your spouse to meet your needs.

The One Who Meets All Needs

That said, let's stop for a quick reality check. Marriage may be a great place to get your needs met, but it cannot meet all your needs. Even on a great day, your spouse has the potential to meet only 30 percent of your needs—which means the remaining 70 percent must be met by other sources. The fact is, you have needs that your mate can never meet, and vice versa. Your mate is not God. You have a foundational need for security and significance that can only be met by your Master, not your mate. Marriage cannot make you whole. Jesus makes you whole. Put your security in God who never changes. Establish your significance in God who always loves you and will never abandon you.

It is only by putting your absolute trust in God for security and significance that you will be able to handle whatever life throws at you. You become emotionally "TUFF" when you realize and accept the biblical truth that God sees you as:

T—Totally accepted

U—Unconditionally loved

F—Fully forgiven

F—Fully pleasing

You can trust God to meet your needs. He loves you with an everlasting "TUFF" love. As Paul says in Romans 8:38–39, "I am convinced that neither death nor life, neither angels nor demons, neither the present nor the future, nor any powers, neither height nor depth, nor anything else in all creation, will be able to separate us from the love of God that is in Christ Jesus our Lord."

THE BONDING OF INTIMACY

Our greatest need in life is for a relationship with God. Next to that, however, our most important need—one that both men and women share—is for a close, intimate relationship with another person. Yet sometimes the very thing we crave we often fight against. As the old song goes:

There is a wall between us
It's not made of stone
The more we are together
The more we are alone[15]

Do you realize it is possible to share a house, a sofa, a bathroom, and even a bed, and yet feel totally isolated and alone? Unfortunately, too many spouses can attest to this sad truth. Emotional isolation and lack of intimacy are like a cancer, destroying an untold number of marriage relationships. In his book *Becoming One,* Joe Beam notes that the "vast majority of marriages, even Christian marriages, have failed to achieve oneness.... People live in marriages that range from empty and unfulfilling to miserable. We often hear the statistic that one in four marriages is happy. If true, this means that 75 percent of married couples exist in a marriage without the intimacy God intended."[16]

The ultimate goal of communication in marriage is intimacy. The Latin word *intimus,* from which we get our word *intimacy,* means "inner or inmost." I like to say that intimacy means "in-to-me-you-see." In marriage, intimacy involves a continual revelation of who you are before God and your spouse. It is a pulling back of the curtains of your life in order to let that special person see inside—the peeling back of your layers of self-protection until you are both unmasked and "naked" before one another. No walls. No secrets. No barriers. No hype.

Genesis 2:25 tells us that the first man and his wife were both naked—physically, mentally, and emotionally—and "they felt no shame." They were safe in the security of their covenant with God and with each other. Only in the safety and security of a sacred marriage covenant are we really free to expose our innermost selves. In covenant, we commit to protect each other's nakedness, knowing that it must never be exploited. We agree to trust ourselves to each other for safekeeping.

When the Bible talks about a husband and wife becoming "one flesh," it is describing intimacy. David Clarke puts it this way: "[Intimacy] is a complete coming together of a man and a woman in three vital areas: (1) physical, (2) emotional, and (3) spiritual. God says that you have complete or ultimate intimacy only when you are bonded in all three areas."[17]

Oftentimes men spell intimacy S-E-X. Great sex is a wonderful result of genuine intimacy in marriage, but we'd be wrong to think intimacy is limited to sex. In fact, to desire only sexual intimacy with your spouse is to set up your marriage for failure. According to Clarke, a marriage built on physical attraction will last six months to a year and a half. Add emotions, and you are good for maybe four to seven years. The fact is, sexual attraction always plateaus eventually, and emotions are notoriously fickle. So what is the secret to genuine intimacy that bonds a couple together for a lifetime? Clarke says:

> The secret to success in every area of life, including relationships with the opposite sex, comes from God and his Word. The secret—God's secret—to having a fulfilling, exhilarating, lasting marriage is spiritual intimacy.... Coming together as a couple spiritually produces passion and energy unmatched in all of human experience. Nothing else can come close to matching it.[18]

Spiritual Beings, Human Experience

It is often said that we are not human beings having a spiritual experience; we are spiritual beings having a human experience! And as spiritual beings, the most important part of our identity, our lives, and our relationships is always spiritual. Clarke continues:

> The love described in Ephesians 5:25 and 1 Corinthians 13 isn't human love! It is God's love.... If you want to love each other with God's love, you must be connected to him as a couple. You must join spiritually.... Spiritual bonding is consistently placing God at the center of your relationship and growing even closer to him as a couple. This means that you include God in everything—you invite him into every nook and cranny of your relationship. It means that your souls come together in the pursuit of God. It is sharing Christ. It is tapping the power of the Holy Spirit and putting him to work in your relationship. It is, without question, the deepest form of intimacy available to a man and a woman. When you spiritually bond, it is no longer the two of you who do the loving. It is God himself who does the loving.[19]

Spiritual intimacy is not available to everyone. To spiritually bond, both partners must first be Christians; and second, they must be growing in Christ. The practical side of growing in Christ involves prayer, Bible study, sharing Christ with others, and serving together in a local church. It may surprise you to know that doing these practical things will improve every area of your married life, including your sex life! For instance, prayer promotes a deeper intimacy and protects you from the attacks of the enemy. Through prayer it is possible to build a shield around your marriage and to tap into the power of God to help you love unconditionally. If your marriage is thriving spiritually, your individual spiritual tracks regularly intersect and become one. You grow spiritually as individuals and as a couple at the same time.[20]

God designed marriage in such a way that it will not work without him in the center. Any other plan is a recipe for disaster. The apostle Paul said of Jesus, "He is before all things, and in him all things hold together" (Colossians 1:17). "All things" includes marriage. Only in a God-centered marriage can you reap the luscious fruit of the Spirit: love, joy, peace, patience, kindness, goodness, faithfulness, gentleness, and self-control (see Galatians 5:22–23).

In the spiritual intimacy of marriage, one plus one equals one. Two become one flesh. In a special way, the husband belongs to the wife, and the wife belongs to the husband. Author Mike Mason says that intimacy is reached "when two people are neither afraid nor ashamed of being possessed by love.... They give themselves freely to the pure joy and liberty of owning and being owned.... Not that a husband and wife own one another outright, entirely, as they are (both) owned by the Lord."[21]

Joseph, my favorite Old Testament character, refused to give in to the tempting come-on of Potiphar's wife and told her, "My master does not concern himself with anything in the house; everything he owns he has entrusted to my care.... My master has withheld nothing from me except you, because you are his wife" (Genesis 39:8–9). Joseph understood that in covenant marriage, a spouse is a possession—but "a possession," Mason writes, "like no other. The most personal of all effects, one that is like one's very own life in that it cannot possibly be given to anyone else.

For marriage is the grafting together of two hearts, the planting of them in one another so that they become interdependent for their very life." Mason continues:

> When a husband looks with love into the eyes of his wife, he may know beyond a shadow of doubt that those eyes, and the person within them, belong to him, in a way that nothing else on earth can—neither his house, nor his car, nor any material thing, nor his insurance policy, nor his children, not any other person. She is his, for life, and anything else that is his can be taken away from him, or estranged, much more easily than she can. So radical is the extremity of this mutual ownership in marriage, and so complete is the symbiosis, that only death can sever it, as only love can confer it.[22]

That's the incredible mystery and beauty of covenant marriage—the place where the deepest communication and the closest intimacy between a man and a woman can be experienced on earth.

Getting *CLOSE*

Intimacy is never automatic. There is no such thing as "instant intimacy." Rather, intimacy is a process that requires determination, patience, and a commitment of time—lots of time. I once heard a psychiatrist say, "If I were going to give ten steps to intimacy, the first nine would be to spend time together." Do you know that the average couple spends about twenty-six minutes per week in conversation, and most of that is superficial talk? Compare that with the nearly seven hours that men spend each week watching sports on television!

In teaching seminars on marriage, I use the acrostic *CLOSE* to describe the components of marital intimacy:

C: Covenant

As we've already said, only in the context of a covenant marriage are you really safe to open up to your spouse. Covenant provides the safety net that enables you to take the risk to communicate freely.

L: Listening

The greatest gift you can give your spouse is to become a wonderful listener—listening not only with your ears but also with your eyes, your mind, and your heart. Listening communicates several important messages to our mate. It says:

- You are important to me.

- You are valuable to me.

- I care about you.

- I want to know you.

- I want to hear what you have to say.

- I want to know how you feel.

Let me say a word here to men. The number one complaint women make against us is that we do not listen. Is listening important? Absolutely! All affairs begin with conversation. Women have to talk; and if *we* don't listen, they will find someone who will. Women fall in love and stay in love with men who have big ears, not big biceps. They choose "top ear" over "top gun" every time. If we care about our marriages, we must learn to listen to our mates!

I realize I'm already in the middle of one acrostic, but since men have such trouble in this area, let me give you another quick acrostic with some practical pointers for improving your listening skills:

L—Lean forward and look into her eyes.

I—Inquire by asking, "Tell me more."

S—Stop interrupting with your "answers."

T—Tell her what you heard her say and ask if you are right.

E—Express comfort: "My, how you have suffered!"

N—Never look at your watch while the two of you are talking.

O: Openness

Intimacy is built on openness—the willingness to be transparent in sharing your feelings, fears, failures, and fantasies with another imperfect human being. True intimacy occurs in an atmosphere of safety that allows you to be who you are and express how you feel. It is only when you feel completely secure, unconditionally loved, and fully accepted that you take the risk of opening up your inner being to your spouse. Indeed, this level of openness is "holy ground" and must be treated as such.

S: Sensitivity

The two major enemies of intimacy—the fear of rejection and the fear of abandonment—can be defeated only by a large dose of sensitivity. The truth is, we are all wounded. We are all insecure and afraid. We all have hurts and needs. Sensitivity demands that you never respond to your mate's communication with rejection, ridicule, or retaliation. Rather, you and your spouse must learn to be acutely sensitive to one another's wants, needs, hurts, and desires, creating a safe place for intimacy to occur.

E: Empathy

Each of us longs to be fully accepted and fully understood by another human being. In marriage, you and your mate can fulfill this need in one another by developing empathy—the capacity to participate in each other's feelings, to see life from the other person's point of view, to understand where each other is coming from. It is no secret that most marriage conflicts stem from misunderstandings. But as someone once said, "The best way to avoid stepping on your mate's toes is to put yourself in his or her shoes."

Some time ago Leigh and I were speaking at a conference in Colorado, and she shared a story that touched every heart in the building—especially mine. Here's what she said:

We were having a very rough time in our ministry, and Fred was really depressed. It just seemed like a cloud of darkness hovered over our home. I was hurting and frustrated, and I had tried everything I knew to encourage my husband. I read books. I prayed. I listened to tapes. I had done everything I knew to do, and nothing worked.

Then one day I went into his closet. I just wanted to be close to him somehow, so I went in and closed the door. I felt so close because his clothes were there. His smell was there. His cologne was there. I felt his presence.

For some reason, I sat down on the floor and began to shine his shoes. (Now guys, don't get excited. I haven't done that since.) I started shining his shoes and boots. And then, sitting in his closet, I put his shoes on my feet and said to the Lord, "Lord, show me how to love this man. Show me what it is like to feel his pressures and carry his burdens. Show me what it is like to walk in his shoes. Help me understand what it's like to pastor a church of over seven thousand members. Help me to know what it's like to have his feelings of rejection and depression."

At that moment God began to reveal to me some incredible things. I realized that it was a great privilege to walk beside this godly man and to be his partner, his best friend, his lover, and his companion. On that day I began to pray for my husband in a way that I have never prayed for him before, and God showed me how to love him in ways I had not known before.

The Bible exhorts husbands to seek to "understand" their wives (1 Peter 3:7 TLB). I know of nothing more vital in building a great marriage than mutual understanding and the kind of empathy that seeks to know what it's like to walk in the other person's shoes and to see life from his or her perspective.

According to authors Les and Leslie Parrott, "Research has shown that ninety percent of our struggles in marriage would be resolved if we did nothing more than see that problem from our partner's perspective." The Parrotts believe that empathy "is the heart of love. Yet loving couples neglect it to their peril. Why? Because it's tough to do. Empathy calls for loving our partner with both our head and heart, concurrently. Years ago poet Walt Whitman said it best in his famous work, *Leaves of Grass:* 'I do not ask how the wounded feels; I myself, become the wounded one.'"[23]

Let me encourage you to seek God on behalf of your mate, and allow him to show you how to recognize, understand, and meet his or her deepest needs. God knows everything there is to know about your spouse, and the Holy Spirit is a wonderful promoter of communication, oneness, and intimacy. Go ahead. Call on divine help!

After all, a marriage will only rise to the level of the communication that transpires within it. There can be no covenant oneness without intimacy. There can be no intimacy without understanding. And there can be no understanding without communication. The good news is that by improving the way you communicate with your spouse, you can turn a low-altitude marriage into one that really soars.

Chapter 13

LEARNING HOW TO MANAGE CONFLICT

The ideas of "me" and "mine" are at the root of all conflict.
—Nisarg Adatta

On Wilma and Harry's fiftieth wedding anniversary, their friends and family threw a big party. Finally, when the festivities were over and the last guest went home, Wilma turned to Harry and said: "You know, Harry, we've been miserable for fifty years. We've fought every day. We've disagreed on nearly everything, and I'm convinced we can't go on this way. So I am making a commitment to pray that God will help us solve this problem. To be honest, I am praying that God will take one of us home. And when he does, I'm going to go live with my sister in Grand Rapids."

Some people believe that a marriage is made in heaven. Yes, but so are thunder and lightning! As one man said, "My wife and I have never had an argument, but the neighbors often complain about hearing us reasoning things out together." Even happily married "super couples" experience conflict. Once Billy Graham's wife, Ruth, was asked if she had ever considered divorce. She replied, "Divorce? No. Murder? Yes!"

Every relationship has its share of rumbles and sparks, no exceptions. Why? First, because we are different, as we've noted in previous chapters. And second, because none of us is perfect. We are all sinners; we are all fallen people who live in a fallen world. Two essentially self-centered lives cannot merge into one without facing a plethora of challenges and conflicts. Temperaments will clash. Egos will engage. That means that conflict in marriage is inevitable. As William Shakespeare said, "The course of true love never did run smooth." What an understatement!

Interestingly, according to Diane Sollee of the Coalition for Marriage, Family, and Couples Education, couples who are happy and stay married have the same number of disagreements and conflicts as couples who are unhappy and get divorced. What makes the still-married couples successful is not the absence of conflict, but their ability to manage conflict when it arises.[1]

In other words, it's not the presence of conflict that will determine the success or failure of your marriage; it's the way you handle that conflict. Marriage does not have to be conflict-free to be good. But as the Bible notes, a house filled with division and conflict destroys itself (see Mark 3:25). That means that in order to have a long-term, happy, and fulfilling marriage, you must keep your house from being overcome by conflict, anger, resentment, and argument. You have to commit yourself to resolving conflicts as soon as they start.

Dr. Howard Markman maintains that the ability to resolve conflicts is the key for staying in love and staying married to one person. Based on twenty years of research, he concludes that if couples would only learn to work through their conflicts successfully, the overall divorce rate would be cut in half. Says Markman: "It's not how much you love one another, how good your sex life is, or what problems you have with money that best predicts the future quality of your marriage.... The best predictor of marital success is the way you handle disagreements."[2]

Unresolved conflict is like a malignant cancer that erodes the joy, intimacy, and commitment of your marriage. The antidote is learning practical skills for dealing with your differences in ways that will develop and not destroy your relationship. I love the story of the elephant and the chicken that somehow got locked up in a room together. "Let's make some rules," the chicken said. "Rule number one: We must not *step* on each other."

When handled successfully, conflict can be a steppingstone—not a stumbling block—to deeper marital intimacy. God tells us in his Word that we will have conflicts and trouble in this world (see John 16:33). But he also tells us that our trials and struggles are the tools he uses to help us change, mature, and grow (see James 1:2–4). That's true in life, and it's true in marriage. Conflicts have the potential to become a best friend and teacher in your marriage or a bitter enemy. The choice is yours. Will you manage your conflicts, or will they manage you?

THE FACTS ABOUT CONFLICT

What do the following subjects have in common: money, sex, communication, and children? They are the four "hot buttons" for conflict in marriage. Ever pressed one of those buttons? Did you remember to duck? Other common areas of conflict include:

- Household chores

- Relatives (especially mothers-in-law)

- Time spent in hobbies

- Competing relationships

- Work

- Religion

Of course, all conflicts are not the same. And some couples struggle with the deeper issues of conflict arising from a spouse's addiction to the Internet, alcohol, pornography, gambling, or drugs. But whether large or small, easy or tough, any of these conflicts has the potential to tear a marriage apart piece-by-piece if not managed correctly.

Let's look at some general facts about conflict that will help us approach our specific conflicts with greater understanding.

Not All Conflicts Can Be Solved

By using rigorous scientific procedures to observe the habits of married couples over many years, Dr. John Gottman has found that "all marital conflicts, ranging from mundane annoyances to all out wars, really fall into one of two categories: Either they can be resolved, or they are perpetual, which means they will be a part of your lives forever, in some form or another." Surprisingly, a whopping 69 percent of marriage conflicts fall into that perpetual category![3] As psychologist Dan Wiles notes, choosing a spouse means that "you will inevitably be choosing a particular set of unsolvable problems that you'll be grappling with for the next ten, twenty or fifty years."[4]

Discouraged? Don't be! The fact is, you don't have to resolve all your major marriage conflicts for your marriage to grow and glow. Psychologists tell us that a person's basic personality is set by age five. This means that the personality of the person you marry—which is often the opposite of yours—will change very little during the course of your marriage. Therefore you must *acknowledge* your differences, *accept* them as reality, and learn to cope with them by *adjusting*—developing strategies to help you deal with them. In other words, you solve what can be solved, change what can be changed, and cope with what can't be solved or changed. To do this successfully you need to develop six characteristics:

- A gracious attitude
- A listening ear
- An understanding heart
- A sense of humor
- A willingness to work
- A patient spirit

Conflicts Don't Solve Themselves

People have a tendency to deny, ignore, or run from conflict. Couples will go so far as to split up or divorce rather than negotiate through the treacherous waters of conflict in marriage. But problems don't dissipate by pretending they don't exist or separating from them; they only get bigger. It's like trying to plug up a water leak with a cork. As the pressure of the water builds, the cork begins to slip. Little incidents become big incidents. Before you realize it, the cork blows out, and the flood rushes in. Issues that were not part of the originally problem get mixed in, causing the real problem to get lost in the deluge.

Conflicts don't solve themselves. When you think they do, they only become more difficult to solve. There is no "quick fix." Solving major or minor conflicts takes time, energy, and megadoses of patience and understanding. But the end result is worth it.

Conflicts Are Often Driven by the Past

So often conflicts have more to do with the past than the present. I'm reminded of the two men who were talking about marriage. One said, "Every time my wife and I argue, she gets *historical*."

"You mean *hysterical*," the second man corrected.

"No," replied the first man, "I mean *historical*. Whenever we argue, she brings up everything I have ever done wrong in the past."

Conflicts are like icebergs—light at the top and heavy at the bottom. When you see an iceberg floating on the water, you are only seeing 10 to 20 percent of the actual mass. The other 80 to 90 percent is under the surface.

Have you ever asked your spouse a simple question, and he or she goes ballistic? Let me give you an example from a male perspective. You walk in the door after a great day at work and see your spouse in the kitchen. Everything looks fine. You say something simple like, "What's for supper?" All of a sudden, a giant storm of rain, thunder, and lightning hits inside your house! You stand there, dumbfounded and without an umbrella, thinking, *Where did this come from?* Unfortunately, your spouse had been suppressing and storing her emotions all day or even longer. As her explosion subsides, you begin to learn that the series of small things that triggered her storm was not above the water but beneath it.

In marriage we must not allow the past—distant or more recent—to color and control the present. God doesn't bring up our past in his relationship with us. Neither should we! When storms occur (and they will!) you need to identify the source of your anger. Are you angry because of the remark your spouse made, or is it a combination of things stored up all day—or even longer? Paul encourages us to forget those things in the past and press on toward the future (see Philippians 3:13). Good advice!

Conflicts Tend to Center on the Small Stuff

You would be surprised to know how many divorces begin in the bathroom over toothpaste. I understand. I squeeze toothpaste from the bottom of the tube and roll it up neatly, the way you're supposed to. Not my wife. With absolutely no respect for a tube of toothpaste, she squeezes it in the middle, leaving it deformed and maimed for life. Thank God for the pump. Mentadent has probably saved hundreds of marriages!

Then there's the toilet tissue roll. Should the paper come out over the top, or should it be pulled from underneath? Perhaps you're thinking, *Who knows and who cares?* It seems like such a small issue, but some people care so much about such things that their marriage is hurt by it. In fact, I bet you've already thought of something your spouse does to irritate you. You know, that "little thing" that just drives you crazy? Go ahead. Admit it! You can't understand why your mate continues to do something so stupid (well, *you* think it's stupid)—especially given that he or she knows that it irritates you to the point of no return. (You *have* told your spouse how you feel, right?)

We have a beautiful oak tree in our front yard that is probably seventy-five years old. A few weeks ago we noticed that many of its leaves were dying and small limbs were breaking off. A closer look revealed hundreds of black carpenter ants around the base of the tree. We sprayed insecticide and killed the ants, but it was too late. The ants had been silently eating on the inside of the tree for who knows how long. A mighty oak will soon fall, victimized by the curse of little things unnoticed and ignored.

Through my dealings with hundreds of couples, I've discovered it is the little things that often do the most damage in relationships. Big problems are easy to recognize, which makes them easier to repair. Small things, on the other hand, eat away on the inside, day in and day out, until the marriage "suddenly" topples. Outside observers wonder, "What happened?"

In marriage, little things make a big difference. You and I need to stop doing the little things that bother our mates and start doing the little things that bless them instead. Our marriages will thrive as a result.

My friend John Maxwell tells about a couple who had been married for sixty-five years. When asked the reason for their long and successful marriage, the man said, "Well, early on my wife went blind, and later I went deaf!" It may be that we all need to become blind and deaf when it comes to the little, irritating quirks in our mates. After all, we have our quirks and idiosyncrasies too, and we want our spouses to overlook *them*, don't we?

Covenant love is neither picky nor touchy. It chooses to overlook the flaws and foibles of others. If you want to turn your marriage from bad to good or from mediocre to magical, sit down with your mate and talk about some of the little things you can do today that will make your marriage better tomorrow. Remember, sometimes the biggest things come in small packages.

The Source of All Conflict Is Self

The Bible tells us that the root cause of all conflicts is selfish pride and ego. James 4:1 says, "What causes fights and quarrels among you? Don't they come from your desires that battle within you?" Self says, "I think of me before I think of you." It turns every argument into a who-is-right and who-is-wrong issue. Self has to be right. Has to win at all cost. Has to be in control. As one extremely frustrated wife complained, "When I married Mr. Right, I didn't realize his middle name was 'Always.'"

Selfishness is critical, condemning, blaming, and judgmental. It is fundamentally destructive to any relationship. The selflessness of covenant, on the other hand, has no driving need to win or always be right. It asks, "What can I do to make this situation better?" It is other-person centered, not self-centered. I love the wisdom and directness of this anonymous verse:

> To keep your marriage brimming
> With love in the loving cup,
> When you're wrong, admit it!
> And when you are not—shut up!

PRINCIPLES OF CONFLICT RESOLUTION

Now that we've established some general facts about conflict, let's look at some key principles that can guide us in resolving conflicts when they arise. As we've said, conflict in marriage is unavoidable, and not all conflicts can be resolved. For that reason, it's important to focus more on the process of resolving conflict than on the conflict itself—more on how you argue than on what you argue about. Your marriage *can* transcend the inevitable turmoil and not only survive but thrive. In his book *Relationship Rescue*, psychologist Phillip McGraw says, "Think about it as though your relationship sits on the limb of a tree overhanging a river. Yet the limb is so high that no matter how much splashing goes on in that river, it cannot splash high enough to reach the relationship."[5]

So how do you keep your marriage high and dry when conflict stirs the waters?

Take a Team Approach

I know you've heard the old saying, "Two heads are better than one." Well, just imagine what would happen if two *individuals* become one. That's what happens in covenant! Remember the description of covenant: Two hearts beating as one, two separate individuals blending together to become one with God's love and protection surrounding them. Conflicts don't like the team approach. They thrive on the selfishness and egos of individuals looking out for "number one." Did you notice that the word *team* does not contain an I? In the bond of covenant marriage, you and your spouse are united. You're a team. That means you approach every conflict asking not, "What's best for me?" but, "What's best for our marriage? What's best for *us?*"

Be Willing to Lose in Order to Win

Many writers promote "win/win" solutions as the goal in conflict resolution. They recommend coming up with a fix that allows both parties to feel as if they won something. But in covenant marriage, win/win may not be the best solution. In his book *To Win at Marriage, Learn to Lose,* Gerry Spence writes, "When couples surrender their desires in the interest of serving each other, they will defuse the battle for control that secretly lurks behind many confrontations. In this way, losing ironically becomes the path to winning for both parties."[6] Mike Mason agrees: "Who 'wins' this battle of wills and whims is not the point; the point is that each tries to surrender as much as possible for the sake of the other so that the love between them may be honored and built up in every way."[7]

You and I must never let ego get in the way of our covenant commitment. In covenant, each person is willing to lose in order for the other person to win. Each is willing to die to self in order for the other to live. Covenant is the antithesis of the competitive mentality that cares more about scoring points and winning the argument than about hearing and understanding what the other person has to say.

In covenant, it's only when both spouses are willing to lose that they both ultimately win. Sometimes we just have to be willing to "give in" in order to "grow up." As Harville Hendricks said, "Conflict is growth waiting to happen."[8]

Focus on the Positive

After years of research, author John Gottman found that "what really separates contented couples from those in deep marital misery is a healthy balance between their positive and negative feelings and actions toward each other." His research found "a very specific ratio that exists between the amount of positivity and negativity in a stable marriage." According to Gottman, that magic ratio is five to one. "In other words, as long as there is five times as much positive feeling and interaction between husband and wife as there is negative…the marriage is likely to be stable."

For this reason, it is important that a couple focus more on what is right with their marriage than on what is wrong. Says Gottman: "To improve or save your marriage, you must remind yourself that your mate's negative qualities do not cancel out all the positives that led you to fall in love. Nor do bad times wipe out all the good times."[9] In stable marriages, the underlying current will always flow along the lines of love and mutual respect.

Take Money Problems into Account

On every marriage survey I've ever seen, "money problems" is always near the top of the list of common conflicts. Money is an accurate barometer of the attitude and atmosphere of a marriage relationship. It is a great revealer. We do not really know another person until we experience how that person deals with money issues.

To keep love in your marriage over the long term, you have to resolve financial conflicts. Money is power; that means you have to take each other's feelings into account when you spend money or make decisions about your finances. "If you make financial decisions easily with mutual consideration," Willard Harley says in his book *Love Busters,* "chances are your love for each other is in good shape. If, on the other hand, you can't seem to agree on how to spend your money, or worse yet you put your individual incomes into separate accounts so you don't have to agree, your love for each other has probably taken a beating."[10]

Control and covenant are contradictory terms. In covenant, you give up control and unselfishly put the interests of your mate above your own—and that includes financial interests. In a covenant marriage, all money, regardless of who made it, belongs in a joint account and should be spent by joint agreement only. A weekly allowance can be taken out of the joint account so that you and your spouse have some "personal" money to spend as you choose. Separate accounts only serve to foster a "my money, your money" mentality. Remember, the two of you are in this together. What belongs to your spouse belongs to you. What belongs to you belongs to your spouse.

Don't Separate Sex from Relationship

The sexual aspect of marriage is so sensitive and emotionally supercharged that the ability to resolve sexual conflicts in a critical key to a lasting marriage. John Gottman reminds us the "no other area of a couple's life offers more potential for embarrassment, hurt, and rejection than sex."[11] As we noted in the last chapter, if sex is going well, it is 10 percent of the marriage; if sex is not going well, it's 90 percent of the marriage.

Sex cannot be separated from the marriage relationship itself. Good sex begins with a good relationship. Conversely, a bad relationship is a great sexual inhibitor. The good news is that by improving the relationship, the sexual part of a marriage usually improves automatically. After all, "the goal of sex," Gottman says, "is to be closer, to have more fun, to feel satisfied, to feel valued and accepted in this very tender area of your marriage."[12]

To achieve this goal, you need to keep the sexual part of your relationship with your spouse free of criticism and negativity. Never argue or fight in the bedroom. Pillow talk should always be loving, affirming, and cherishing. Make a concerted effort to learn about the sexual likes, dislikes, and needs of your spouse without taking any differences personally, and learn to communicate your own sexual needs and feelings in a nonthreatening way. You can do it! Clifford and Joyce Penner, authors of six books on sexual adjustment in marriage, were asked, "What percentage of couples can attain a mutually satisfying sexual relationship?" Their response? "One-hundred percent of them. We've never worked with a single married couple whom we felt were incapable of attaining a high level of sexual satisfaction with each other."[13]

Covenant is the key. The best sexual relationship, says marriage counselor Neil Clark Warren, "is one that proceeds out of a couple's deep and intimate 'soul bonding.' It is spiritual bonding that characterizes the finest marital relationships.... Spiritual bonding comes from hard work that is carried out in an atmosphere of deep trust. When spiritual bonding is established, sex is a lot more than the merging of body parts. What really happens is that the souls of two people are woven together."[14] What a beautiful description of covenant marriage!

Ultimately, sex is a critical area where taking the covenant "walk of death" is of supreme importance. To put it bluntly, if you insist on being selfish in your sex life, you are not going to build a lasting and fulfilling marriage. The Bible tells husbands and wives not to deprive each other sexually except for brief periods of time devoted to prayer (see 1 Corinthians 7:3–5). If you refuse to meet your spouse's sexual needs, you set up a vulnerability to major temptation.

Let me say a word now to the men reading this book. In an earlier chapter we discussed the role of the man in covenant. We said that the husband is the initiator of covenant and has the greater responsibility for the protection and success of the marriage relationship. This initiating role is important when it comes to sex. According to the Penners, "The most vital factor in producing a great sexual relationship in marriage revolves around the role of the man. The marriage changes drastically when the man changes, even when the woman is the one hindering the sexual relationship. The man must move in the direction of the woman's needs. He needs to be acutely aware of as many of her spiritual and emotional needs as he possibly can. Mutual satisfaction is the expectation of every sexual experience."[15] Covenant love requires you, as the husband, to be sensitive to your wife's sexual needs. The more you are tuned in to your wife, the better sex will be for *you*.

Deal with Your Anger

A lady went to a gun dealership and told the man behind the counter, "I want to buy a gun for my husband."

"What model of gun does your husband want?" the man asked.

"I don't know," said the woman. "He doesn't know that I'm going to shoot him!"

One of marriage's most deadly enemies is unresolved anger. Someone has said that anger is the "noise of the soul." It irritates. It poisons. It increases in volume until it's the only sound you hear. It colors everything red. In my years of counseling, I've noted that most struggling couples have unresolved anger issues. They talk about other problems, but those problems are merely symptoms of a more serious illness—warning signals that something lurks just beneath the surface of their married life that is bigger and uglier.

Anger is born whenever conflicts are internalized rather than resolved. But as Gary Smalley says, "when we bury anger inside us...it's always buried alive."[16] Listen carefully: Anger is too powerful and too revealing an emotion to handle by denial, blame, or justification. It cannot be ignored; it must be dealt with.

One of the best things Leigh and I did early on to protect our marriage was to make a commitment to each other to never let the sun go down on our anger. In other words, we agreed that we would not go to sleep mad at each other. We also agreed that we would pray together and tell each other "I love you" every night before we nodded off. Has it always been easy? No. There have been times when I have not wanted to "work it out" before dark. I've wanted to pout for a week and make Leigh suffer. But I made a commitment—and that decision has paid wonderful dividends over the years.

The truth is, unresolved anger is the quickest way for Satan to get into a marriage. The Bible tells us, "Do not let the sun go down while you are still angry," because, if you do, you give Satan an opportunity to get a foothold in your relationship (Ephesians 4:26–27). Satan is anti-marriage and desires to alienate you from your mate. If you give him a foothold, he will make it a stronghold—and your marriage will be in jeopardy.

Watch Your Words

Think about the last fight you had with your spouse. What did you say? What did your mate say? What was the issue? More than likely, you don't remember what the fight was about—but you do remember a verbal missile launched by your spouse that landed in your heart. Unfortunately, we all know what "hot buttons" to push that will light fireworks within our mates. We know how to hurt the ones we love. We know how to take delicate information given to us by our mates and use it as a platform to launch our verbal attacks.

The Bible says that the power of life and death is in the tongue (see Proverbs 18:21). That means that the words you use can bring life to your marriage or kill it stone dead. Words are powerful for good or evil. They can curse or cure. As wise King Solomon said, "Reckless words pierce like a sword, but the tongue of the wise brings healing" (Proverbs 12:18). And, "A gentle answer turns away wrath, but a harsh word stirs up anger" (Proverbs 15:1).

Recently I have counseled unsuccessfully with a couple who is going ahead with a divorce. Both have said to me, "Nothing has happened in our marriage that warrants a divorce, but I'm tired of being miserable. I'm tired of fussing and fighting. I don't think he (or she) loves me." In this situation, the husband and wife have continually stuffed conflicts rather than resolving them. The words they have used to hurt each other have crushed the spirit of the marriage and cursed their relationship. It is as if scar tissue from all the verbal bullets has covered their hearts and killed their marriage.

I remember reading a poem some time ago about a man who took his "city" wife out West. Although she struggled with frontier life, she loved her husband and was determined to try her best to adapt. One day the husband came home and found the fence gate open and the cattle gone. He rushed into the cabin, screaming at his wife for leaving the gate open. Like verbal bullets, his words pierced her heart: "A storm is coming, and now I have to try to find the cattle. How could you do this? I'm out there working hard, and what do you do? You leave the gate open!" Then he stomped out, slamming the door behind him.

When he returned after dark, his meal was on the table, and there was a note that read: "I am so sorry. I didn't know the gate was open. If I had known it was open, I would have closed it. I am so sorry. Please forgive me. I have gone to look for the cattle."

Suddenly the man realized he had made a terrible mistake. He knew that his wife knew nothing about the frontier and would never survive the night in the newly falling snow. He searched and searched for her until morning to no avail. When he finally returned to their cabin, he saw her lying on the porch—dead.

Words! They have the power to build up or tear down, to heal or to kill. In the book *Being Married Happily Ever After,* Tova Borgnine includes a list of words and phrases that you never want to say or hear in your home because they can destroy a loving marriage. Here they are (plus a few of my own):

- I told you so.

- If only you had…

- You should have…

- You promised me that…

- You don't respect me.

- You never tell me…

- My mother told me you'd…

- My mother warned me about you.

- You always say…

215

- I hate when you do that.

- I'll tell you what kind of man (woman) I think you are.

- You never take me out.

- You never tell me you love me.

- Have you gained weight?

- You're just like your mother.

- You're not going to make me.

- I wish I'd never met you.

- I wish I'd never married you.

- If you do that again, I'll divorce you.[17]

Escalating a conflict is always as easy as opening our mouths. It takes little effort. Most of us know how to stir the pot, but we are not so good at calming the storm. For that reason, let me give you seven fight-stopping phrases that are painfully difficult—but extremely important—to say:

- I am being insensitive.

- I am wrong.

- I am sorry.

- How can I make it up to you?

- I need you.

- I love you.

- Will you forgive me?

Fight Fairly

Did you know that you can disagree without being disagreeable? Take exception without taking aim? To manage conflict in your marriage successfully, experts agree you need to learn how to fight right! In an article in

Focus on the Family magazine, authors Richard and Mary Strauss say they try to turn all their conflicts into "love fights"—"exchanges that not only resolve the conflict, but actually increase their love for each other."[18] That's possible if you always find ways to show acceptance, admiration, respect, and love for your partner—whatever the issue you're fighting about. It's not possible if you resort to one of the negative actions I've listed below. I call it my "Top Ten Inappropriate Behaviors" list:

1. Calling your spouse inappropriate names

2. Making assumptions

3. Trying your hand at mind reading

4. Laying on guilt

5. Bringing up the past

6. Attacking your spouse's family

7. Making fun of or putting down your spouse

8. Using the "you" word ("you always," "you never")

9. Assigning blame

10. Rejecting or discrediting your spouse

Perception can be the worst form of cruelty. "If either (or both) of you feel judged, misunderstood, or rejected by the other," John Gottman says in *The Seven Principles for Making a Marriage Work*, "you will not be able to manage the problems in your marriage."[19] Any of the ten inappropriate behaviors will lead to the kinds of perceptions that erode trust and damage a relationship. And yet they are all so easy to slip into!

What every married couple needs is a set of rules that both spouses can agree upon for fighting fairly, respectfully, and lovingly. Here are twenty basic rules I have gleaned over the years from research and from my own work with couples. We have already talked about many of them in this chapter.

Twenty Rules for Fair Fighting

1. Accept the reality that conflict is inevitable.

2. Practice conflict resolution in a nonthreatening situation. Don't wait until sparks are flying.

3. Agree together that the time is appropriate to discuss the issue. Always let things cool down before you talk.

4. Be specific when you make a complaint. Identify and define the conflict.

5. Share feelings without blaming.

6. Consider the possibility that you could be wrong. It may be *your* problem to deal with.

7. Be honest and show mutual respect.

8. Attack the problem but never the person.

9. Deal with the problem at hand and refuse to bring up the past.

10. Don't say friends or relatives agree with you.

11. Don't use sarcasm or degrading language.

12. Avoid "you always" or "you never" statements.

13. Do not resist the other person's viewpoint.

14. Surrender personal desires and choose to serve your spouse.

15. Do not assume you know what your partner is thinking or feeling or that you know how he or she will react.

16. Do not try to tell your partner how he or she feels or should feel or try to override the thoughts and feelings of your mate.

17. Always leave room for compromise—your partner's perception of reality is as real as your own.

18. Don't fight in public.

19. Complete the fight phase before offering a positive solution. It doesn't work to insist on a solution while you are still upset.

20. Agree to try the solution for a while. Leave the door open for the possibility that it might not work. Be flexible and go back to the drawing board if necessary.

To these I add an important rule from God's Word: Pray! Pray about everything, and that will get you through anything.

Practice Forgiveness

Ultimately, there is one key to the resolution of every conflict: forgiveness. As Josh McDowell writes, "Forgiveness is the oil of relationships. It reduces the friction and allows people to come close to each other." Unforgiveness, on the other hand, blocks people from being open and vulnerable to one another. "An unforgiving person is incapable of developing deep, lasting, and intimate relationships," McDowell says. Therefore, "an unforgiving partner in a marriage destroys the possibility of fulfilling the potential for intimacy in that relationship."[20]

We are not angels! Two imperfect human beings, living together 24/7, are bound to cause hurt and pain—sometimes intentional, sometimes not. As Tim LaHaye writes in an article titled "How to Live Happily Ever After":

> Who of us is not subject to bad moods, ill temperaments, a negative spirit, and a critical attitude? Admittedly these things should not exist in a Christian marriage, but they do. There is no married couple who, in the daily life of marriage, does not have a host of "complaints." Yet we see many such couples enjoying love, harmony, and peace in their relationship. Invariably, their secret is forgiveness.[21]

The failure to forgive and receive forgiveness sabotages all our relationships and leaves us prisoners of our own emotions, guaranteeing a life of misery. When we choose not to forgive, bitterness is automatic, freedom becomes bondage, joy turns to sadness, and frustration leads to depression.

Les Parrott makes a good point when he says, "If forgiveness is not given to cleanse the marriage soul, condemnation hovers over the relationship. Resentment piles on top of resentment until we blame our partners not just for their wrongdoing, but also for our failure to forgive them."[22]

Forgiveness is God's release valve for the pain, pressure, and poison within our hearts. It is a choice, an act of the will. In covenant marriage, we are to forgive when we feel like it and when we don't feel like it, when we want to and when we don't want to.

We shouldn't think, however, that we haven't forgiven something if we haven't forgotten it. "Forgive and forget," the old saying goes. But the truth is, forgiveness is not forgetting. (And forgetting is not forgiveness; it's just stuffing the pain.) You may choose to cancel a person's debt against you, but that doesn't mean you suddenly forget that it ever existed. In fact, it's because it's so hard to forget that we have to forgive. Then, if we have truly forgiven, time will ultimately cause the pain to subside until it no longer exerts control over us.

Let me open the door to my bedroom for a moment and tell you something my wonderful wife does that frustrates me. I'll be lying in bed with a cold, coughing, and Leigh will reach over and pat me, saying, "Honey, try not to cough! Try not to cough!" What's the deal? Does she think I'm lying there trying to cough? I don't want to cough more than she doesn't want me to cough. But the harder I try not to cough, the more I cough.

The same is true with forgetting. It is hard to forget something you are trying to forget. However, you can choose not to focus on it. The best way to develop a good "forgetory" is to build a good memory. When you focus your thoughts on remembering the good times and the special things that bless your marriage, all the bad things—the things you've chosen to forgive—will eventually fade into insignificance.

Recently I heard a beautiful story about a grandmother celebrating her fiftieth wedding anniversary. Surrounded by friends and family, she was asked, "What is the secret of your long marriage?"

"Oh, it's very simple," she said. "Before Henry and I got married, I was determined to write down a list of ten things that I would always forgive him quickly for and then forget about. After we got married, Henry would do certain things and I would think, 'Lucky for him—that one is on the list.'"

The young wives in the room scrambled to find pens and paper, anxious to copy down the ten items on the old woman's list. "So tell us, Grandma," one of them said, "what were those ten things?"

The grandmother smiled. "To be honest," she said, "I never got around to making that list. So every time Henry did something I didn't appreciate, I would just say, 'Lucky for him—that one is on the list.'"

Wow! That woman knew one of the secrets of covenant love: It doesn't make lists. As the Bible says, love "keeps no record of wrongs" (1 Corinthians 13:5). Covenant love always forgives.

Draw on the Spirit of Reconciliation

God intended marriage to bring out the *best* in us. But leave God out, and marriage brings out the *beast* in us. The truth is, conflict resolution always begins with God and us. We are spiritual beings who were disconnected from God because of our sins. But by accepting through faith what Jesus did on the Cross—believing that he died to pay the price for our sins—we are reconnected and reconciled to God. As a result, we have the spirit of reconciliation in our hearts. We have received forgiveness, and now we desire to forgive others by the power of God's Holy Spirit that resides within us.

Earlier in this book we said that every marital problem is first a spiritual problem. That means that the first step to resolving any conflict is getting right with God. Once your differences with God are settled, you will have the power and grace to settle your differences with your spouse. Peace is not the absence of problems—it's the presence of the Lord!

Remember, God took the initiative in conflict resolution by sending his Son. Now he wants you to mirror his action by taking the initiative to go to your spouse and reconcile. He wants you to take that "walk of death" that lies at the core of covenant. You will have to die to being right, die to getting your way, and die to being in control. But by dying to self, as Jesus died on the cross, you will open the way for true reconciliation. And reconciliation is your ministry as a believer in Christ (see 2 Corinthians 5:18). You may not be able to resolve every problem, but you can always reconcile every relationship. As someone once said, "You can walk hand in hand without seeing eye to eye."

Marriage and the Stock Market

I remember a *Peanuts* cartoon in which Charlie Brown is listening to Lucy bemoan her plight. "Lucy, life is a series of ups and downs, and you can't change that," Charlie Brown says. To which Lucy replies: "All I want is ups and ups."

We may share Lucy's sentiments, but the truth is, Charlie Brown is right. No relationship is problem-free or consistently satisfying. Leonard Pitts, a columnist for the *Miami Herald,* says an old friend told him that "90 percent of the time, his marriage makes him glad he's alive. The other 10 percent makes him want to beg, 'Please kill me now.'" Pitts concludes: "The trick is to get through the 10 by trusting the 90."[23] Marriage is a lot like the stock market—unpredictable and constantly changing. The ups and downs in marriage are like the ups and downs in the market. They are normal and natural. Nothing is broken. There is no need to bail out. Just stay the course. Conventional wisdom says that investors do best when they do not focus on day-to-day swings in market performance but keep a long-term view. The same is true with marriage. "Unending bliss is just not what marriage is like for most people," writes Howard Markman in *Fighting for Your Marriage.* "It's wonderful at times and very hard at other times. Sometimes it's wonderfully hard. That's why it takes commitment—and a long-term view."[24]

Covenant marriage has that kind of commitment. It takes the long-term view. That's why covenant pays the greatest dividends in a marriage relationship. As a covenant partner, your goal is to add value to your spouse and to your marriage in everything you say and do.

Conflict will always be a part of marriage. Some problems will be resolved easily; others will require a greater sacrifice of love, acceptance, and forgiveness. Either way, the presence of conflict is never a reason to give up. It's a reason to *look* up—to God. In Christ, the ultimate example of conflict resolution, we find our hope and our answer every time.

Epilogue

WOULD YOU DO IT ALL OVER AGAIN?

A frantic mother was trying to control her three small children in the grocery store with little success. The children definitely had the upper hand. Mom was losing the battle—it showed on her face and could be heard in her voice. About that time a man standing nearby who had been observing the entire fiasco asked this question: "If you had it to do all over again, would you have kids?"

"Yes," the mom shouted back, "but not the same ones!"

What if someone asked that question about your marriage? Would you do it all over again? If you knew what you know now, would you still marry the same person? I want to go on record and answer an emphatic yes! If I could go back to June 2, 1973, knowing what I know today, I would stand at that same altar and say those same covenant vows and take Leigh to be my wife.

Listen to how Mike Mason describes what it means to wake up every morning beside the one you love:

> There is a woman in bed beside me. Right this moment I could reach out my hand and touch her, as easily as I touch myself, and as I think about this, it is more staggering than any mountain or moon. It is

even more staggering, I think, than if this woman happened instead to be an angel (which, come to think of it, she might well be).

And so, practicing already for heaven, it is with an expectancy of grace that I look over in the awakening light of this brand new day at the woman lying next to me, breathing lightly, like an organ of my own body. She is more beautiful to me than the light itself, more present than this towering mountain, her form under the covers is more elementary than any horizon, and she is closer to me than the air I breathe. She is "bone of my bones, and flesh of my flesh." There are other people in my life, but no one like her. More than anyone else on earth, more even than my own self, she represents the vessel into which I must and will be poured. She will have all the very best, the cream, of my love.

She is as close as anyone in the world can come to being for me, in that mournful, radiant flesh of hers, what Christ is to me in the spirit.[1]

Wow! Double wow! I wish I had said that about my precious bride—and you know what? I just did, through Mike Mason.

THE FINAL WORD: *SEMPER FI*

Marty Manning is a former Marine who has lived his life by the Marine Corps motto, *Semper Fi* ("always faithful"). These days all that tough-as-nails resolve and commitment are being gently and lovingly applied to the care of his wife, Lynn, who has Alzheimer's disease. Lynn has lost most of her memory but not her song. She has seven devoted children but can only remember their names if she sings them out. On occasion she surprises Marty with a flash of remembrance—usually in the form of a song. "Good night, sweet Mickey," she'll sing.

Clearly, Marty knows something about covenant. "It's hard, and it's not gonna get any easier," I heard Marty tell the hosts of *Good Morning America* some time ago. "My intent is to keep my wife at home as long as I possibly can." Marty wants to take care of Lynn at home so they can battle the disease side by side. He is absolutely intent upon keeping his promise of covenant love and commitment to his wife and companion of forty-two years.

Are you willing to work on your marriage with the same tough-as-nails Marine resolve as Marty Manning? That's what covenant marriage is all about. With God's grace and power in your life, you can build a relationship with your spouse that is lasting, satisfying, and fulfilling—come rain or shine, in good times and in struggles. Covenant marriage is a perfect union, not because it is a union of two perfect people, but because it is God's perfect design for a man and woman in marriage.

Semper Fi!

Appendix 1

A Covenant Wedding Ceremony

Introductory Words

Minister:

_____ (groom's name) and _____ (bride's name) have fallen in love. More importantly, they have chosen to love each other, unconditionally, for the rest of their lives.

Such love is unnatural. It is a continual process and requires hard work and unselfish sacrifice. It demands that _____ (groom) and _____ (bride) rely on God's supernatural presence, provision, and power.

There are two passages in the Bible that beautifully describe this special and unique love that God has designed to bond a husband and wife together and to sustain the relationship over time. The first one is found in 1 Corinthians 13.

_____ (groom) and _____ (bride), listen carefully as God's word defines the kind of love God wants you to have for each other:

Love never gives up.
Love cares more for others than for self.
Love doesn't want what it doesn't have.
Love doesn't strut,
Doesn't have a swelled head,
Doesn't force itself on others,

Isn't always "me first,"
Doesn't fly off the handle,
Doesn't keep score of the sins of others,
Doesn't revel when others grovel,
Takes pleasure in the flowering of truth,
Puts up with anything,
Trusts God always,
Always looks for the best,
Never looks back,
But keeps going to the end.
(1 Corinthians 13:4–7 MSG)

_____ (groom) and _____ (bride), you have heard love defined and described. You have heard what it does and what it does not do.

Always remember that love is a verb. It requires action. It is not just something you feel, but something you do. Listen now to the lyrics of a love song found in the eighth chapter of the Song of Songs that sings of love in action.

Place me like a seal over your heart,
like a seal on your arm;
for love is as strong as death…
It burns like blazing fire, like a mighty flame.
Many waters cannot quench love;
rivers cannot wash it away. (Song of Songs 8:6–7)

Isaiah 54:10 (NLT) says, "For the mountains may depart and the hills disappear, but even then I will remain loyal to you." Even then I will love you.

_____ (groom) and _____ (bride), I encourage you to model the love described in these passages. Today and always, let your love for each other come from God.

(*Minister leads in prayer.*)

PRESENTATION OF THE BRIDE

There is an old proverb that says, "A thousand-mile journey begins with the first steps." With this in mind, let this journey of marriage begin by taking a first important step, a step of separation away from parental control and provision and a step toward your two independent lives being merged into one.

Who presents this beautiful bride to be married to this man?

(Father or presenter responds.)

Since the beginning of time, God has dealt with mankind on the basis of covenant. Our God is a covenant God; the Bible is a covenant book; and we are a covenant people. From Genesis to Revelation, the Bible clearly links God's covenant marriage to his people with our marriage covenant to our spouse.

Marriage is much more than a legally binding contract written on a piece of paper. It is a permanent commitment that is engraved upon the heart. In covenant, two become one, never to be separated again.

> It is the merging of hearts—
> Two beating as one.
> It is the blending of lives—
> Two becoming one.

> In covenant, you promise to give
> Your life
> Your love
> Your loyalty…until death.

Are you, _____ (groom) and _____ (bride), ready to enter into a sacred marriage covenant that is binding for the rest of your lives? If so, please join right hands.

COVENANT PROMISES AND VOWS

Groom speaking to bride:

(Minister may lead groom through these statements.)

_____(bride), who could imagine a more perfect mate than you, except for our perfect Lord and Savior? In my heart I know that you are the woman for whom I have prayed to be my wife, my lover, my partner, my companion, and my best friend. You alone are the one with whom I want to spend the rest of my life—serving God, establishing a home, and raising godly children.

I promise to hug you, hold you, listen to you, care for you, and encourage you. I promise to love you, cherish you, pray for you, and never forsake you—all the days of my life.

In our marriage I promise to be open with you, to communicate honestly with you, and to work through any conflicts. I will always seek to show you unconditional love, gentleness, kindness, forgiveness, and patience.

_____(bride), I joyfully make this covenant with you as my loving wife and promise to keep it for as long as I shall live. May our Lord truly make us one.

Minister:

_____(groom), will you take _____ (bride's) left hand and make this sacred vow to her?

(Minister leads groom in saying this vow.)

"I _____ (groom) covenant with you _____ (bride) to be my wedded wife, to have and to hold from this day forward; for better, for worse; for richer, for poorer; in sickness and in health. I covenant to love you and to cherish you 'till we are separated by death."

Bride speaking to groom:

(Minister may lead bride through these statements.)

_____ (groom), who could imagine a more perfect mate than you, except for our perfect Lord and Savior? In my heart I know that you are the man for whom I have prayed to be my husband, my lover, my partner, my companion, and my best friend. You alone are the one with whom I want to spend the rest of my life—serving God, establishing a home, and raising godly children.

I promise to respect you, listen to you, encourage you, and honor your God-given role as my husband. I promise to love you, cherish you, pray for you, and never forsake you—all the days of my life.

In our marriage I promise to be open with you, to communicate honestly with you, and to work through any conflicts. I will always seek to show you unconditional love, gentleness, kindness, forgiveness, and patience.

_____(groom), I joyfully make this sacred covenant with you as my loving husband and promise to keep it for as long as I shall live. May our Lord truly make us one.

Minister:

_____(bride), will you take _____(groom's) left hand and make this sacred vow to him?

(Minister leads the bride in saying this vow.)

"I _____(bride) covenant with you _____(groom) to be my wedded husband, to have and to hold from this day forward; for better, for worse; for richer, for poorer; in sickness and in health. I covenant to love you and to cherish you until we are separated by death."

Bride and groom together:

(May be led by the minister.)

We surrender our marriage to the Lord as together we seek to glorify him as husband and wife. Together we will serve the Lord and build a household of faith.

THE GIVING AND RECEIVING OF RINGS

Minister:

(To best man)

May I have the bride's ring, please?

(To groom)

_____(groom), every time you look at this ring on _____ (bride's) finger, let it remind you that on _____(date), you gave this ring to her as a tangible symbol of a spiritual commitment. Let it remind you that your love is endless and your commitment is forever.

_____(groom), place this ring on the finger of your bride and say this to her:

(Minister leads groom in following statement.)

"_____(bride), this ring is a symbol and seal of my covenant commitment to you as your husband. As Jesus molds my love for you into the kind of love he has for the church, I promise to love you with a Christlike love.

Wear this ring for me every day. I believe with all my heart that my love for you is forever. I give this ring to you as my loving wife."

(To matron of honor)

May I have the groom's ring, please?

(To bride)

_____(bride), every time you look at this ring on _____ (groom's) finger, let it remind you that on _____(date), you gave this ring to him as a tangible symbol of a spiritual commitment. Let it remind you that your love is endless and your commitment is forever.

_____(bride), place this ring on the finger of your groom and say this to him:

(Minister leads bride in following statement.)

"_____(groom), this ring is a symbol and seal of my covenant commitment to you as your wife. As Jesus molds my love for you into the kind of love he has for the church, I promise to love you with a Christlike love.

Wear this ring for me every day. I believe with all my heart that my love for you is forever. I give this ring to you as my loving husband."

(To couple)

_____(groom) and _____(bride), in the presence of God and before family and friends as witnesses, you have committed yourselves to each other by covenant, and you have sealed your covenant vows by the giving and receiving of rings. Therefore it is my privilege to pronounce you husband and wife—one in covenant, together in the Lord.

What God has joined together in covenant, let no man break apart.

Note: The lighting of the unity candle, communion, or the salt covenant tradition can be added to this ceremony as a beautiful symbol of the couple's covenant commitment.

Appendix 2

A COVENANT RECOMMITMENT CEREMONY

THE WELCOME

Minister:

Church family, friends, guests, and those who have come to renew their marriage covenant, we welcome you to this special service of covenant renewal. This is a time of ceremony, recommitment, and celebration. It is also a time of introspection for those of us who are married as we carefully and prayerfully examine our own lives to see if we are standing strong and fulfilling the marriage covenant we have made with our spouse and with Holy God.

(An optional processional can take place at this time, with participating couples proceeding to the front of the church. If there is no processional, couples can be asked to come to the altar or to stand at their seats.)

INTRODUCTORY WORDS

God is a covenant God. The Bible is a covenant book. We are a covenant people. In Genesis 2, we see clearly that God designed marriage as a covenant relationship: "and they [the man and his wife] will become one flesh" (Genesis 2:24). Two become one, never to be separated again. That is covenant. This basic description of marriage is quoted by Jesus and reported in the Gospels. It is used by Paul in Ephesians 5 as the biblical foundation for marriage. It is evident that the Bible portrays marriage as a sacred and permanent covenant, witnessed and protected by God himself.

Marriage is a contract, but it is so much more. A contract is based on limited liability; a covenant is based on unlimited responsibility. A contract calls for the signing of names; a covenant calls for the binding of hearts.

Marriage is designed by God as a binding covenant—broken only by death.

(Minister leads in prayer.)

THE WEDDING CHARGE

Before God and these witnesses, we acknowledge marriage as a divine institution and celebrate what God is doing in the lives of these couples. We charge you—church family, friends, and loved ones—to stand behind these couples with your prayers and encouraging words as they reaffirm and renew their marriage covenant.

In the words of Christ, stated as a command: "Therefore what God has joined together, let man not separate"(Mark 10:9).

THE VOWS

(To couples)

Do you, as husbands and wives, understand that God designed marriage as a serious and sacred covenant that is to be broken only by death? If so, please join hands as we come to this serious and sacred time of renewing covenant vows to each other.

(To husbands)

Husbands, face your wives and repeat after me:

Husbands speaking to wives:

(Minister leads husbands through these statements.)

I thank God for our covenant marriage and for the gift of your love. In the presence of God, family, and friends, I renew my covenant marriage vows to you as my loving wife.

I joyfully renew my vow to placing our relationship above all earthly relationships. I promise to love you, to honor you, to cherish you, and to care for you at all times and in all ways for as long as you live.

I covenant to validate your needs and to give myself to unselfishly meeting your needs. I will be faithful to you and to you alone and will always treasure you as God's special gift to me.

With God as my helper, I joyfully make a covenant vow that I will keep every one of these promises.

Minister (To wives):

Wives, face your husbands and repeat after me:

Wives speaking to husbands:

(Minister leads wives through these statements.)

I thank God for our covenant marriage and for the gift of your love. In the presence of God, family, and friends, I renew my covenant marriage vows to you as my loving husband.

I joyfully renew my vow to placing our relationship above all earthly relationships. I promise to love you, to honor you, to cherish you, and to care for you at all times and in all ways for as long as you live.

I covenant to validate your needs and to give myself to unselfishly meeting your needs. I will be faithful to you and to you alone and will always treasure you as God's special gift to me.

With God as my helper, I joyfully make a covenant vow that I will keep every one of these promises.

EXCHANGE OF RINGS (OPTIONAL)

(If couples want to exchange rings as a symbol of their recommitment, the following ceremony can be added.)

Minister:

"Your wedding ring is an outward and visible sign of the marriage covenant you made with your mate. The ring has been used for centuries by kings and rulers to seal important covenants. As the most lasting symbol of marriage, your ring is a constant reminder of your commitment to this one who stands next to you. The refined precious metal in your ring represents the purity of faithful, untarnished covenant-keeping. Your ring's unending, circular design represents the permanence of covenant commitment. As you once again place your mate's ring on his or her hand, remember the blessings of God as your covenant promises have been honored and pledge anew to keep the solemn covenant you made and now renew to the honor of God."

(Minister leads husbands and wives alternately through the following statement as rings are exchanged.)

I give you this ring as a symbol of my forever commitment to you, and, thereby, seal this covenant of marriage.

(Optional: The following words can also be repeated.)

"You are mine, my love, and I am yours, as ordained by God from the beginning of time. He brought us together and he has kept us together, to love and be loved, to cherish and be cherished, for all the days of our lives. You are God's gift to me, my priceless treasure, my blessing for life. May he bless us as we come together today to renew our pledge of love to one another."

(To couples)

As your pastor, it is my privilege to declare your marriages:

bound and blessed

solid and sound

happy and holy

What God has joined together in covenant, let nothing separate.

Appendix 3

RECOMMENDED READING

A Marriage without Regrets by Kay Arthur

Becoming One by Joe Beam

Covenant Relationships by Keith Intrator

Communication by Norman Wright

His Needs, Her Needs by Willard Harley

Making Love Last Forever by Gary Smalley

Making Sense of the Men in Your Life by Kevin Leman

Our Covenant God by Kay Arthur

One Home at a Time by Dennis Rainey

Sacred Marriage by Gary Thomas

Sex Begins in the Kitchen by Kevin Leman

Surrendering to Marriage by Iris Krasnow

Take Back Your Marriage by William Doherty

The Abolition of Marriage by Maggie Gallagher

The Case for Marriage by Maggie Gallagher and Linda Waite

The Five Love Languages by Gary Chapman

The Marriage Covenant by Samuele Bacchiocchi

The Mystery of Marriage by Mike Mason

The Triumphant Marriage by Neil Clark Warren

The Unexpected Legacy of Divorce by Judith Wallerstein,
    Julie Lewis, and Sandra Blakesler
To Have and to Hold by David Atkinson
We Still Do by Dennis Rainey
When Bad Things Happen to Good Marriages by Les and Leslie Parrott
Why Marriage Succeeds or Fails by John Gottman

NOTES

Introduction: What Do You Want for Your Marriage?

    1.   Barbara DeFoe Whitehead, *The Divorce Culture* (New York: Random House Publishers, 1996), 44.

    2.   Blaine Fowers, *Beyond the Myth of Marital Happiness* (San Francisco: Jossey-Bass, 2000), 13–14.

    3.   Joe Brown, *Battle Fatigue* (Nashville: Broadman & Holman Publishers, 1995), 95.

    4.   Fowers, *Beyond the Myth of Marital Happiness,* 96.

    5.   Henry Brandt, *Marriage God's Way* (Nashville: Broadman & Holman Publishers, 1999), 13.

    6.   Quoted in David Atkinson, *To Have and to Hold* (Grand Rapids, Mich.: Eerdmans Publishing Company, 1979), 75.

    7.   Quoted in Bill O'Reilly, *The O'Reilly Factor* (New York: Broadway Publishers, 2000), 109.

    8.   George Barna, *The Frog in the Kettle* (Ventura, Calif.: Regal Books, 1990), 46.

    9.   Atkinson, *To Have and to Hold,* 75.

  10.   Ibid., 72.

  11.   Ibid., 76.

12. Fowers, *Beyond the Myth of Marital Happiness*, 72.

13. Samuele Bacchiocchi, *The Marriage Covenant* (Berrien Springs, Mich.: Biblical Perspectives, 1991), 40.

Chapter 1: Marriage American Style

1. Maggie Gallagher, *Abolition of Marriage* (Washington, D.C.: Regnery Publishing, Inc., 1996), 5.

2. Whittney Gleaves, "America's Divorce Revolution Has Failed," *Crisis Online,* May 1996, 1.

3. Jim Smoke, *Growing Through Divorce* (Eugene, Ore.: Harvest House Publishers, 1995), 121.

4. Linda Waite and Maggie Gallagher, *The Case for Marriage* (New York: Doubleday Publishers, 2000), 125.

5. Judith Wallerstein, *The Good Marriage* (New York: Warner Books, 1995), 125.

6. Ibid., 139–40.

7. Waite and Gallagher, *The Case for Marriage,* 147–48.

8. Barbara Whitehead, *The Divorce Culture* (New York: Random House Publishers, 1996), 3.

9. Chuck Colson, "Numbers Don't Lie," *Breakpoint,* 21 May 2000.

10. Ralph Steed, "Just Married," *USA Today,* 13 December 1999.

11. Whitehead, *The Divorce Culture,* 7.

12. Kingsley Davis, "The Meaning and Significance of Marriage in Contemporary Society," Kingsley Davis, ed., *Contemporary Marriage* (New York: Russell Sage Foundation, 1985), 21.

13. Ibid., 21.

14. Nancy Saunders, "Heard on the Street," *On the Record-Monitor Online,* 30, no. 3, March 1999.

15. Bill O'Reilly, *The O'Reilly Factor* (New York: Broadway Publishers, 2000), 108.

16. Debbie Ford, *Spiritual Divorce* (New York: HarperCollins Publishers, 2000), 43.

17. Martin Miller, "To Have and to Hold: Till Divorce Do Us Part," *The Times,* (Shreveport, La., 11 September 2001).

18. William J. Bennett, *The Broken Hearth* (New York: Doubleday Publishers, 2001), 165.

19. Whitehead, *The Divorce Culture,* 4.

20. Bennett, *The Broken Hearth,* 11–12.

21. Whitehead, *The Divorce Culture,* 4.

22. Sheila Muto, "From Here to Immodesty: Milestones in the Topping of TV's Taboos," *Wall Street Journal,* 15 September 1995.

23. Ibid.

24. Dennis Rainey, *One Home at a Time* (Wheaton, Ill.: Tyndale House Publishers, 1997), 23.

25. Bennett, *The Broken Hearth,* 13.

26. Waite and Gallagher, *The Case for Marriage,* 96, 44–45.

27. Barbara Whitehead, "The Christian Divorce Culture," *Christianity Today,* 4 September 2000, 47.

28. David Atkinson, *To Have and to Hold* (Grand Rapids, Mich.: Eerdmans Publishing Company, 1979), 91–92.

29. Paul R. Stevens, *Married for Good* (Downers Grove, Ill.: Regent College Publishing, 1986), 17.

30. Gary Smalley, *Always* (Wheaton, Ill.: Tyndale House Publishers, 1999), 102.

31. James Dobson, "Staying Together," *Focus on the Family,* June 2000, 2.

32. Terry Hargrave, www.smartfamilies.com/hargrave.html.

Chapter 2: When Marriage Is Not What You Expected

1. *Martha Stewart Living,* September 2000, 113.

Chapter 3: Making "I Do" Harder to Undo

1. Steven Nock, "Marriage Movements Today: The Politics of Matrimony," Council on Contemporary Families, http://www.contemporaryfamilies.org/fact11.htm.

2. Blaine Fowers, *Beyond the Myth of Marital Happiness* (San Francisco: Jossey-Bass, 2000), 71–73.

3. Maggie Gallagher, *The Abolition of Marriage* (Washington, D.C.: Regnery Publishing, Inc., 1996), 150.

4.   Iris Krasnow, *Surrendering to Marriage* (New York: Talk Miramax Books, 2001), 198–199.

5.   Chuck Colson, "Numbers Don't Lie," *Breakpoint,* 21 May 2000.

6.   Linda Waite and Maggie Gallagher, *The Case for Marriage* (New York: Doubleday Publishers, 2000), 148–49.

7.   Kendall Hamilton and Pat Wingert, "Can Gen Xers Make Their Own Marriages Last?" *Newsweek,* 20 July 1988.

8.   Joe Loconte, *The Samaritan: How Government Contracts Are Reshaping Social Services* (Boston: Pioneer Institute, 1977), 46.

9.   Martha Williamson, *Invite God to the Wedding* (New York: Harmony Books, 2000), 3.

10.   "Virginity Pledge Helps Teens Delay Sexual Activity," National Institutes of Health press release, 5 January 2001.

11.   Thomas S. Dee, "Until Death Do You Part," www.economics.harvard.edu/ statistics.

12.   Maggie Gallagher, "What Can Covenant Marriage Do for a Couple?" *SmartMarriages,* 9 February 2001, The Coalition for Marriage, Family, and Couples Education, www.smartmarriages.com.

Chapter 4: What Is Covenant?

1.   Kay Arthur, *Our Covenant God* (Colorado Springs: Waterbrook Press, 1999), 12–14.

2.   Martha Williamson, *Invite God to the Wedding* (New York: Harmony Books, 2000), 44.

3.   Dannah Gresh, *And the Bride Wore White* (Chicago: Moody Press, 1999), 128.

4.   Ibid.

5.   Arthur, *Our Covenant God,* 34.

6.   William Miller, *The Joy of Feeling Good* (Minneapolis, Minn.: Augsburg Fortress Publishers, 1986), 167.

Chapter 5: The Blessing of Covenant Marriage

1.   Quoted in Barrie Richardson, *How to Get Extraordinary Results from Ordinary People: The 10 Percent Principle* (San Diego: Pfeiffer & Company, 1993), 81.

2. Samuele Bacchiocchi, *The Marriage Covenant* (Berrien Springs, Mich.: Biblical Perspectives, 1991), 41–50.

3. R. Paul Stevens, *Married for Good* (Downers Grove, Ill., Regent College Publishing, 1986), 20.

4. Bacchiocchi, *The Marriage Covenant,* 42.

5. Ibid., 41.

6. Andre Maurois, BrainyQuotes, http://www.brainyquotes.com/quotes/quotes/a/q115809.html.

7. David Atkinson, *To Have and to Hold* (Grand Rapids, Mich.: Eerdmans Publishing Company, 1979), 71.

8. Ibid., 72.

9. Les and Leslie Parrott, *Saving Your Marriage Before It Starts* (Grand Rapids, Mich.: Zondervan Publishers, 1995), 139.

10. Scott Stanley, Howard Markham, and Susan Blumberg, *A Lasting Promise* (San Francisco: Jossey-Bass, 1994), 15.

11. David Jeremiah, *Home Improvement: Tools to Rebuild Your Family* (San Diego: Turning Point, 2000).

12. Keith Intrator, *Covenant Relationships* (Shippensberg, Penn.: Destiny Image Publishers, Inc., 1995), 13–14.

13. Ibid.

14. G. R. Dunstan, *Theology* (1975), 102–103.

15. Iris Krasnow, *Surrendering to Marriage* (New York: Talk Miramax Books, 2001), 200.

16. Dennis Rainey, *One Home at a Time* (Wheaton, Ill.: Tyndale House Publishers, 1997), 48.

17. Atkinson, *To Have and To Hold,* 72.

18. Intrator, *Covenant Relationships,* 19.

19. Rainey, *One Home at a Time,* 82.

20. Mike Mason, *The Mystery of Marriage* (Grand Rapids, Mich.: Zondervan Publishers, 1985), 93–105.

21. Kay Arthur, *Our Covenant God* (Colorado Springs: Waterbrook Press, 1999), 76.

22. Diane Warner, *The Complete Book of Wedding Vows* (Franklin Lakes, N. J.: Career Press Publishers, 1996), 174.

23.   Ibid., 159.

24.   "Covenant of Salt," *International Standard Bible Encyclopaedia* (Grand Rapids, Mich.: Eerdmans Publishing Company, 1939), 729.

25.   Larry Crabb, *The Marriage Builder* (Grand Rapids, Mich.: Zondervan Publishers, 1982), 14.

26.   Parrott, *Saving Your Marriage Before It Starts,* 145.

27.   Bob Moeller, *For Better for Worse for Keeps* (Sisters, Ore.: Multnomah Books, 1993), 75–76.

28.   Harriet Beecher Stowe, BrainyQuotes, http://www.brainyquotes.com/quotes/quotes/h/q126390.html.

Chapter 6: Is Your Marriage a Contract or a Covenant?

1.   Samuele Bacchiocchi, *The Marriage Covenant* (Berrien Springs, Mich.: Biblical Perspectives, 1991), 41.

2.   Paul E. Palmer, "Christian Marriage: Contract or Covenant?" *Theological Studies,* 33, no. 4 (December 1972), 639.

3.   Paul and Evelyn Mochoschetta, *The Marriage Spirit* (New York: Simon & Schuster, 2000), 168–69.

4.   Les and Leslie Parrott, *Saving Your Marriage Before It Starts* (Grand Rapids, Mich.: Zondervan Publishing House, 1995), 148.

5.   Gary Smalley and John Trent, *The Language of Love* (Grand Rapids, Mich.: Zondervan Publishers, 1996), 17.

Chapter 7: Is "I Do" Your Final Answer?

1.   Ruth Harms Calkin, *Hold Me Close: Prayer Poems that Celebrate Married Love* (Wheaton, Ill.: Tyndale House Publishers, 1996), 54.

2.   Gary Thomas, *Sacred Marriage* (Grand Rapids, Mich.: Zondervan Publishers, 2000), 35–36.

3.   Donald Harvey, "Bonds of Steel," *Marriage Partnership,* Winter 1996, 13, no. 4, 50.

4.   Douglas C. Minson, "Love and Its Counterfeits," *Breakpoint Online,* February 2001, no. 11.

5.   Derek Prince, *The Marriage Covenant* (New Kensington, Penn.: Whitaker House Publishers, 1978), 34.

6. Terry Hargrave, "The Essential Humility of Marriage," www.smartmarriages.com/hargrave.html. Keynote address presented at the Fourth Annual Smart Marriages Conference in Denver, Colorado, 1 July 2000.

7. Mike Mason, *The Mystery of Marriage* (Sisters, Ore.: Multnomah Books, 1985), 88.

8. Iris Krasnow, *Surrendering to Marriage* (New York: Hyperion Publishing, 2001), 13–15.

9. Ibid., back cover.

10. Mason, *The Mystery of Marriage,* 72.

11. Thomas, *Sacred Marriage,* 68.

12. Helen Rowland, "Interesting Quotes," www.geocities.com/bornhoney/quotes.htm.

13. David Edwards, "Happiness Is Dissent: The Truth About Looking Out for Number One," *Medialens,* August 2001, http://www.medialens.org/articles/de_number_one.html.

14. Katherine Porter, *The Days Before* (New York: Harcourt Brace, 1952), 134–35.

15. "Happy Marriage Contest," *Good Housekeeping,* November 1993, 63.

16. Diane Sollee, "Shifting Gears: An Optimistic View of the Future of Marriage," The Coalition for Marriage, Family, and Couples Education, http://www.smartmarriages.com/optimistic.html.

Chapter 8: A Covenant Wedding

1. Scott Stanley, *The Heart of Commitment* (Nashville: Thomas Nelson Publishers, 1998), 4.

2. Ibid., 5.

3. "In the Game," 14 September 2000, FindWhat.com, www.findwhat.com/investor relations.

4. E. J. McGregor, "Chris Spielman's Family Tackles Breast Cancer," September 17, 1999, CNN/*Sports Illustrated,* www.sportsillustrated.cnn.com/caring/spielman.html.

5. Suzanne Lainson, "What Are You Trying to Accomplish as an Athlete?" *The Creative Athlete,* June 1997, http://onlinesports.com/sportstrust/creative1.html.

6. Ray Vander Laan, "His Body, His Blood," *Focus on the Family* magazine, April 1999, 7.

7. Dannah Gresh, *And the Bride Wore White* (Chicago: Moody Press, 1999), 130–31.

8. Ray Vander Laan, "His Body, His Blood," *Focus on the Family* magazine, April 1999, 8.

9. T. D. Jakes, *Celebrating Marriage: The Spiritual Wedding of the Believer* (Tulsa, Okla.: Albury Publishing, 1988), 38.

10. Martha Williamson, *Inviting God to Your Wedding* (New York: Harmony Books, 2000), 87.

11. David Atkinson, *To Have and to Hold* (Grand Rapids, Mich.: Eerdmans Publishing Company, 1979), 84.

Chapter 9: The Power of Covenant Love

1. Douglas Minson, "Love and Its Counterfeits," *Breakpoint Online,* February 2001, www.breakpoint.com.

2. Gary Smalley, *Making Love Last Forever* (Nashville: Word Publishing, 1996), 135.

3. Gary Thomas, *Sacred Marriage* (Grand Rapids, Mich.: Zondervan Publishers, 2000), 16.

4. Bob Moeller, *For Better for Worse for Keeps* (Sisters, Ore.: Multnomah Books, 1993), 24.

5. Thomas Jones, *Sex and Love When You're Single Again* (Nashville: Thomas Nelson Publishers, 1990), 93–96.

6. Marjorie Holmes, *A Time to Love* (Wheaton, Ill.: Tyndale House Publishers, 1990), 45.

7. Josh McDowell, *The Secret of Loving* (Wheaton, Ill.: Tyndale House Publishers, Inc., 1990), 17–18.

8. Norman Wright, *Secrets of a Lasting Marriage* (Ventura, Calif.: Regal Books, 1995), 14.

9. Jeanette and Robert Lauer, "Marriages Made to Last," *Psychology Today,* June 1985, 22–26.

10.   Gary and Barbara Rosberg, *The Five Love Needs of Men and Women* (Tyndale House Publishers, Wheaton, Ill.: 2000), 235.

11.   Mike Mason, *The Mystery of Marriage* (Sisters, Ore.: Multnomah Books, 1985), 98.

12.   Elizabeth Achtemeier, *The Committed Marriage* (Philadelphia: Westminster Press, 1976), 57.

13.   Janis Abrahms Spring, *After the Affair* (New York: Harper-Perennial, HarperCollins Publishers, 1996), 66.

14.   Mason, *The Mystery of Marriage,* 102.

15.   Madeline L'Engle, *The Irrational Season* (San Francisco: Harper Publishers, 1983), 88.

Chapter 10: Do You Have a Purpose-Driven Marriage?

1.   Ed Shea, "Love on Purpose," Life on Purpose Institute, www.lifeonpurpose.com/love_on_purpose.html.

2.   Susan Dixon, "Marriage: What's the Point?" *Friends and Lovers,* Summer 1985, 33.

3.   Neil Clark Warren, *The Triumphant Marriage* (Colorado Springs: Focus on the Family Publishing, 1995), 29.

4.   Gary Thomas, *Sacred Marriage* (Grand Rapids, Mich.: Zondervan Publishers, 2000), 33–35.

5.   "Quotations on the Virtues of Making Mistakes," Wilton High School Chemistry Web Site, www.chemistrycoach.com/quotatio.htm.

6.   Warren, *The Triumphant Marriage,* 5.

Chapter 11: Covenant Companionship

1.   John Gottman, *Why Marriages Succeed or Fail* (New York: Simon & Schuster, 1994), 13.

2.   William Glasner, *Reality Therapy* (Nashville: Thomas Nelson Publishers, 1999), 47.

3.   Gary and Barbara Rosberg, *The Five Love Needs of Men and Women* (Wheaton, Ill.: Tyndale House Publishers, 2000), 111.

4. Steve Carr, *Married and How to Stay That Way* (Phoenix, Ariz.: ACW Press, 1998), 15.

Chapter 12: The Critical Role of Communication

1. Paul Tournier, "John Powell's Contributions to Human Trinity Hypnotherapy," http://www.durbinhypnosis.com/powell.htm.

2. Norman Wright, *Communication: The Key to Your Marriage* (Ventura, Calif.: Regal Publishing, 2000), 62–63.

3. John Bachcom, "Convenience Less Communication," *Family Notes,* vol. 1, no. 1, March 1998, http://lfa.lcms.org/famnot01.htm.

4. Virginia Slims opinion poll conducted in 1990 by the Roper Organization, Inc., Roper Center, University of Connecticut.

5. Gary Smalley, *Making Love Last Forever* (Nashville: Word Publishing, 1996), 141.

6. Gary Smalley and John Trent, *The Language of Love* (Pomona, Calif.: Focus on the Family Publishing, 1988), 10.

7. Nancy Reagan, *I Love You, Ronnie* (New York: Random House Publishers, 2000), 76–77, 137.

8. Gary Chapman, *The Five Love Languages* (Chicago: Northfield Publishing, 1995), 36.

9. David Clarke, *Men Are Clams, Women Are Crowbars* (Tempe, Ariz.: Evangelical Christian Publishers Association, 1998), 19.

10. Josh McDowell, *The Secret of Loving* (Wheaton, Ill.: Tyndale House Publishers, 1985), 71.

11. Willard Harley, *His Needs, Her Needs* (Grand Rapids, Mich.: Fleming H. Revell Publishers, 1994), 45–46.

12. Ibid., 76–78.

13. Barbara and Allen Pease, *Why Men Don't Listen and Women Can't Read Maps* (New York: Welcome Rain Publishers, 2000), 212.

14. Harley, *His Needs, Her Needs,* 96, 106.

15. Quoted in Joe Beam, *Becoming One* (West Monroe, La: Howard Publishing Company, 1999), 27.

16. Ibid.

17. David Clarke, *A Marriage after God's Own Heart* (Sisters, Ore.: Multnomah Books, 2001), 23.

18. Ibid., 33, 45.

19. Ibid., 38–39.

20. Ibid., 75.

21. Mike Mason, *The Mystery of Marriage* (Sisters, Ore.: Multnomah Books, 1985), 88.

22. Ibid., 89–90.

23. Les and Leslie Parrott, *When Bad Things Happen to Good Marriages* (Grand Rapids, Mich.: Zondervan Publishers, 2001), 136.

Chapter 13: Learning How to Manage Conflict

1. Diane Sollee, "The Emerging Field of Marriage Education," Coalition of Marriage, Family, and Couples Education, 1997 (revised October 2000), www.smartmarriages.com.

2. Howard Markman, *Fighting for Your Marriage* (San Francisco: Jossey-Bass, 1994), 6.

3. John Gottman, *The Seven Principles for Making a Marriage Work* (New York: Three Rivers Press, 1999), 129.

4. Ibid., 131.

5. Phillip McGraw, *Relationship Rescue* (New York: Hyperion Publishing, 2000), 177.

6. Gerry Spence, *How to Argue and Win Every Time* (New York: St. Martin's Press, 1995), 49.

7. Mike Mason, *The Mystery of Marriage* (Sisters, Ore.: Multnomah Books, 1985), 152.

8. Harville Hendricks, *Getting the Love that You Want* (Harper Perennial, A Division of HarperCollins Publishers, 1990), 109.

9. Gottman, *The Seven Principles for Making a Marriage Work*, 135–36.

10. Willard Harley, *Love Busters* (Grand Rapids, Mich.: Fleming H. Revel Publishers, 1992), 124.

11. Gottman, *The Seven Principles for Making a Marriage Work*, 200.

12. Ibid.

13.   Neil Clark Warren, *The Triumphant Marriage* (Colorado Springs: Focus on the Family Publishing, 1995), 123.

14.   Ibid., 121–25.

15.   Ibid., 131.

16.   Gary Smalley, *Making Love Last Forever* (Nashville: Word Publishing, 1984), 20.

17.   Tova Borgnine, *Being Married Happily Forever* (New York: G. P. Putnam & Sons Publishers, 1997), 42–43.

18.   Richard and Mary Strauss, "Resolving Conflicts," *Focus on the Family* magazine, March 1998, 3.

19.   Gottman, *The Seven Principles for Making a Marriage Work,* 146.

20.   Josh McDowell, *The Secret of Loving* (Wheaton, Ill.: Tyndale House Publishers, 1985), 122.

21.   Tim LaHaye, "How to Live Happily Ever After," *Christian Life,* September 1979, 26.

22.   Les and Leslie Parrott, *Saving Your Marriage Before It Starts* (Grand Rapids, Mich.: Zondervan Publishers, 1995), 140.

23.   Leonard Pitts, *Miami Press Herald,* found in *The Times,* Shreveport, in a Letter to the Editor, 10 March 2000.

24.   Markman, *Fighting for Your Marriage,* 152.

Epilogue: Would You Do It All Over Again?

1.   Mike Mason, *The Mystery of Marriage* (Sisters, Ore.: Multnomah Books, 1985), 182.